3.

乙己 Cerre
11/14

4?

D1402064

Recruitment, Retention and Retirement in Higher Education

Building and Managing the Faculty of the Future

Edited by

Robert L. Clark

North Carolina State University, USA

Jennifer Ma

TIAA-CREF Institute, USA

Edward Elgar

Cheltenham, UK • Northampton, MA, USA

© TIAA-CREF, 2005

All rights reserved. No part of this publication may be reproduced, stored in a retrieval system or transmitted in any form or by any means, electronic, mechanical or photocopying, recording, or otherwise without the prior permission of the publisher.

Published by
Edward Elgar Publishing Limited
Glensanda House
Montpellier Parade
Cheltenham
Glos GL50 1UA
UK

Edward Elgar Publishing, Inc.
136 West Street
Suite 202
Northampton
Massachusetts 01060
USA

A catalogue record for this book
is available from the British Library

ISBN 1 84542 185 X

Printed and bound in Great Britain by MPG Books Ltd, Bodmin, Cornwall

Contents

List of figures   vii
List of tables   ix
List of contributors   xi
Foreword   xiii
Herbert M. Allison, Jr

1   Changing faculty demographics and the need for new policies   1
   Robert L. Clark
2   Filling the gap: finding and keeping faculty for the university
   of the future   23
   Molly Corbett Broad
3   The changing nature of faculty employment   32
   Ronald G. Ehrenberg and Liang Zhang
4   The growing postdoctorate population at US research
   universities   53
   Jennifer Ma and Paula E. Stephan
5   Planning for the generational turnover of the faculty:
   faculty perceptions and institutional practices   80
   Jerry Berberet, Betsy E. Brown, Carole J. Bland, Kelly R. Risbey
   and Carroll-Ann Trotman
6   The future of retiree health benefits in higher education in the
   United States   101
   Sylvester J. Schieber
7   Impact of retiree health plans on faculty retirement decisions   135
   John Rust
8   Faculty recruitment, retention and retirement: a case study
   of human resources policymaking at Syracuse University   170
   John L. Palmer, Michael A. Flusche and Myra Z. Johnson
9   The value of phased retirement   185
   Steven G. Allen
10   Faculty retirement incentives by colleges and universities   209
   John Pencavel
11   To phase or not to phase: the dynamics of choosing phased
   retirement in academe   239
   David W. Leslie and Natasha Janson

12 Phasing out of full-time work at the University of California   252
    Ellen Switkes
13 The costs and benefits of early retirement plans   259
    John B. Shoven
14 Recruitment, retention and retirement: institutional research
    and the need for data   267
    Michael A. Baer, Deborah A. Freund, Charlotte V. Kuh,
    David E. Shulenburger and Richard R. Spies
15 Developing new employment and compensation policies
    in higher education   276
    Robert L. Clark and Madeleine B. d'Ambrosio

Index   287

Figures

1.1	Aging of the tenure-track faculty of the University of North Carolina	5
1.2	Age structure of Canadian faculty	5
4.1	Median length (in months) of total post-doc experience for ten fields by PhD year	68
4.2	Median length (in months) of total post-doc experience by field for those who received a PhD between 1965 and 1990	68
4.3	Median length (in months) of total post-doc experience for four fields by PhD year	69
6.1	Percentage of total personal health care expenditures paid out-of-pocket and percentage of GDP spent on personal health care, 1960 to 2002	108
6.2	Compound annual growth rates by decade in GDP per capita and medical expenditures per capita for the US population, 1960 to 2002	109
6.3	Employer contributions to private health benefit plans as a percentage of cash wages paid to employed workers for selected years	111
6.4	Rough characterization of health care utilization under a typical employer-sponsored health plan in the United States in 2003	113
6.5	Age profile of average expenditures on health care in the United States during 2000	114
6.6	Ratio of current employees to number of employees in 1968 for selected industries, compared to faculty in higher education, by year	128
6.7	Percentage of faculty in higher education and employees in selected industries aged 50 or over, by year	130
7.1	Results of simulations of the model in the 'base case' (1)	147
7.2	Results of simulations of the model in the 'base case' (2)	149
7.3	Results of simulations of the model in the 'base case' (3)	150
7.4	Results of simulations of the model in the 'base case' (4)	151
7.5	Comparisons of base case and case 0: effects of shifting 50 per cent of retiree health insurance premiums to retirees (1)	154

7.6   Comparisons of base case and case 0: effects of shifting
      50 per cent of retiree health insurance premiums to
      retirees (2)   155
7.7   Comparisons of base case and case 0: effects of shifting
      50 per cent of retiree health insurance premiums to
      retirees (3)   156
7.8   Comparisons of base case and case 0: effects of shifting
      50 per cent of retiree health insurance premiums to
      retirees (4)   157
7.9   Comparisons of base case and case 1: effects of canceling
      retiree health insurance (1)   158
7.10 Comparisons of base case and case 1: effects of canceling
      retiree health insurance (2)   159
7.11 Comparisons of base case and case 2: effects of canceling
      retiree health insurance after age 65 (1)   161
7.12 Comparisons of base case and case 2: effects of canceling
      retiree health insurance after age 65 (2)   162
10.1 The relationship between each verip's replacement ratio
      and the acceptance rate by age   228
10.2 Tenured faculty employment by age at the University of
      California before and after the buyouts   232
13.1 FRIP participant age distribution, FY1994–FY2002   265
13.2 S&P500 Index vs. per cent of faculty retiring,
      FY1991–FY2002   266

Tables

1.1   Age structure of full-time and part-time instructional faculty and staff in degree-granting institutions   2

1.2   Age distribution of tenure-track faculty in the UNC system: 1982–2000, selected years   4

1.3   Type of pension plan offered by institutions of higher education   11

1.4   Percentage of colleges and universities with phased retirement plans by type of institutions   13

1.5   Percentage of institutions that had one or more financial incentive programs since 1995 to encourage faculty members to retire prior to age 70   15

3.1   Ratio of full-time non-tenure-track faculty/total full-time faculty   34

3.2   Ratio of part-time faculty/total full-time faculty   36

3.3   Ratio of non-tenured new hires/total new hires   37

3.4   Logarithmic faculty demand functions estimates: instructors excluded   41

3.5   Logarithmic faculty demand functions: tenure-track status correctly assigned   42

3.6   Number of new hire faculty, institutional fixed effects   45

3A.1 Full-time non-tenure-track faculty/total full-time faculty   51

4.1   Postdoctorate population in science and engineering at US universities, 1987–2001   55

4.2   Summary statistics of explanatory variables for the propensity model, 1981–99   58

4.3   Logit model results for those who received a PhD between 1981 and 1999   60

4.4   Logit results for those who received a PhD between 1981 and 1995   63

4.5   Relationship of taking a postdoctoral position to number of PhDs in cohort by field, 1981–95   65

4.6   Summary statistics for the full sample and postdoctoral sample, SDR, 1975–90   70

4.7   OLS regression results of postdoctoral length model, 1975–80 PhD cohorts   72

4.8	Duration and OLS regression results	75
5.1	Demographic characterisations of respondents	83
5.2	Professional profile of respondents	84
5.3	Faculty work patterns	85
5.4	Work allocation vs. perception of institutional expectations	85
5.5	Sources of motivation and satisfaction	86
5.6	Retirement plans	88
5.7	Financial profile of respondents	88
5.8	Retirement planning issues	89
5.9	Institutional relationships in retirement	90
6.1	Number of institutions of higher learning in survey sample providing retiree health benefits to retired faculty by indication of coverage	123
6.2	Cost and cost-sharing of retiree health benefits provided by private and public colleges and universities in 2004	125
6.3	Utilization of minimum service requirements to qualify for health benefits provided to retired faculty by institutions of higher learning in 2004	126
7.1	Expected discounted compensation under alternative scenarios	165
9.1	Percentage of colleges and universities with phased retirement plans, by institutional characteristics	191
9.2	Probit analysis of odds that a campus will have a phased retirement program	194
9.3	Retirement rates for University of North Carolina system faculty, by year	197
9.4	Percentage of eligible faculty entering retirement, University of North Carolina system, by year and age group	199
9.5	Faculty workload on campus, before and after entering phased retirement	200
10.1	Type of pension and private–public status: percentage of all institutions	214
10.2	The percentage of institutions offering various benefits to retired faculty	218
10.3	Maximum likelihood estimates of institutional variables associated with the incidence of phased retirement programs and the incidence of faculty buyouts	220
13.1	Schedule of one-time payments	264

Contributors

Steven G. Allen is Associate Dean for Graduate Programs and Research for the College of Management, and Professor of Business Management and Economics at North Carolina State University. He is also a Research Associate with the National Bureau of Economic Research.

Herbert M. Allison, Jr is Chairman, President and Chief Executive Officer of TIAA-CREF.

Michael A. Baer is Senior Vice President for Programs and Analysis at the American Council on Education.

Jerry Berberet is Executive Director of the Associated New American Colleges.

Carole J. Bland is Research Director of Family Practice and Community Health at the University of Minnesota Medical School.

Molly Corbett Broad is President of the 16-campus University of North Carolina.

Betsy E. Brown is Associate Vice President for Academic Affairs in the Office of the President of the 16-campus University of North Carolina.

Robert L. Clark is Professor of Economics and Professor of Business Management at North Carolina State University.

Madeleine B. d'Ambrosio is Vice President and Executive Director of the TIAA-CREF Institute.

Ronald G. Ehrenberg is the Irving M. Ives Professor of Industrial and Labor Relations and Economics at Cornell University. He is also Director of the Cornell Higher Education Research Institute.

Michael A. Flusche is Associate Vice Chancellor at Syracuse University.

Deborah A. Freund is Vice Chancellor for Academic Affairs and Provost at Syracuse University. She is also Distinguished Professor of Public Administration and Economics in the Maxwell School of Citizenship and Public Affairs at Syracuse University and Adjunct Professor of Orthopedics at the State University of New York Upstate Medical University.

Natasha Janson is a graduate student at The College of William and Mary.

Myra Z. Johnson is Director of Benefits and Human Resources Services at Syracuse University.

Charlotte V. Kuh is Deputy Executive Director of the Policy and Global Affairs Division at the National Research Council.

David W. Leslie is Chancellor Professor of Education at The College of William and Mary.

Jennifer Ma is Senior Research Fellow at the TIAA-CREF Institute.

John L. Palmer is University Professor at the Maxwell School of Citizenship and Public Affairs at Syracuse University. He is also currently a public trustee for the Medicare and Social Security programs.

John Pencavel is the Levin Professor of Economics at Stanford University.

Kelly R. Risbey is a Research Assistant at the Minnesota Postsecondary Education Research Institute at the University of Minnesota.

John Rust is Professor of Economics at the University of Maryland.

Sylvester J. Schieber is Vice President of Research and Information at Watson Wyatt Worldwide.

John B. Shoven is the Charles R. Schwab Professor of Economics at Stanford University and Director of the Stanford Institute for Economic Policy Research.

David E. Shulenburger is Provost and Executive Vice Chancellor of the University of Kansas.

Richard R. Spies is Executive Vice President for Planning and Senior Advisor to the President at Brown University.

Paula E. Stephan is Professor of Economics at the Andrew Young School of Policy Studies at Georgia State University.

Ellen Switkes is Assistant Vice President for Academic Advancement at the University of California, Office of the President.

Carroll-Ann Trotman is Associate Professor of Dentistry at the University of North Carolina at Chapel Hill.

Liang Zhang is Assistant Professor of Educational Policy and Administration at the University of Minnesota.

Foreword

Herbert M. Allison, Jr

Chairman, President and Chief Executive Officer, TIAA-CREF

Over the last century, American colleges and universities have been the world leaders in higher education. Our campuses have also generated the theoretical and applied research that has helped fuel our nation's remarkable long-term economic growth. Today, however, this position of global prominence is being tested, as higher education faces a range of financial and human resources challenges: budget reductions, soaring health-care costs, the aging of faculty, and declining endowments. The chapters in this volume examine these challenges and how they are causing academic administrators to rethink their employment and compensation policies.

For over 85 years, TIAA-CREF has partnered with colleges and universities to promote the well-being of faculty and help ensure the academy's vitality. Throughout its history, TIAA-CREF has produced research and analyses to help higher education address its challenges effectively. In 1998, we deepened our commitment to our core market by establishing the TIAA-CREF Institute. It serves as a bridge between our business and the business of higher education, striving to enhance our knowledge of the issues confronting institutions, administrators and the individuals they employ. The April 2004 conference on which this volume is based is one example of the Institute's work.

TIAA-CREF is proud to have sponsored *Recruitment, Retention and Retirement in Higher Education.* The Institute's Three R's conference reflects our dedication to doing all we can to assist colleges and universities maintain their position as world leaders. The conference brought together prominent scholars and university decision makers to debate the current problems and identify potential solutions. It addressed both broad macro issues as well as specific concerns of front-line administrators.

For example, the conference looked at one of the most significant trends in employment and compensation policies: the increasing use of part-time instructors, contract faculty, and post-doctoral fellows instead of traditional tenure-track faculty. While research has documented and accounted for the trend, we are just beginning to learn about its impact on student learning, and the quality of teaching and research.

Another issue addressed was how to craft salary and benefit packages competitive enough to retain top faculty. Several chapters in this volume illustrate the importance of strong benefit plans, and show how various national trends are affecting the ability of universities to maintain the level of benefits they provide.

The conference also considered the implications of the aging of the professoriate, as faculty delay retirement. Pension plans, phased retirement plans, and retiree health plans all play central roles in faculty retirement decisions; these plans also constitute a significant component of labor costs.

We have received much positive feedback about the Three R's conference, and this provocative and useful volume expands on its findings. We hope this collection's insights help administrators confront the challenges they face, while giving scholars fertile research ideas. We at TIAA-CREF stand ready to work closely with campus leadership and other stakeholders in academia to seek innovative solutions to the issues surrounding faculty recruitment, retention, and retirement.

1. Changing faculty demographics and the need for new policies

Robert L. Clark

Colleges and universities are facing a series of challenges and opportunities that demand immediate action if American institutions of higher education are to remain the best in the world. Public universities must confront financial difficulties associated with substantial reductions in the growth rate of state appropriations and, in many instances, the absolute reductions in operating budgets. Public and private institutions are concerned with fluctuations in endowments and escalating costs of employing faculty, especially the increasing cost of providing health insurance to active and retired faculty. In addition, faculties are growing older and low retirement rates limit the number of new hiring opportunities.

The importance of these issues varies between public and private institutions, between those where human resource polices are collectively bargained and those that are non-union, across differing local economic environments, and by Carnegie classification. However, colleges and universities of all types are facing a series of common challenges that will shape higher education in the twenty-first century. In order to maintain high quality faculty in the coming years, colleges and universities must carefully consider their compensation policies and working conditions. The primary questions facing presidents, chancellors, provosts, deans and department heads are:

- How do they continue to recruit the best faculty?
- Having hired the best, how do they retain them?
- How can the faculty be restructured in the coming years through the orderly retirement of older professors and the hiring of appropriate replacements?

This volume addresses the key issues associated with recruiting, retaining, and retiring of faculty across all types of institutions. The chapters examine the increasing reliance on non-tenure-track faculty to staff classes, the role of health insurance in attracting, maintaining, and retiring faculty, and the development of retirement policies that produce an orderly transition from full-time work to complete retirement. This chapter provides a framework for examining these issues by describing the aging of the professoriate and examining the implications of the demographic changes that are occurring. Faculty aging presents both challenges and opportunities for institutions of higher education. Developing appropriate employment and compensation policies will be the key to successfully aligning the age structure of the faculties of the future.

1.1   AN AGING FACULTY

Faculty are aging. Data from the National Center for Educational Statistics (NCES), shown in Table 1.1, illustrate how quickly the American professoriate has aged. The table reports the age structure of full-time and part-time instructional faculty and staff in two- and four-year, degree-granting institutions (NCES 2002, Table 234 and unpublished data provided by Thomas Snyder of NCES).[1] In 1987 the age structure could be described as uniform with 25 per cent of the full-time instructional staff less than 40 years old, 25 per cent were 55 years or older, and 50 per cent were between the ages of 40 and 54. However, the professoriate aged rapidly during the next decade. By 1998, only 18 per cent of faculty was less than age 40 while

Table 1.1   Age structure of full-time and part-time instructional faculty and staff in degree-granting institutions

Age	1987	1992	1998
Less than 30	1.6	1.5	1.6
30–34	8.4	6.6	5.7
35–39	14.7	12.7	10.7
40–44	16.8	17.0	14.6
45–49	18.8	18.6	17.3
50–54	15.1	18.0	18.7
55–59	12.1	12.7	16.1
60–64	12.7*	8.5	9.8
65 and older		4.5	5.5

Note: * This entry is for faculty aged 60 years and older

Source: NCES (2002). The data for 1987 was provided by Thomas Snyder of NCES

over 31 per cent were aged 55 years or older. The changing age structure of faculties is due to past hiring patterns, low turnover rates, low retirement rates, and the end of mandatory retirement.

This rapid aging of the faculty reflects past hiring patterns, turnover rates, and retirement decisions. A relatively large number of faculty were hired in the 1960s and 1970s. These faculty are now in their 50s and 60s. Slow growth in the number of new faculty positions and relatively low exit rates from the academy have produced the aging of the professoriate shown in Table 1.1. As the large cohort of older faculty approaches traditional retirement ages, many academic leaders have expressed concerns over the elimination of mandatory retirement policies a decade ago and the prospects that senior faculty will remain on the job into their 70s. These concerns are at the heart of the debate over early and phased retirement plans and the continued offering of retiree health insurance.

Ultimately these relatively large cohorts of older faculty will retire and this will create a unique opportunity for institutions of higher education to restructure their faculties. Large number of retirements will allow academic administrators to reallocate positions across their institutions. Past trends indicate that many colleges and universities have been replacing retiring tenured faculty with non-tenure-track instructors, post-doctoral fellows, and part-time staff. Advantages associated with replacing retiring tenured professors with contract staff, post-doctoral fellows, and part-time faculty include greater staffing flexibility and lower employment costs. The wisdom of this trend was one of the topics of discussion for this conference. These staffing decisions will be even more important in the next decade with the expected large number of retirements. Academic leaders should recognize the long-run importance of today's employment decisions on the faculty of the future.

While Table 1.1 illustrated the aging of the American professoriate, decisions are made at individual institutions. Each institution should examine its current faculty age structure and begin to plan for the future. Development of long-term faculty planning models would enable chancellors, presidents, and provosts to predict the expected number of retirements and thus new hiring opportunities. A better understanding of future retirements should guide today's hiring decisions.

For the past six years, I have been working in the University of North Carolina (UNC) Office of the President to evaluate new and existing retirement programs.[2] As part of this effort, we have examined the changing age structure of the faculties at the 15 campuses of the UNC system. Therefore, to assess the implications of faculty aging in a specific institution, we can review data from the UNC as an example of the aging of the faculty in one institution. Overall, the UNC faculty aged considerably from 1982 to 2001.

Table 1.2   Age distribution of tenure-track faculty in the UNC system:
           1982–2000, selected years

Age	1982	1986	1990	1994	1998	2000
<35	15.2	10.7	8.1	6.3	5.7	5.9
35–39	20.2	18.0	14.5	12.1	10.5	10.2
40–44	18.4	20.5	19.4	18.0	15.6	14.2
45–49	14.9	17.2	20.4	20.1	19.3	18.7
50–54	13.7	13.4	15.0	18.9	20.2	20.3
55–59	10.0	11.4	12.2	13.2	16.7	17.9
60–64	7.1	6.9	7.5	8.5	8.7	9.1
65–69	0.5	1.9	2.8	2.8	2.9	3.1
70+	0.0	0.0	0.0	0.2	0.5	0.8
Total	6796	7094	7533	7849	7906	7848

Note: Entries are rounded to nearest tenth

Source: Clark and Ghent (2004)

The age distribution of the entire tenure-track and tenured UNC faculty for selected years is shown in Table 1.2. For the combined UNC faculty, there are substantial decreases in the proportion of the faculty in each age category younger than age 40 and large increases in the proportion of all faculty who are in each age group above age 55. For example, the proportion of the faculty aged 35 to 39 fell from 20.2 per cent in 1982 to 10.2 per cent in 2000. During the same period, the proportion of faculty aged 55 to 59 increased from 10.0 per cent to 17.9 per cent. The trend in faculty aging is dramatically shown in Figure 1.1 as the proportion of the faculty under age 40 declines from 35.4 per cent 1982 to 16.1 per cent in 2000, while the proportion of faculty over age 55 increases from 17.6 per cent to 30.9 per cent. The picture reveals what might be described as an 'aging cross' of university faculty. Does the age structure of your institution over the past 20 years also exhibit this aging cross?

The aging cross is observed for each class of institutions (research, doctoral, masters, and baccalaureate) in the UNC system. The crossing point occurs between 1988 and 1991 as each of the four types of institutions changes from universities with primarily young faculties to universities with primarily older faculties. Examining each of the campuses separately reveals a similar crossing pattern in the age distribution of faculty.

Interestingly, faculties at Canadian colleges and universities are also aging rapidly. Figure 1.2 presents data complied by Robert Giroux (1999), President of the Association of Universities and Colleges of Canada.

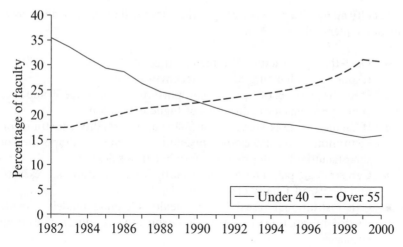

Source: Clark and Ghent (2004)

Figure 1.1   Aging of the tenure-track faculty of the University of North Carolina

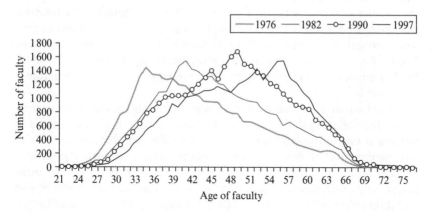

Source: Giroux (1999)

Figure 1.2   Age structure of Canadian faculty

These demographic profiles show the aging of the Canadian professoriate from 1976 to 1997. Giroux highlights the challenges and opportunities associated with the current age structure including the possibility of hiring large numbers of younger faculty in the coming years that will dramatically alter the age structure of the Canadian professoriate.

Faculty aging raises a series of questions that will be discussed in subsequent chapters. These include:

- Does the age structure of a faculty affect its quality or its ability to respond to a changing educational environment?
- Does the prospect of a growing proportion of faculty age 70 and over create problems for institutions of higher education?
- If faculty aging is viewed as a financial and quality constraint on institutions, can colleges and universities alter the age composition of their faculties by adopting new retirement policies?
- Can strategic planning be improved by better institutional research and the use of faculty planning models?
- Can institutional research and faculty planning models provide needed information to assess the long-run impact of alternative hiring strategies?

1.2 ENDING MANDATORY RETIREMENT

Federal legislation outlawing mandatory retirement significantly altered the human resource policies of many academic institutions. At the time this change became effective in 1994, the faculties of colleges and universities around the country were aging rapidly; however, most institutions had only a small proportion of their total faculty aged 60 and older. Thus, the full impact of ending mandatory retirement on faculty age structure is only now being felt.

The elimination of mandatory retirement has the potential of exacerbating faculty aging if older faculty choose to remain on the job instead of retiring at the traditional ages. Continued employment beyond age 70 also has the potential of slowing promotional prospects, reducing the number of new hires, and increasing labor costs.[3] However, delayed retirement might help institutions respond to increased numbers of students and maintain an important resource. The importance of the positive and negative aspects associated with delayed retirement can be debated; however, this conference focuses on the actual retirement response of individual faculty members to the newly available option of continuing employment beyond age 70.

Ashenfelter and Card (2002) and Clark et al. (2001) found that age-specific retirement rates at age 70 and older declined after the ending of mandatory retirement.[4] Initially, this had a relatively small effect on faculty age structures as the number of faculty still working in their late 60s was comparably small. However, in the coming decade, large numbers of professors will be aging into this group. If their average age of retirement is substantially higher than that of previous cohorts, institutions will confront the prospect of a growing number of faculty remaining on the job past age 70. Thus, a central question of our deliberations should be how colleges and universities will respond to low retirement rates, aging faculties in general, and the emergence of an increasing number of faculty in excess of age 70.

Ashenfelter and Card (2002) find a sharp decline in the probability of retiring at age 70 after mandatory retirement policies were eliminated in their sample of 104 colleges and universities. Retirement rates at age 70 were found to be 45 percentage points higher prior to 1994 than in the post mandatory retirement period (75.6 per cent between 1987 and 1993 compared to less than 29.1 per cent between 1994 and 1996). Retirement rates at age 71 fell by almost 37 percentage points.

Clark and Ghent (2004) estimated retirement equations using UNC faculty employment data for years before and after the ending of mandatory retirement. Similar to Ashenfelter and Card (2002), they found that after the end of mandatory retirement, the probability UNC faculty retiring at age 70 dropped sharply. These findings indicate that the change in mandatory retirement laws had a dramatic effect on retirement decisions at age 70. This research implies that in the future a growing number of faculty will continue on the job past age 70.

It is extremely unlikely that colleges and universities will be allowed to re-impose mandatory retirement policies in the future. Thus, academic administrators must carefully consider their retirement policies and assess their desire to achieve certain patterns of retirement. Key questions include:

- Can phased retirement plans be used to achieve a more desirable age pattern of retirement among faculty?
- Are early retirement plans a cost-effective means of altering retirement decisions?
- How do retiree health insurance plans affect retirement decisions?
- Can institutions continue to provide retiree health plans in the face of rapidly rising health care costs?

1.3 PLANNING FOR THE FACULTY OF THE FUTURE: THE ROLE OF INSTITUTIONAL RESEARCH

The most important job of academic administrators is to maintain a high quality faculty. This requires the development of appropriate human resource policies and levels of compensation consistent with recruiting, retaining, and then retiring faculty. Understanding future needs for hiring new faculty is central to adequate planning within the university, as is the concern over the changing composition of faculty. Strategic planning should include the development of a faculty-planning model that would enable academic administrators to project the number of faculty who can be expected to leave the institution over the coming years. Such a model could predict the annual need for new faculty as existing faculty retire or leave the university.

A faculty-planning model should be based on demographic models of population growth and employment records of individual institutions. Using the planning model, academic administrators would be able to observe the changing age structure of their faculty, expected turnover rates and retirement rates, and the need for new faculty. The model will also be able to address the changing composition of the faculty between full-time tenure-track faculty and other types of faculty appointments.

A computer simulation model could be developed to show how the current age structure of the faculty will evolve under alternative scenarios. Using historical employment records, the model would be built using the current size of the faculty and its age structure. Projections into the future would employ past age-specific turnover and retirement rates of the faculty, the desired strategy for new hires (hire only at the assistant professor level, hire at all ranks, etc.), and the projected change in faculty size (growing, declining, or stable). The simulations would trace out the changes in faculty age structure and the year-by-year hiring rates that could be expected.

The simulation model would allow administrators to alter their hiring strategy and change the growth rate of faculty size. In addition, one could model the impact of changes in human resource policies. For example, early retirement policies would increase the number of retirements. Based on past experiences at other universities, the model would show the impact of implementing such a policy on age-specific retirement rates. Higher retirement rates would provide greater future hiring possibilities. The impact of other human resource policies such as phased retirement, alternative tenure policies, and higher compensation could be included in the model. In each of these cases, the impact of hiring policies on faculty composition could be determined. For example, retirees are replaced by new assistant professors or, alternatively, retirees are replaced by several part-time, temporary instructors.

Assessing the impact of alternative compensation and employment policies should be guided by faculty preferences. Periodic surveys to determine faculty attitudes toward retirement, the importance of pension and health plans, desire for new transitions into retirement, and expected retirement ages would be useful. Jerry Berberet and his colleagues (Chapter 5) examine the findings from two faculty surveys concerning workloads, career development, and retirement plans.

Faculty planning and development models would be useful tools for academic administrators concerned about the significant changes in faculty age structure, size, and composition. Such models could be used by institutions of all classifications and could address a variety of perceived challenges in the twenty-first century. The models would help university planners to better understand the long-run implications of their policies and would enable them to assess the impact of changes in retirement policies such as early retirement plans.

Why do academic leaders not devote more resources to research and evaluation of their own strategic decisions? On most campuses, electronic data are available that would allow analysts to predict future retirements and other terminations. Through the use of a faculty-planning model, one could then determine future hiring opportunities and the long-run impact of alternative hiring strategies such as greater use of contract and part-time faculty. These models could also be used to estimate the impact of adopting early retirement or phased retirement plans, the elimination of retiree health insurance, shifting to defined contribution pension plans, or other significant policy changes. Should academic organizations and foundations be encouraged to support the development of such a planning model that could be used widely by institutions of higher education?

The value of institutional research to colleges and universities and the need for adequate data to compare compensation policies to those of other institutions are explored in Chapter 14. Questions for consideration include: would it be helpful to have a national database that contained plan descriptions of phased and early retirement plans that had been adopted? Would it be useful to those institutions considering implementing such plans to know whether comparable colleges and universities have established these types of retirement plans? Have institutions evaluated the impact of such plans on their faculty quality and costs? If there is a need for greater information and coordination among colleges and universities, where can we find the resources to establish such a database?

1.4 TRANSITIONS TO RETIREMENT

In many colleges and universities, the retirement of older faculty is the primary mechanism by which faculty positions become available.[5] Vacant positions resulting from retirements of existing faculty can be used to hire new, younger faculty. Retirements provide universities with the opportunity to reallocate positions across disciplines and, thus increase the number of faculty in areas of high student demand or respond to opportunities to develop programs in emerging areas.[6] Some analysts argue that academic administrators are using retirements as an opportunity to reduce costs and long-term commitment of faculty by replacing retiring faculty with part-time instructors or fixed-term lecturers instead of new tenure-track assistant professors. Still others believe that retirements do not result in cost savings because institutions replace retiring professors with similar, high-salaried senior professors from other institutions. The impact of retirements and new hiring on faculty age structure and labor costs varies across institutions and depends on the objectives and cost constraints facing individual campuses.

The importance of retirements to the age distribution of faculty is greater in institutions that have stable or declining enrollments. Such institutions do not have the opportunity to restructure their faculties through net new hiring but must depend on retirements to create vacancies. Successful academic administrators must assess the potential for enrollment growth and determine how this translates into demand for faculty. Next, they must consider the current age structure of their faculty and determine current and projected patterns of age-specific retirement rates.

Transitions from full-time work to full-time retirement are influenced by basic retirement plans and whether the institution offers phased or early retirement incentives to senior faculty. Virtually all institutions offer basic retirement plans to their full-time faculty (Anderson 2002).[7] Let us consider how each type of retirement plan influences the work decisions of senior faculty.

1.4.1 Basic Retirement Plans

Retirement rates differ between the faculty members enrolled in the defined benefit plans and those who are participating in defined contribution plans. Defined benefit plans have specific retirement incentives associated with certain ages, such as the ages of eligibility for early and normal retirement. Studies examining retirement decisions by participants in defined benefit plans find that retirements are clustered around these ages.[8] Defined contribution plans are more age-neutral in their retirement incentives. In general, we expect that retirement rates will be greater for participants in defined benefit plans.

Among institutions of higher education, public colleges and universities typically offer defined benefit plans while private colleges and universities

Table 1.3   Type of pension plan offered by institutions of higher education
         (by percentage)

	Pension plan type offered				
	Defined benefit only	Defined contribution only	Combination plan	Choice of defined benefit or defined contribution	N
Total	15.3	41.1	7.6	35.9	607
Public	20.9	12.7	10.9	55.2	392
Private	5.1	93.0	1.4	0.5	215
AAUP school classification *Four-year institutions:*					
Doctoral I	11.4	35.0	11.4	42.3	123
Masters	12.0	42.1	6.6	39.3	183
Baccalaureate	6.5	75.2	3.9	14.4	153
Two-year institutions:					
w faculty ranks	15.5	8.5	7.0	69.0	71
w/o faculty ranks	46.8	11.7	11.7	29.9	77

Note: Entries are rounded to nearest tenth

Source: Ehrenberg (2003a), Table 2

tend to offer only defined contribution plans (see Table 1.3). Nationally, private sector firms are rapidly moving away from defined benefit plans and toward greater use of defined contribution plans (Clark and McDermed 1990; Purcell 2002). Even public employers are now considering shifting to defined contribution plans. The future seems clear. More and more individuals will be included in defined contribution plans and fewer will be in defined benefit plans. In addition, many public institutions allow faculty to choose between a state defined benefit plan and optional defined contribution plans.

Ashenfelter and Card (2002) find that, among faculty who are participants in defined contribution plans, those with larger account balances are more likely to retire. Thus, we can expect retirement rates to fluctuate with economic conditions. The proportion of older faculty retiring will be higher when equity markets have been rising but retirement rates are likely to decline during periods when stock prices have fallen. UNC provides a choice to all new employed faculty members. Clark, Ghent and McDermed

(2004) found that faculty in the defined contribution plan had significantly lower age-specific retirement rates than comparable faculty who were participants in the defined benefit plan. Higher retirement rates for those in the state plan reflect the economic incentives to retire that are part of the defined benefit state retirement plan.

When given the choice between the state defined benefit plan and a defined contribution plan, faculty overwhelmingly tended to select the defined contribution plan.[9] Thus, colleges and universities must be prepared for a future that for the most part will include faculty covered by defined contribution plans and without any required or mandatory retirement age. Without the retirement incentives that are imbedded in defined benefit plans, faculty who are participating in defined contribution plans tend to retire at later ages.

The discussion thus far indicates that in the next decade, many colleges and universities will have an increasing number of their faculty reaching age 70 and, without mandatory retirement, many of these faculty will choose to stay on the job. Institutions with defined contribution plans will have higher retention rates among their older faculty. It is in this context, chapters in this volume consider the desirability and impact of adopting phased retirement plans (Chapters 9, 10, 11 and 12) and early retirement plans (Chapters 10 and 13). In addition, Sylvester Schieber (Chapter 6) and John Rust (Chapter 7) assess the pros and cons of retaining retiree health plans.

As the prevalence of defined contribution plans continues to grow, academic leaders must consider their obligations as plan sponsors. Questions concerning appropriate plan design must be addressed. How much choice should faculty be given? How many plan providers should be allowed and how many individual funds should each be permitted to offer? Finally, how should these decisions be made – through faculty committees or benefits offices?

Institutions must also consider their obligation to provide financial education to their faculty and other employees. Faculty must plan for their retirement. Participants in defined contribution plans have greater responsibility for their retirement income. Clark and d'Ambrosio (2003) have shown that participation in financial planning seminars alters saving behavior and retirement goals. As retirement transitions change so must retirement planning.

1.4.2 Phased Retirement Plans

Recently, many colleges and universities have introduced phased retirement programs. Ehrenberg (2003a) describes the incidence of phased retirement plans in the Survey of Changes in Faculty Retirement Policies. He reports the following percentage of institutions with phased retirement plans:

Table 1.4   Percentage of colleges and universities with phased retirement plans by type of institution

Category	Private	Public	Total
Research and doctoral	50	31	35
Masters	38	23	29
Baccalaureate	30	24	29
Total	35	26	30

Source: Ehrenberg (2003a)

This study finds that about one third of responding institutions have phased retirement plans, that phased retirement plans are most common in private institutions, and that phased retirement plans are most prevalent in research and doctoral institutions. These are also the institutions that have been most concerned about the impact of ending mandatory retirement and the aging of their faculties.

These plans provide senior faculty with new employment/retirement options. Many plans provide prorated compensation for faculty who give up tenure and accept a fixed-term contract for part-time employment. The value of these plans to the institution is that they provide information concerning the total retirement date thus eliminating the uncertainty of when senior faculty will finally leave the university. The value to faculty members is that they have a new option, typically half-time work instead of full time. Individual deals for part-time employment have always been available to selected faculty; however, formal phased retirement programs usually provide this option to all qualified faculty at a pre-set level of compensation.

If appropriately structured, phased retirement plans can be win–win situations as faculty can more easily transition into retirement and institutions gain flexibility. Plans can be arranged to be basically cost neutral, say half-time work for half-time pay. The attractiveness of phased retirement plans is related to their generosity. More generous terms, say 75 per cent pay for half-time work, will induce more faculty to enroll in the plan. Of course, the more generous the terms, the higher the costs.

There have been relatively few studies of the effects of phased retirement plans. Ghent et al. (2001) and Allen et al. (2004) provide the best available evidence to date on the response to phased retirement plans.

They have studied the impact of a phased retirement program at UNC. Their results indicate that about one in every four retirees chose to enter phased retirement. This program was begun as an experiment but after careful review the UNC Board of Governors made this program a permanent policy. Steven Allen (Chapter 9) provides new evidence of the effectiveness of phased retirement. Ellen Switkes (Chapter 12) reports on consideration of a phased retirement plan at the University of California, and David Leslie and Natasha Janson (Chapter 11) describe the results from interviews with nine colleges and universities that have adopted phased retirement plans.

I anticipate that phased retirement plans will become increasingly popular in the future and that a larger proportion of retiring faculty will choose to be part of these programs. I also believe that similar programs will be adopted throughout the economy. It is even possible that phased retirement will become the normal or preferred transition to retirement among university faculty.[10] With the emergence of phased retirement, are new financial products needed or do we simply need new and better retirement planning? Our discussions should highlight how pension payouts need to be structure for phased retirees and how phased retirees should plan for their income during and after their part-time employment.

1.4.3 Early Retirement Plans

Over the years, a number of institutions have adopted early retirement plans in an effort to reduce the size of their faculty and reduce costs. These plans tend to offer specific incentives to qualified faculty to retire within a specified time period. These plans are often linked to defined benefit plans in those public institutions that have these types of pension plans. Faculty are often treated as if they were older thus reducing early retirement penalties and they are often given credit for extra years of service to increase their annual retirement benefit. To take advantage of this offer, faculty must retire during the enrollment window. Such plans are often successful at attracting many older faculty to enroll in the early retirement plan. The more generous the plan is, the greater the number of faculty that will accept the offer.

Ehrenberg (2003a) presents results from the Survey of Changes in Faculty Retirement Policies showing that almost half of all reporting institutions had adopted at least one early retirement incentive program since 1995 (see Table 1.5). The survey showed that among four-year institutions, private colleges and universities were more likely to have established these programs and that doctoral institutions were most likely to have offered early retirement plans to their faculty. Unfortunately, relatively few

Table 1.5   *Percentage of institutions that had one or more financial*
              incentive programs since 1995 to encourage faculty members to
              retire prior to age 70

Institutional category	Private (%)	Public (%)	Total (%)
I (Doctoral)	60	42	46
IIA (Masters)	42	41	41
IIB (Baccalaureate)	45	37	43
III (2 yr. w faculty ranks)	0	67	66
IV (2 yr. w/o faculty ranks)	0	44	42
Overall	46	46	46

Source: Ehrenberg (2003a), Table 5

institutions seek to review and evaluate these plans after they have been
completed.

Perhaps the most studied early retirement program in higher education
was the one instituted by the University of California in the 1990s. This
was a three-part program that generated a substantial increase in faculty
retirements. Switkes (2001) and Pencavel (2001) provide statistical evidence
on response to this early retirement plan. John Pencavel (Chapter 10) provides a further discussion of the impact of early retirement plans on faculty
retirement rates and John Shoven (Chapter 13) examines the cost and
benefits of offering early retirement buyouts to senior professors.

Generous early retirement plans can induce many senior faculty members
to retire; however, the costs of these programs should be carefully studied.
If the objective is to permanently reduce faculty size, early retirement plans
can be a cost-effective method of achieving this result allowing faculty to
self-select retirement rather than having the institution resort to layoffs. If,
however, the institution quickly replaces the retiring faculty, the university
ends up paying higher retirement benefits and still must pay the salary of the
new professor. In such cases, institutions may rather quickly regret their
decision to offer early retirement plans.

Key questions that need to be considered include:

- Should early retirement plans be used to address faculty aging or only
  when the objective is to reduce the total number of faculty?
- Should early retirement plans be targeted at faculty in their 50s and
  60s only or should such plans also attempt to increase retirements
  among those past the traditional retirement ages?
- Yes, early retirement plans can induce retirements, but are they cost-
  effective?

● How should institutions with defined contribution plans use early retirement plans?

1.5   HEALTH INSURANCE

In the United States, most individuals between the ages of 22 and 65 are enrolled in employer-based health insurance plans provided by either their employer or that of their spouse. However, there are millions of working Americans who do not have health insurance. Medicare provides broad-based health insurance to individuals aged 65 and over, but older persons still face the prospect of substantial medical bills. Some companies extend their health care plans to retirees thus reducing out-of-pocket costs. Throughout the economy, employers have been reassessing their health insurance plans. In the face of rapidly rising costs, employers have been raising employee premiums to participants in company plans, increasing deductibles, and establishing higher co-payments. In addition, some organizations have been eliminating health plans as an employee benefit and many companies have terminated retiree health insurance plans. The health care system in the United States is a major focus of political debate and proposals for reform are being considered.

1.5.1   Health Insurance for Active Faculty

In higher education, most full-time faculty are covered by health insurance but many part-time faculty are not. Anderson (2002) examines data from the 1999 National Study of Postsecondary Faculty and reports that virtually all institutions provide health insurance to full-time active faculty. In contrast, only 36 per cent of institutions offer health insurance coverage to part-time faculty.

Colleges and universities are not immune to the rising cost of health care. Medical insurance costs in academic institutions rose from 6.5 per cent of the average faculty salary in 2001–02 to 7.3 per cent of the average salary in 2002–03. The one-year increase in the cost of health insurance added the equivalent of 0.8 percentage points to the increase in average faculty salary (Ehrenberg 2003b). This higher cost to the institution does not indicate an increase in medical benefits but simply reflects the higher cost of health insurance and medical cost inflation in general. In addition to the increased costs borne by the institution, faculty often had larger amounts deducted from their paychecks to pay for their portion of the insurance premium.

Quality medical insurance is one of the most important benefits that faculty receive. The promise of health insurance coverage helps institutions recruit and retain faculty. If medical inflation continues to be more rapid than the increase in the Consumer Price Index, how will colleges and universities cope with these added costs? John Palmer, Michael Flusche, and Myra Johnson (Chapter 8) present a case study of how Syracuse University reexamined its health care plans. They provide an interesting overview of the process that Syracuse used to evaluate and modify its health plans.

1.5.2   Retiree Health Insurance

After the passage of Medicare in 1965, many large companies and public employers adopted retiree health insurance plans. Medicare is the primary payer for retirees covered by employer-provided health insurance. Thus, the adoption of Medicare significantly reduced the cost of offering these plans. Economic research has shown that retiree health insurance provides an important inducement for early retirement to those younger than 65 and who are not yet eligible for Medicare.

Retiree health insurance is a disappearing benefit in the private sector. This decline began in the 1990s with the introduction of new accounting rules, the rapid increase in health care costs, and the increase in the ratio of retirees to workers in many companies (Clark et al. 1994). According to a survey by Mercer Human Resource Consulting, only 36 per cent of companies with 500 or more workers provided retiree health insurance to current workers in 2003. This was down from 50 per cent in 1993 (Freudenheim 2004). All indications are that this trend will continue.[11] In addition, those employers that continue to offer retiree health insurance are requiring greater worker contributions or are converting their plans to medical savings accounts that typically require worker contributions.

Educational institutions are also facing the rising cost of health insurance for their retirees. How will they respond? Sylvester Schieber (Chapter 6) presents findings from a new survey by Watson Wyatt Worldwide of colleges and universities and their retiree health plans. Many colleges and universities are engaged in revising and eliminating their plans. How will this affect retirement decisions of older faculty? John Rust (Chapter 7) examines the retirement decisions of faculty and how they are influenced by retiree health insurance.

This volume provides important new information on the future of retiree health plans in higher education. Will retiree health insurance plans continue to exist? Will they be restructured into medical savings plans? If retiree health plans are maintained, how will institutions pay for them? If they are eliminated, will faculty delay retirement to even later ages?

1.6   ACADEMIC LABOR MARKET: CONTRACT FACULTY

Each time a faculty member retires, an institution must decide whether it will hire a new full-time, tenure-track faculty member or fill the vacancy with a full-time contract instructor, post-doctoral fellow, or some type of part-time lecturer. This choice will be a function of the current funding status of the institution and its longer range staffing plan. Recently there has been a trend toward greater reliance on part-time staffing choices and the use of non-tenure-track faculty.

The American Association of University Professors (AAUP) (2004) reports that 44.5 per cent of all faculty are now employed part-time and in total, non-tenure-track positions account for more than 60 per cent of all faculty appointments. Between 1998 and 2001, the number of part-time and full-time non-tenure-track appointments grew by 35.5 per cent. Benjamin (2002) finds that 'the proportion of all faculty who teach part-time virtually doubled from 22 per cent in 1970 to 43 per cent in 1997.'

Once again it is useful to look at trends at specific institutions as well as the aggregate data. Shapiro (2002) reports that the ratio of full-time tenured and tenure-track faculty to total faculty in the California State University system typically averaged 70 to 75 per cent until 1990. Under significant budgetary pressure, the California State system adopted a policy of not replacing most of the tenured faculty who left through retirement, resignation, and death. Instead, many 'temporary' part-time instructors were hired. 'The result of these actions and trends was that by 2001 the ratio of tenured and tenure-track to total faculty lines in the system had dropped to 52 per cent' (Shapiro 2002).

After reviewing the national trends, the AAUP concluded that 'The proportion of faculty who are appointed each year to tenure-line positions is declining at an alarming rate' (AAUP 2003). This conference began with an examination of why colleges and universities are opting to replace retiring tenured faculty with shorter-term contract staff using a variety of different types of contracts. Key questions for discussion included:

- Whether this trend is temporary or can be expected to continue in the coming years?
- Should the AAUP be alarmed by the trend?
- Does a decline in the proportion of faculty who are tenure-track adversely affect the teaching and research missions of colleges and universities?
- Is the use of contract faculty driven by the financial realities of higher education?

- How is the recruitment of new tenure-track faculty related to the greater use of contract faculty?

These and other questions are addressed in chapters by Ronald Ehrenberg and Liang Zhang (Chapter 3) and Jennifer Ma and Paula Stephan (Chapter 4).

1.7   CHALLENGES AND OPPORTUNITIES

Considerable challenges are confronting institutions of higher education as their faculties age, budgets stagnant, retirement rates are low, and employment costs are rising. In this climate, academic administrators must reconsider their personnel policies and engage in strategic planning. The primary objective of this volume is to provide the framework for an in-depth analysis of the primary challenges associated with changes that are occurring in the academic labor market and to identify solutions and opportunities. Senior academic administrators should find the data and analysis presented in the following chapters very informative as they consider amending employment and compensation policies. Members of boards of trustees, state legislators, and federal policy-makers should also carefully consider the findings of these chapters as they attempt to provide the climate that will enable American colleges and universities to remain the best in the world.

NOTES

1. Full-time, tenured and tenure-track faculty tend to be older than part-time and full-time, non-tenure-track faculty. Anderson (2002) reports that the average age of full-time tenure-track faculty was 50 compared to 48 for part-time faculty and 46 for full-time, non-tenure-track staff. Thus, data for only full-time tenure track faculty would indicate an even older professoriate.
2. This research has been conducted in conjunction with Linda Ghent, Steven Allen, Ann McDermed, and Betsy Brown.
3. Ehrenberg et al. (2001) provide a useful description of these effects using Cornell as an example.
4. A series of early studies (Hammond and Morgan 1991, Holden and Hansen 1989, and Rees and Smith 1991) predicted that most faculty would continue to retire around traditional retirement ages; however, faculty at research institutions would tend to remain on the job longer now that they were not forced to retire.
5. Of course, some younger faculty are not awarded tenure and are required to leave the university and others leave voluntarily for employment at other institutions.
6. Ehrenberg et al. (2001) provides a thorough discussion of the impact of delayed retirement on annual hiring rates.
7. However, only about half of the colleges and universities extend pension coverage to their part-time faculty (Anderson 2002).

8. The incentives inherent in most defined benefit plans are clearly illustrated in Kotlikoff and Wise (1989) and Quinn et al. (1990).
9. Clark et al. (2004) found that 85 per cent of all new hires aged 45 years or younger by UNC between 1983 and 2000 selected a defined benefit plan instead of the state plan. Among faculty hired in 2000, 91 per cent opted for the defined contribution plans.
10. A survey by Watson Wyatt (1999) provides information on the incidence of phased retirement plans throughout the economy and finds that educational institutions are at the forefront of introducing phased retirement plans.
11. A survey by Hewitt Associates found that in 2003 10 per cent of companies with retiree health plans were eliminating coverage for future retirees, and 71 per cent were increasing retirees' contributions for coverage. A separate Hewitt survey found that 57 per cent of employers with 1000 or more employees offered health insurance to Medicare eligible retirees, down from 80 per cent in 1981 (*News and Observer* 2004).

REFERENCES

Allen, Steven G., Robert L. Clark and Linda S. Ghent (2004), 'Phasing into retirement', *Industrial and Labor Relations Review*, **58** (1), 112–27.
American Association of University Professors (AAUP) (2003), 'Contingent appointments and the academic profession', accessed February 2004 at www.aaup.org/statements/SpchState/contingent.htm.
American Association of University Professors (AAUP) (2004), 'Contingent faculty appointments', accessed February 2004 at www.aaup.org/Issues/part-time/index.htm.
Anderson, Eugene (2002), *The New Professoriate: Characteristics, Contributions, and Compensation*, Washington: American Council on Education Center for Policy Analysis.
Ashenfelter, Orley and David Card (2002), 'Did the elimination of mandatory retirement affect faculty retirement?', *American Economic Review*, **92** (4), 957–80.
Baldwin, Roger and Jay Chronister (2001), *Teaching Without Tenure: Policies and Practices for a New Era*, Baltimore, MD: Johns Hopkins University Press.
Benjamin, Ernst (2002), 'How over-reliance on contingent appointments diminishes faculty involvement in student learnings', accessed February 2004 at www.aacu.org/peerreview/pr-fa02/pr-fao2feature1.cfm.
Bowen, William and Julie Ann Sosa (1989), *Prospects for Faculty Retirement in the Arts and Sciences*, Princeton, NJ: Princeton University Press.
Clark, Robert and Madeleine d'Ambrosio (2003), 'Ignorance is not bliss', *Research Dialogue*, December, **78**, 1–14.
Clark, Robert and Linda Ghent (2004), 'Ending mandatory retirement: Its impact on retirement rates and faculty aging', unpublished working paper, North Carolina State University, Raleigh.
Clark, Robert and Brett Hammond (2001), *To Retire or Not? Retirement Policy and Practice in Higher Education*, Philadelphia: University of Pennsylvania Press.
Clark, Robert and Ann McDermed (1990), *The Choice of Pension Plans in a Changing Regulatory Environment*, Washington: American Enterprise Institute.
Clark, Robert, Linda Ghent and Alvin Headen (1994), 'Retiree health insurance and pension coverage: Variations by firm characteristics', *Journal of Gerontology*, **49** (2), S53–61.

Clark, Robert, Linda Ghent and Juanita Kreps (2001), 'Faculty retirement at three North Carolina universities', in Robert Clark and Brett Hammond (eds), *To Retire or Not? Retirement Policy and Practice in Higher Education*, Philadelphia: University of Pennsylvania Press, pp. 21–38.

Clark, Robert, Linda Ghent and Ann McDermed (2004), 'Pension plan choice among university faculty', unpublished working paper, North Carolina State University, Raleigh.

Conley, Valerie, David Leslie and Linda J. Zimbler (2002), 'Part-time instructional faculty and staff: Who they are, what they do, and what they think', *Education Statistics Quarterly*, **4** (2) (Summer), accessed at nces.ed.gov/programs/quarterly/vol 4/42/4-2.asp.

Ehrenberg, Ronald (2003a), 'The survey of changes in faculty retirement policies', American Association of University Professors, accessed January 2004 at http://www.aaup.org/Issues/retirement/retrpt.htm.

Ehrenberg, Ronald (2003b), 'Unequal progress: The annual report on the economic status of the profession, 2002–2003', accessed at http://www.aaup.org/surveys/zrp.htm.

Ehrenberg, Ronald, Michael Matier and David Fontanella (2001), 'Cornell confronts the end of mandatory retirement', in Robert Clark and Brett Hammond (eds), *To Retire or Not? Retirement Policy and Practice in Higher Education*, Philadelphia: University of Pennsylvania Press, pp. 81–105.

Freudenheim, Milt (2004), 'Companies limit health coverage of many retirees', *New York Times*, 3 February, p. 1.

Ghent, Linda, Steven Allen, and Robert Clark (2001), 'The impact of a new phased retirement option on faculty retirement decisions', *Research On Aging*, **23** (6), 671–93.

Giroux, Robert (1999), 'Faculty renewal: the numbers, the director', speech presented at the Association of Universities and Colleges of Canada general meeting, Brandon, Manitoba, accessed at www:aucc.ca/pdf/english/speeches/1999/faculty.

Hammond, Brett and Harriet Morgan (eds) (1991), *Ending Mandatory Retirement for Tenured Faculty*, Washington, DC: National Academy Press, pp. 21–38.

Holden, Karen and Lee Hansen (eds), (1989), *The End of Mandatory Retirement in Higher Education*, San Francisco: Jossey-Bass.

Kotlikoff, Laurence and David Wise (1989), *The Wage Carrot and the Pension Stick*, Kalamazoo, MI: Upjohn Institute for Employment Research.

National Center for Education Statistics (2002), *Digest of Education Statistics*, Washington, DC: US Department of Education.

News and Observer (2004), 'Retirees losing health benefits', 15 January, p. D2.

Parsad, Basmat, Denise Glover and Linda Zimbler (2002), *Tenure Status of Postsecondary Instructional Faculty and Staff: 1992–1998*, Washington, DC: National Center for Education Statistics, July accessed at http://nces.ed.gov/pubs 2002/2002210.pdf.

Pencavel, John (2001), 'The response of employees to severance incentives: The University of California's faculty, 1991–1994', *Journal of Human Resources*, **36** (1), 58–84.

Purcell, Pat (2002), 'Pensions and retirement savings plans: Sponsorship and participation', *CRS Report for Congress*, October 7.

Quinn, Joseph, Richard Burkhauser and Daniel Myers (1990), *Passing the Torch: The Influence of Economic Incentives on Work and Retirement*, Kalamazoo, MI: Upjohn Institute for Employment Research.

Rees, Albert and Sharon Smith (1991), *Faculty Retirement in the Arts and Sciences*, Princeton, NJ: Princeton University Press.

Robinson, Ira and Everett Lee (1993), 'The aging of faculty in American colleges and universities: Demographic trends and implications', in Nancy Julius and Herbert Krauss (eds), *The Aging Work Force*, Washington, DC: College and University Personnel Association, pp. 41–58.

Shapiro, Mark (2002), 'Irreverent commentary on the state of education in America today', *The Irascible Professor*, 27 March, accessed at www.irascibleprofessor.com/comments-03-27-02.

Switkes, Ellen (2000), 'The University of California voluntary early retirement incentive programs', in Robert Clark and Brett Hammond (eds), *To Retire or Not? Retirement Policy and Practice in Higher Education*, Philadelphia: University of Pennsylvania Press, pp. 106–21.

Watson Wyatt (1999), *Phased Retirement: Reshaping the End of Work*, Watson Wyatt Consulting research report, Lake Oswego, OR.

2. Filling the gap: finding and keeping faculty for the university of the future

Molly Corbett Broad

Never before in the history of America has a university education been more important since, in a knowledge-based global economy, our only competitive advantage is our people and the skills, innovation, and know-how they bring to the table. That truth has considerable implications as our nation's universities seek to find and retain the faculty needed to serve future generations of students.

The most important and distinguishing characteristic of American universities is the social compact that connects the people, their government, and their universities. American universities serve the nation's interests through a unique three-part mission: excellent teaching, research, and practical service to our citizens. The manifestations of these components have evolved over time in response to new social and economic challenges, yet the core missions have remained intact.

2.1 FORCES OF GLOBAL CHANGE

Several powerful forces of global change are dramatically impacting higher education, however. The evolution and integration of technology, knowledge, and economics is fast creating a single global market. As the Internet and emerging technologies proliferate, they will continue to drive globalization forward. They ensure that how we communicate, how we invest, and how we look at the world will be increasingly global.

Prosperity now requires more than seizing, holding, and exploiting land and natural resources. The competition for the best information and knowledge workers has replaced the competition for the best farmland or oilfield. As a result, we are facing a boom in the demand for education and training, as well as the need to rethink the way in which that education is delivered. The transition to a knowledge-based economy is creating a fertile environment for innovation and change in the education sector. Universities are being viewed as major economic resources to an extent never witnessed before. And not surprisingly, the US model of investing in education and research as a mechanism for economic development is rapidly being adopted around the world, creating a globally competitive knowledge economy.

Increasingly powerful computing applications have helped facilitate an explosion of new knowledge. As a result, we within the higher education community are being forced to adapt, not only to the sheer volume of new knowledge, but also to the velocity of change. Lyman and Varian (2001) of the University of California at Berkeley are involved in an ongoing research project that attempts to measure how much information is produced in the world each year. Based on their findings, they estimate that:

> the people of the world generate an estimated two billion gigabytes of information each year. This massive amount of information represents the aggregate total of all new printed, film, optical, magnetic, and Internet media. Divided among the world's six billion people, this averages to approximately 250 megabytes of new data per person per year. What's more, 93 per cent of new data is stored digitally. If all of this information were placed onto standard floppy disks, the stack would reach two million miles high.

Nowhere is the impact of this knowledge explosion more apparent than in the life sciences, particularly the interrelated fields of genomics and bioinformatics. Genomics has been described as the 'new Internet', the next industry that will undergo the explosive growth and world-altering impact that has accompanied the rise of information technologies. And like computer power, genomics is expected to grow exponentially. Yet whereas we once believed that our mapped genetic code would offer up a detailed 'blueprint of humanity', we now know that at best it provides an index or table of contents to a vast encyclopedia of biological information. We have barely scratched the surface.

These forces of global change are transforming our economy as well. Information technology now plays a central role in the American economy. More Americans now make computers than make cars. More spend their days processing data than processing petroleum. Knowledge jobs are growing three-to-six times as fast as economy-wide job growth (Moe and Blodget 2000). It is increasingly clear that those who are adequately educated will be positioned economically to survive and thrive in the global economy. Those who are not risk becoming economically obsolete. For that reason, adults aged 25 and over now represent half of all postsecondary enrollments in the USA.

A study by the Business-Higher Education Forum (1999), an organization of US business and university CEOs, found that to succeed in an environment of continuous change, American business leaders say they need workers who have learned *how* to learn, to think critically, work in teams, reason analytically, communicate effectively, use information technologies, and perform in diverse settings. What does this mean for American higher education? Gone forever is the time when mastering a body of knowledge in your early 20s could suffice for a lifetime. In the global economy, a four-year degree is just a prerequisite to participating in the industries of the future. Lifelong learning is now required for survival and economic longevity, and technology has emerged as the great facilitator. Consequently, higher education is facing new expectations and demands from several different directions, including high school graduates who have spent much of their lives on the Internet; employers and employees looking to bolster their competitiveness; and government leaders looking to universities as economic catalysts.

The pending retirement of baby boomers will only heighten the growing demand for highly trained workers in the USA. Between 2000 and 2020, the percentage of the US population over age 60 is projected to rise from 16 per cent to nearly 23 per cent. The median age of the population will rise to 38.6 years during that period. By 2020, even the nation's youngest boomers will be well beyond their prime working years. It is noteworthy that countries such as China, Brazil, Mexico, and India – all countries that are on the verge of creating a middle-class in their economies – have populations that are significantly younger (Population Division 2001).

The 'graying of America' and the baby-boomer retirements that accompany it will have a major impact on workforce preparedness. In fact, we arguably are on the verge of a critical shortage of workers with college-level skills. If US employers cannot find skilled workers at home, they will be forced to look overseas, a strategy that already is causing economic consequences for the USA. On the other hand, if we can produce a workforce proficient in the learning skills needed to adapt to job changes, enormous economic benefits could result.

The percentage of newly created US jobs requiring high levels of skills and education has been escalating rapidly in recent years, now approaching 85 per cent. Given our aging workforce, if the USA maintains current levels of educational attainment, and if trends in the growth of jobs requiring at least some college training continue, by 2020 the USA will face a shortage of about 12 million college-educated workers (Business – Higher Education Forum 2003). This disconnect underscores the need to boost the percentage of our citizens seeking higher education.

2.2 THE GRAYING OF THE PROFESSORIATE AND TRENDS IN EARNED DOCTORATES

University faculty are aging along with the general population, with dire implications for the future. Large numbers of faculty hired in the 1960s and 1970s – in response to the baby boom – are now in their 50s and 60s and approaching traditional retirement age, just as the 'echo boomers' are enrolling in unprecedented numbers.

According to the National Center for Education Statistics, in 1987 roughly half of US college faculty were between the ages of 40 and 54. The remainder were fairly equally divided between those who were under age 40 and those who were age 55 or older. That distribution shifted quite dramatically over the next decade, however. By 1998, the percentage of instructional faculty at US two- and four-year institutions who were under age 40 had declined to below 20 per cent, while the percentage over age 55 had soared to nearly 40 per cent (US Department of Education 2002). This trend is continuing at a time when, in most parts of the country, we are experiencing significant increases in university enrollment.

While there are no comprehensive national analyses that examine projected faculty retirements versus production of new PhDs, the data that are available offer ample cause for concern. According to the 2002 Survey of Earned Doctorates, US universities conferred just under 40 000 doctorates during the 2001–02 year, marking a 6-per cent decline since 1998. The 2002 total was the lowest since 1993.

As the survey reveals, some fields have gained in relative share of doctorates awarded in recent decades, while others have lost ground. In the humanities and social sciences, most fields barely held their own over the past three decades, with PhD production in many fields now below 1972 levels. Fields experiencing steady or significant gains include the biological sciences, computer sciences, health sciences, and engineering. Conversely, in chemistry, mathematics, physics and astronomy, the number of doctorates awarded in 2002 fell to below 1972 levels.

The survey also highlights significant shifts in the citizenship of the potential faculty pool. US citizens received only 70 per cent of all doctorates earned in 2002 by individuals who identified their citizenship status, continuing a steady increase in foreign doctoral enrollment. The percentage of new doctorates awarded to individuals on temporary visas rose from 9 per cent in 1972 to 26 per cent in 2002. Over the past three decades, these foreign students on temporary visas have accounted for virtually all of the overall growth in the number of doctorates awarded. The five leading countries of origin for foreign students are China, South Korea, India, Taiwan, and Canada. China alone accounts for 7 per cent of all US doctorates awarded. These foreign students are concentrated in the natural sciences and engineering fields, accounting for more than half of all US enrollments in those key fields.[1]

Nearly three-quarters of 2002 doctoral recipients had definite post-graduation commitments for employment or continued study. Some 31 per cent – the highest level ever recorded in the Survey – planned post-doctoral studies. Those pursuing postdoctoral study were more likely to be non-citizens on temporary visas, concentrated in the physical and life sciences. Among US citizens, only 55 per cent of new doctoral recipients with firm employment commitments cited education as their intended work sector – a cause for some concern as we prepare to replace large numbers of retiring faculty.

The US model of investing in education and research as a mechanism for economic development is rapidly being adopted around the world, creating a globally competitive knowledge economy. For developing countries, replicating the industrial infrastructure needed to compete in the global marketplace is prohibitively expensive. So they are increasingly focusing on achieving economic success through developing better educated work-forces, which a networked economy will allow them to use to their competitive advantage.

For example, Abdul Khan, former rector of the Open University of New Delhi and now with UNESCO, has noted that software engineering has become the path out of poverty and into wealth for his country. Some of the wealthiest people in India today have achieved that status by riding the IT revolution. They have eclipsed centuries in which traditional family wealth has been handed from one generation to the next.

Ireland is another country that is leveraging strategic investments in education and research in order to leapfrog the industrial age right into the knowledge age. This small country is investing heavily in university-based training and research, particularly in the biotechnology field.

Like Ireland, China is investing heavily in developing a skilled workforce. About a year ago, I was with some officials for the Education Ministry of China, who were talking about economic development and some of their goals and strategies. It became clear that China's primary economic development strategy is to increase its college-going rate from 2 per cent in 1990 to 20 per cent by 2020. Imagine how many millions of individuals that represents in a population the magnitude of China! Perhaps some of the post-docs who are today working in the finest American laboratories will be drawn back to their own counties to help meet their growing demand for higher education.

2.3 THE UNIVERSITY OF NORTH CAROLINA RESPONSE

What do such national and global trends mean for the future of American higher education? The experience of my own institution – the 16-campus University of North Carolina – offers a case study of the issues facing colleges and universities across the nation. The first public university in America to open its doors, UNC encompasses all public institutions in the state that grant baccalaureate degrees or higher, and enrolls more than 183 000 students. We are moving from a period of relatively stable enrollment into a sustained period of unprecedented growth. Our campuses have absorbed an additional 20 000 students over the past three years alone, and expect to add another 50 000 students within a decade. This growth is driven not only by a surge in the number of students graduating from North Carolina high schools, but also by a growing number of older students returning to the University to upgrade their job skills.

A recent analysis of faculty aging trends within UNC over the period 1982–2000 confirms that our age distribution is shifting in a manner that mirrors national data. In fact, somewhere around 1990 the age composition of UNC's faculty reversed itself. Across all UNC campuses – regardless of size and mission – there have been substantial decreases in the proportion of faculty under age 40 and large increases in the proportion of faculty over 55, including those aged 70 and over.

While national data on future supply and demand in the academic labor market do not offer a coherent picture of the impact of an aging faculty and escalating enrollment, UNC has made some projections related to our growth. In 2001, we concluded that we would need to hire more than 10 000 additional faculty over the decade to meet enrollment growth needs and replace faculty who retired or resigned. By 2003–04, enrollment growth was already higher than projected, such that we have had to hire about 300 more faculty than anticipated at this point.

Some UNC campuses – particularly our two research-extensive institutions – report increasing difficulty in retaining faculty who receive offers of higher salaries, better benefits, and more extensive research support than UNC can match. Because we have not received new state funding for salary increases in three years, other UNC campuses report increasing difficulty in hiring new faculty because of non-competitive salary and benefits. This is exacerbated by the growing salary gap between public and private universities.

We know there is no single solution that can solve the growing set of challenges with ensuring a sufficient pool of faculty for the university of the future. Within UNC, we are pursuing several strategies grouped around greater management flexibility, more competitive personnel policies and programs, a phased retirement program for faculty, and the use of surveys targeted at faculty in varying stages of their careers.

To help our campuses become more nimble in addressing the faculty challenge, we are delegating greater authority in hiring and compensation to our local boards of trustees. We also are monitoring non-tenure-track hiring patterns across the University, and are targeting funds generated by recent tuition increases to reduce class size, add course sections, and increase tenure-track appointments.

In the human resources arena, we are developing new benefit policies (e.g., disability, parental leave), more flexible leave options, and cafeteria plans. We also have been successful in expanding faculty eligibility for participation in the state's Optional Retirement Program. Looking to the future, we hope to secure authority from the state to establish our own UNC Human Resource System, one that would be separate and apart from a cumbersome state bureaucracy.

Since 1998, UNC has had in place a Phased Retirement Program that allows tenured faculty to retire and be rehired on a half-time basis for a three-to five-year period. Over the six-year life of the program, about one-third of all eligible faculty have participated in this program. As reflected in recent surveys, satisfaction with the program is extremely high. Nearly 95 per cent of participants indicate that, given the choice, they would choose to enter the program again. However, a large majority also indicated that they would have continued working full-time had the phased-retirement option not been available.

With support from the TIAA-CREF Institute, UNC is conducting a number of targeted surveys to gauge faculty attitudes and intentions. We recently concluded a survey of senior faculty (age 50+) that produced a number of interesting findings. The mean age of respondents was 58, and their average projected retirement age was 66. Yet the anticipated time to retirement tended to rise in step with respondents' age. Among respondents 60 and older, for example, the projected retirement age was 68. About one-third of all respondents anticipated entering UNC's Phased Retirement Program, consistent with current experience.

On average, UNC's senior faculty anticipate needing about three-quarters of their current income in retirement, and the economy – including stock market performance – is clearly a factor in retirement decisions. Health benefits are their overwhelming concern as they plan for retirement.

UNC is preparing to conduct a parallel survey of newly hired and newly tenured faculty to identify issues related to recruitment and retention of this faculty cohort. It is anticipated that a number of factors will be identified – in addition to salary and benefits – that UNC campuses can use to improve faculty recruitment and retention during the next decade.

If UNC – and other colleges and universities across the nation – are unable to figure out the right combination of programs and policies that will ensure our ongoing ability to attract and retain the finest faculty, the excellence that defines American higher education may be at great risk. Our economic prosperity as a nation hinges on the outcome. We are not alone in that realization. As noted earlier, other nations are systematically executing economic development strategies founded on increasing their college-going rates and investing in technology and research infrastructure.

Two decades after *A Nation at Risk* (US Department of Education 1983) warned of a 'rising tide of mediocrity' within the US educational system, we must admit that we have not risen to the education challenge posed by globalization with the same commitment – or the same focused passion and leadership – that characterized our 1950s reaction to Sputnik and the threat it posed to our scientific and technological superiority. Sputnik spurred American universities to develop extraordinary capabilities in basic scientific research, advanced educational partnerships with government and industry, and propelled US universities into an unquestioned leadership position for the remainder of the twentieth century. That superiority may soon be challenged.

If the American university is to survive and prosper in the years ahead, we must embrace change and explore new ways of recruiting and retaining high-quality faculty. We must develop better models for analysing the academic labor market, and must address serious policy issues related to recruitment, retention, and retirement. But at every step of the process, we must ensure that we remain true to our three-part mission and to the pursuit of excellence.

NOTE

1. More recently, federal Student and Exchange Visitor Information System (SEVIS) regulations appear to have had a dramatic negative impact on foreign student applications at the graduate level, especially those from China. According to a survey conducted by the Council of Graduate Schools, total international applications to responding graduate schools for fall 2004 declined 32 per cent from fall 2003. More than three-quarters of responding schools reported declines in applications from China.

REFERENCES

Business-Higher Education Forum (1999), *Spanning the Chasm: Corporate and Academic Cooperation to Improve Work-force Preparation*, Washington, DC: American Council on Education, June.

Business-Higher Education Forum (2003), *Building a Nation of Learners*, Washington, DC: American Council on Education, June.

Lyman, Peter and Hal Varian (2001), University of California at Berkley, March, accessed at www.sims.berkley.edu/how-much-info.

Moe, Michael T. and Henry Blodget (eds) (2000), *The Knowledge Web*, Merrill Lynch Knowledge Enterprises Group presentation, May.

Population Division (2001), Department of Economic and Social Affairs of the United Nations Secretariat.

US Department of Education (1983), *A Nation at Risk: the Imperative for Educational Reform*; an open letter to the American people, National Commission on Excellence in Education report, April.

US Department of Education (2002), *Digest of Education Statistics*, Washington, DC: National Centre for Education Statistics.

3. The changing nature of faculty employment

Ronald G. Ehrenberg and Liang Zhang

3.1 INTRODUCTION

The last two decades of the twentieth century saw a significant growth in the shares of faculty members in American colleges and universities that are part-time or are full-time without tenure-track status (Anderson 2002, Baldwin and Chronister 2001, Conley et al. 2002). Growing student enrollments faced by academic institutions during tight financial times, and growing differentials between the salaries of part-time and full-time non-tenure-track faculty on the one hand, and tenured and tenure-track faculty on the other hand, are among the explanations given for these trends. However, surprisingly, there have been few econometric studies that seek to test whether these hypotheses are true.[1]

Our chapter begins by presenting information, broken down by form of control (public/private) and 1994 Carnegie category, on how the proportions of full-time faculty at four-year American colleges and universities that are tenured, on tenure tracks and are not on tenure tracks have changed since 1989, using information for a consistent sample of institutions from the annual IPEDS Faculty Salary Surveys and the biennial IPEDS Fall Staff Surveys.[2] The latter source also permits us to present similar estimates of the proportions of faculty that are employed part-time and the share of new full-time faculty appointments that are not on tenure tracks.

To analyse the role that economic variables play in causing changes in faculty employment across categories, we conduct two types of econometric analyses. First, in section 3.3, we use panel data to estimate demand functions for tenure and tenure-track faculty on the one hand, and full-time non-tenure-track faculty on the other hand, to learn how changes in revenues per student and the average salaries of different types of full-time faculty influence the distribution of faculty across categories of full-time faculty. We do this using both models that assume instantaneous adjustments of employment of different types of faculty to changes in revenues and salaries of different types of faculty and models that permit adjustments of faculty employment to these changes to take place over a number of periods.

Second, in section 3.4, we estimate models that seek to explain the flow of new hires of each type of faculty member (rather than the levels of faculty employment) using data on new hires that are available from the IPEDS Fall Staff Surveys. To explain new hires, in addition to information on changes in revenues per student, changes in enrollment and the levels of faculty salaries, we require information on the number of vacant faculty positions that are potentially available to be filled. We construct information on the latter using data on the number of continuing full-time faculty members at an institution each year that the American Association of University Professors (AAUP) collects (but does not publish) as part of its annual salary survey.

Continuing faculty members in a rank are defined as the number of faculty members in a rank one year, who also are on the payroll of the institution in the next year, regardless of their rank in the second year. Summing up an institution's continuing faculty members across ranks in a year and subtracting that number from the institution's total faculty employment in the previous year provides us with an estimate of the number of full-time faculty vacancies that an institution could have filled in a year if it had replaced each of its departing full-time faculty members.

A brief concluding section summarizes our findings and discusses their implications for American colleges and universities and their students.

3.2 CHANGES IN FACULTY COMPOSITION

Table 3.1 provides annual data on the share of full-time faculty members that are not employed in tenured or tenure-track positions at four-year colleges and universities in the United States for the 1989 to 1999 period. The data come from the annual IPEDS Faculty Salary Surveys and are tabulated separately by form of control and 1994 Carnegie category. Because a few institutions fail to report survey data each year, we restrict our attention to a sample of 504 public and 854 private colleges and universities that responded to the survey each year.

In the aggregate, the ratio of full-time non-tenure-track faculty to total full-time faculty rose from 0.110 to 0.137 at the public institutions in the sample, and from 0.142 to 0.197 at the private institutions in the sample. Contrary to what one might have expected, given the well-known budget problems of public higher education during the period, the increased usage

Table 3.1   Ratio of full-time non-tenure-track faculty/total full-time faculty

	1989	1990	1991	1992	1993	1994	1995	1996	1997	1998	1999*
Public (sample size)											
Research I (59)	0.099	0.100	0.099	0.099	0.097	0.101	0.099	0.102	0.112	0.121	0.128
Research II (26)	0.109	0.105	0.100	0.095	0.094	0.096	0.096	0.102	0.112	0.120	0.123
Doctoral I (28)	0.117	0.117	0.114	0.110	0.116	0.119	0.121	0.124	0.128	0.149	0.160
Doctoral II (38)	0.121	0.126	0.129	0.125	0.121	0.128	0.121	0.132	0.133	0.139	0.149
Comprehensive I (246)	0.111	0.117	0.108	0.111	0.107	0.109	0.111	0.114	0.124	0.128	0.138
Comprehensive II (25)	0.148	0.138	0.129	0.153	0.133	0.129	0.129	0.127	0.135	0.131	0.160
Liberal arts I (7)	0.213	0.220	0.203	0.180	0.157	0.116	0.120	0.125	0.103	0.092	0.103
Liberal arts II (75)	0.134	0.131	0.134	0.140	0.147	0.138	0.139	0.135	0.141	0.153	0.165
Total	0.110	0.112	0.108	0.108	0.107	0.109	0.109	0.112	0.121	0.128	0.137
Private (sample size)											
Research I (29)	0.124	0.173	0.148	0.171	0.167	0.159	0.166	0.172	0.151	0.156	0.154
Research II (11)	0.065	0.083	0.078	0.089	0.095	0.108	0.113	0.118	0.121	0.128	0.127
Doctoral I (23)	0.092	0.105	0.107	0.102	0.088	0.161	0.141	0.154	0.163	0.180	0.194
Doctoral II (22)	0.123	0.096	0.107	0.102	0.141	0.123	0.090	0.107	0.115	0.132	0.141
Comprehensive I (180)	0.146	0.171	0.165	0.182	0.190	0.181	0.189	0.193	0.203	0.193	0.221
Comprehensive II (65)	0.186	0.258	0.253	0.265	0.260	0.215	0.223	0.223	0.225	0.233	0.226
Liberal arts I (156)	0.109	0.102	0.095	0.097	0.098	0.099	0.102	0.109	0.115	0.119	0.130
Liberal arts II (368)	0.226	0.244	0.250	0.259	0.275	0.284	0.275	0.277	0.288	0.295	0.306
Total	0.142	0.165	0.158	0.169	0.175	0.176	0.176	0.182	0.184	0.187	0.197

Note: *The estimates for 1999 are based on preliminary data released by NCES (2004)

Source: National Center for Educational Statistics (NCES) IPEDS Faculty Salary Survey

of full-time non-tenure-track faculty was larger at the private than at the public institutions. Moreover, for almost all Carnegie categories, the share of full-time faculty that is not on tenure tracks was higher in 1999 at private institutions than it was at public institutions.[3]

Appendix A provides similar tabulations for the 1989 to 2001 period using data from the biennial IPEDS Fall Staff Surveys.[4] There are a number of important differences in the definition of faculty in the two surveys. The Staff Survey includes faculty on visiting appointments, while the Faculty Salary Survey does not. Inasmuch as visitors are non-tenure-track appointments (from the perspective of the reporting institution) this will cause the shares of non-tenure-track employees to be higher in the Staff Survey. The Faculty Salary Survey is restricted to instructional faculty, while the Fall Staff Survey also includes faculty without any instructional responsibilities who are entirely on research or public service appointments. This also probably leads the share of full-time faculty that is on non-tenure-track appointments to be higher in the Staff Survey data.

The tabulations in Appendix Table A.1 are for a sample of 319 public and 761 private four-year colleges and universities that participated in the Staff Survey each year. While the share of full-time faculty on non-tenure tracks is also higher at private institutions than at public institutions in this sample, the increase was greater during the period at the publics than at the privates, due primarily to large increases at the public Research I and Research II institutions. This suggests that a growing usage of full-time non-tenure-track faculty positions for full-time researchers may be responsible for the increases at these institutions.

In Table 3.2, we provide some evidence on the growing usage of part-time faculty members. Part-time faculty data are available in the Fall Staff Survey but not in the Faculty Salary Survey. The numbers presented in the table represent the ratio of total part-time faculty members to total full-time faculty members at a set of institutions that were both in the sample each year and reported positive numbers of part-time faculty members in each year.[5] The ratios are calculated using a sample of 352 public and 483 private institutions.

During the 1989 to 2001 period, the ratio of part-time to full-time faculty members rose from 0.269 to 0.377 at the public institutions in the sample and from 0.499 to 0.686 at the private institutions in the sample. In 2001, the share of part-time faculty was higher for each Carnegie category of institution at private institutions than it was at public institutions.

Finally, the Fall Staff Survey also contains information on whether faculty members who are newly hired during the academic year are on tenured, tenure-track or non-tenure-track appointments. Remembering

Table 3.2   Ratio of part-time faculty/total full-time faculty

	1989	1991	1993	1995	1997	1999[a]	2001[a]
Public (sample size)							
Research I (50)	0.211	0.195	0.229	0.222	0.285	0.268	0.260
Research II (22)	0.153	0.214	0.175	0.197	0.201	0.224	0.219
Doctoral I (23)	0.304	0.316	0.364	0.358	0.348	0.394	0.352
Doctoral II (34)	0.335	0.234	0.329	0.380	0.407	0.455	0.503
Comprehensive I (174)	0.350	0.352	0.397	0.415	0.454	0.478	0.541
Comprehensive II (10)	0.372	0.387	0.383	0.373	0.456	0.557	0.484
Liberal arts I (2)[b]	–	–	–	–	–	–	–
Liberal arts II (37)	0.484	0.558	0.611	0.658	0.674	0.667	0.631
Total	0.269	0.263	0.298	0.306	0.347	0.365	0.377
Private (sample size)							
Research I (22)	0.215	0.300	0.387	0.440	0.494	0.329	0.416
Research II (8)	0.430	0.351	0.410	0.418	0.406	0.464	0.420
Doctoral I (12)	0.792	0.631	0.694	0.702	1.043	1.127	0.923
Doctoral II (13)	0.551	0.634	0.633	0.780	0.816	0.643	0.643
Comprehensive I (109)	0.909	0.882	0.945	1.032	1.016	1.045	1.186
Comprehensive II (36)	0.708	0.745	1.083	1.116	1.239	0.903	0.949
Liberal arts I (111)	0.309	0.330	0.367	0.349	0.391	0.320	0.358
Liberal arts II (172)	0.685	0.766	0.852	0.887	0.947	0.788	0.885
Total	0.499	0.532	0.599	0.643	0.697	0.622	0.686

Notes:
[a] The numbers for 1999 and 2001 are from preliminary data released by the NCES
[b] Proportions not reported because of the small sample size

Source: National Center for Educational Statistics, IPEDs Fall Staff Survey (2004)

that these data include visiting faculty members and faculty members on research or public service appointments who do not have any instructional responsibilities, Table 3.3 presents information for the 1989 to 2001 period on the shares of new faculty appointments that are neither tenured nor on tenure-tracks. These tabulations are for a set of 383 public and 516 private institutions that reported data on new faculty hires each year.

Overall, the share of new full-time faculty appointments not on tenure tracks increased from 0.460 to 0.515 at public institutions and from 0.452 to 0.573 at private institutions in the sample during the period. Increasingly, new faculty members at four-year colleges and universities in the United States are being appointed to positions that are not on tenure tracks.[6]

Table 3.3   Ratio of non-tenured new hires/total new hires

	1989	1991	1993	1995	1997	1999*	2001*
Public (sample size)							
Research I (53)	0.543	0.546	0.575	0.558	0.622	0.684	0.573
Research II (25)	0.411	0.372	0.501	0.475	0.545	0.524	0.523
Doctoral I (22)	0.481	0.565	0.495	0.461	0.495	0.564	0.514
Doctoral II (31)	0.377	0.418	0.509	0.516	0.536	0.505	0.502
Comprehensive I (191)	0.395	0.382	0.410	0.410	0.429	0.435	0.429
Comprehensive II (17)	0.410	0.357	0.385	0.314	0.415	0.488	0.532
Liberal arts I (3)	0.449	0.577	0.559	0.382	0.531	0.339	0.451
Liberal arts II (41)	0.404	0.398	0.393	0.450	0.411	0.435	0.566
Total	0.460	0.460	0.494	0.485	0.529	0.565	0.515
Private (sample size)							
Research I (25)	0.636	0.594	0.630	0.602	0.708	0.656	0.700
Research II (10)	0.409	0.511	0.536	0.459	0.460	0.457	0.423
Doctoral I (16)	0.528	0.466	0.562	0.568	0.528	0.413	0.641
Doctoral II (13)	0.328	0.324	0.456	0.588	0.416	0.452	0.499
Comprehensive I (117)	0.351	0.476	0.416	0.507	0.418	0.526	0.461
Comprehensive II (39)	0.310	0.351	0.477	0.451	0.359	0.441	0.443
Liberal arts I (119)	0.427	0.447	0.494	0.508	0.556	0.563	0.583
Liberal arts II (177)	0.281	0.302	0.386	0.360	0.405	0.448	0.547
Total	0.452	0.473	0.503	0.518	0.526	0.542	0.573

Note: *The numbers for 1999 and 2001 are from preliminary data released by NCES

Source: National Center for Education Statistics, IPEDs Fall Staff Survey (2004)

3.3   THE DEMAND FOR TENURE-TRACK AND NON-TENURE-TRACK FACULTY MEMBERS

Consider an academic institution which, for simplicity, hires only two types of faculty members – tenure and tenure-track (F_T) and non-tenure-track (F_N). The latter category includes both full-time and part-time faculty members. The academic institution is assumed to derive benefits from hiring more of each type of faculty member relative to the number of full-time equivalent students that are enrolled at the institution (E). Mathematically, this is expressed by saying that it derives utility from its employment of each category relative to its number of full-time equivalent enrolled students.

$$U(F_T/E, F_N/E) \tag{3.1}$$

Tenured and tenure-track faculty members are important to the academic institution because, in addition to teaching, they: advise students about their courses of study and provide advice and letters of recommendation for postgraduate education and employment opportunities; conduct research; share governance responsibilities with the administration and the trustees; and provide long-term stability to the institution. Full-time non-tenure-track faculty may be important to the institution because, in the absence of the responsibility to produce research, they can be assigned higher teaching loads and can specialize in teaching. Part-time non-tenure-track faculty are valuable because, in areas in which there is a large supply of people willing to work in such positions, they provide the institution with an inventory of instructors who can be hired at the last moment to meet fluctuations in demand. In fields that deal directly with 'real world' matters, such as engineering and business, full-time employed profession-als willing to teach part-time also provide a type of specialized instruction that institutions might otherwise not be able to offer. In a world in which revenue sources are increasingly uncertain, both types of non-tenure-track faculty members provide the academic institution with flexibility in meeting rapid changes in its financial situation that the tenure system would otherwise constrain it from doing.

Suppose that the average salary per full-time tenured and tenure-track faculty member to the institution is S_T and the average salary per non-tenure-track faculty member is S_N. If the funds, per full-time equivalent student, that the institution has available to employ faculty are B/E and the institution seeks to maximize its utility from hiring faculty members subject to the constraint that the employment budget is exhausted, then the employment demand curves (3.2) and (3.3) will result.

$$F_T/E = F_T/E(S_T, S_N, B/E) \qquad (3.2)$$

$$F_N/E = F_N/E(S_T, S_N, B/E) \qquad (3.3)$$

The employment of each type of faculty per full-time equivalent student will depend upon the salaries for both types of faculty members and the funds that are available to employ faculty members. Other factors held constant, when a faculty type's average salary level rises an institution will hire fewer of that type of faculty member and, if its demand for that type of faculty members is elastic with respect to the faculty type's average salary, substitute more faculty members of the other type.[7] An increase in the per full-time equivalent student faculty employment budget will usually lead to an increase in both types of faculty members per full-time equivalent student. This is likely to be true for institutions that do not have a strong research component in their faculty members' portfolio of responsibilities. However institutions that value research highly might employ fewer non-tenure-track faculty members as their faculty employment budget expands.

In this section, we employ nine years of institutional level data that span the fall 1989 to fall 1997 period to estimate variants of equations (3.2) and (3.3) for a national sample of four-year colleges and universities. Because no information is available to us on the salaries paid to part-time faculty members, we confine our attention only to the employment of full-time faculty members. Initially, we treat all professorial level faculty (professors, associate professors and assistant professors) as tenured and tenure-track faculty, all lecturers as non-tenure-track faculty and exclude instructors from the analyses.[8] These assumptions allow us to easily compute average faculty salary variables for tenured and tenure-track and for non-tenure-track faculty members at each institution. However, nationally a small percentage of professorial faculty are actually not on tenure-track lines and a small percentage of lecturers are tenured or on tenure-track lines. Hence, we relax these assumptions below and also include instructors in the analyses.

Table 3.4 provides estimates of four different specifications of models based upon equations (3.2) and (3.3). All are estimated in logarithmic form and include institutional level dichotomous $(0, 1)$ variables to control for differences in the nature of the curriculum, the research intensity of the institution and other omitted forces that might influence the usage of different types of faculty members. Inasmuch as the funds available to employ faculty depends upon the revenues coming into the institution, in each equation we replace the per full-time equivalent student faculty employment budget of an institution by its revenues per full-time equivalent student that are available to hire faculty members.[9]

Panel A provides baseline estimates. The elasticities of both professorial faculty and lecturers with respect to revenue per student are both close to unity – a given percentage change in revenue per student leads to approximately the same percentage changes in employment of both types of faculty. Professorial faculty members' employment is very sensitive to their own salaries – a given percentage change in professorial faculty members' average salaries is associated with approximately an equal but opposite percentage change in their employment level – but is insensitive to the salary levels of lecturers. In contrast, lecturers' employment levels are not very sensitive to their own salary levels – a given percentage change in lecturers' salaries leads to a much smaller percentage change in the opposite direction in their employment level – and is negatively related to the salary levels of professorial faculty. As we shall show, the latter result does not continue to hold in models that allow for gradual adjustment of faculty employment levels to faculty salary levels.

Panel B presents similar estimates for equations that also include dichotomous (0,1) variables for each year. The latter are included to control for omitted variables that may vary systematically over time and influence the demand for faculty members. For example, in years in which students' financial need is high, colleges and universities may have to use more funds for institutional grant aid and thus have fewer resources available to employ faculty members. While the inclusion of the year dichotomous variables marginally reduces the magnitudes (in absolute value) of the responsiveness of faculty employment levels to faculty salaries, in the main the results are similar to those in panel A.

The estimates in panels A and B assume that faculty employment levels adjust instantaneously to changes in faculty salaries. However, there may be lags in the adjustment process due to the presence of tenured faculty members and tenure-track and non-tenure-track faculty members who are on multiyear contracts. To allow for only partial adjustment of faculty employment levels to changes in faculty salaries and revenue in a year, panels C and D present estimates of models that include lagged (one year) values of the logarithm of the faculty category's employment level as an additional explanatory variable.[10] These models are estimated using dynamic estimation methods that control for the endogeneity of the lagged dependent variables (see Arellano and Bond, 1991).

The coefficient of the lagged dependent variable in the professorial employment equation is very close to zero, which implies that an almost immediate adjustment of tenure and tenure-track faculty employment levels to changes in their salary levels occurs. This implies that normal voluntary turnover creates sufficient vacancies each year that adjustment to new desired employment levels can rapidly occur, even when desired employment levels are falling. In contrast, there is evidence of somewhat slower adjustment in the demand for non-tenure-track faculty members.[11] Moreover, once we allow for only partial adjustment to changing salaries and revenue to occur, the demand for both tenure and tenure-track faculty members on the one hand, and non-tenure-track faculty members on the other hand, become relatively insensitive to changes in their own salaries – a given percentage increase in the salary of each group leads to a smaller per cent change in the opposite direction of employment of the group. In addition, higher salaries for tenured and tenure-track faculty are now seen to lead to an increase in the employment of non-tenure-track faculty.[12]

The estimated coefficients in Table 3.4 come from models in which all professorial faculty are assumed to be tenure or tenure-track and all

Table 3.4 Logarithmic faculty demand functions estimates: instructors excluded* (t statistics in parentheses)

	Log (all professorial faculty per student)	Log (lecturers per student)
(A) Without year effects		
Log (ave. all prof. faculty salary)	−1.0667 (−27.27)	−0.7244 (−5.65)
Log (ave. lecturer salary)	0.0154 (0.64)	−0.1933 (−2.48)
Log (revenue per student)	0.8216 (58.55)	0.8375 (18.23)
R^2	0.9428	0.9109
N	2019	2019
(B) With year effects		
Log (ave. all prof. faculty salary)	−0.9645 (−22.89)	−0.5435 (−3.88)
Log (ave. lecturer salary)	0.0157 (0.67)	−0.1853 (−2.38)
Log (revenue per student)	0.8409 (59.6)	0.8586 (18.32)
R^2	0.9449	0.9117
N	2019	2019
(C) Without year effects		
Lagged dependent variable	0.0430 (2.23)	0.1461 (4.07)
Log (ave. all prof. faculty salary)	−0.2291 (−3.08)	0.6330 (1.99)
Log (ave. lecturer salary)	−0.0041 (−0.20)	−0.1911 (−2.21)
Log (revenue per student)	0.6659 (21.09)	0.5510 (4.09)
Wald chi squared	459	43
N	1326	1291
(D) With year effects		
Lagged dependent variable	0.0079 (0.46)	0.1527 (4.31)
Log (ave. all prof. faculty salary)	−0.2986 (−4.08)	0.6437 (2.00)
Log (ave. lecturer salary)	−0.0011 (−0.06)	−0.1856 (−2.15)
Log (revenue per student)	0.6561 (21.27)	0.5670 (4.19)
Wald chi squared	480	51
N	1326	1291

Note: *All professorial faculty are considered tenured, and tenure-track faculty and all lecturers are considered non-tenure-track faculty. Instructors are excluded from the analyses

lecturers are assumed to be non-tenure-track. In actuality there is a small percentage of non-tenure-track faculty members in the professorial groups, a small percentage of tenured and tenure-track faculty members in the lecturer group and instructors, excluded from the analyses in Table 3.4, are in both groups. It is straightforward for us to accurately compute the employment of tenured and tenure-track faculty members at each institution and the employment of non-tenure-track faculty members at each institution from the Faculty Salary Survey data. However, additional assumptions must be made to enable us to obtain estimates of the average salaries of the two different types of faculty at each institution. Specifically, we assume that the average salary of non-tenure-track faculty at each rank at an institution is a multiple of the average salary of tenure and tenure-track faculty at the rank at the institution. This multiple is allowed to vary across institutions and over time but is assumed to be constant across ranks at an institution at a point in time.[13]

Making this assumption, Table 3.5 presents estimate similar to those found in Table 3.4 for the more accurately defined measures of tenured

Table 3.5   Logarithmic faculty demand functions: tenure-track status correctly assigned (t statistics in parentheses)

	Log (tenure & tenure-track per student)	Log (non-tenured per student)
(A) Without year effects		
Log (ave. ten. and ten.-track fac. sal.)	−0.1791 (−5.26)	0.9869 (11.12)
Log (ave. non-ten.-track fac. sal.)	0.0198 (0.75)	−1.0508 (−15.24)
Log (revenue per student)	0.2482 (17.48)	0.3157 (8.52)
R^2	0.9166	0.8012
N	7654	7654
(B) With year effects		
Log (ave. ten. and ten.-track fac. sal.)	−0.0748 (−2.1)	1.1071 (11.86)
Log (ave. non-ten.-track fac. sal.)	0.0222 (0.85)	−1.0438 (−15.17)
Log (revenue per student)	0.2921 (19.63)	0.3620 (9.28)
R^2	0.9179	0.8024
N	7654	7654
(C) Without year effects		
Lagged dependent variable	0.0809 (2.00)	0.3314 (12.57)
Log (ave. ten. and ten.-track fac. sal.)	−0.0797 (−1.48)	2.0236 (11.21)
Log (ave. non-ten.-track fac. sal.)	−0.0416 (−1.53)	−0.8309 (−8.92)
Log (revenue per student)	0.3831 (14.89)	0.3157 (3.76)
Wald chi squared	227	311
N	5224	5061
(D) With year effects		
Lagged dependent variable	0.1280 (3.27)	0.3317 (12.82)
Log (ave. ten. and ten.-track. fac. sal.)	−0.0979 (−1.79)	2.0331 (11.27)
Log (ave. non-ten.-track fac. sal.)	−0.0415 (−1.50)	−0.8373 (−9.01)
Log (revenue per student)	0.3920 (14.99)	0.3299 (3.92)
Wald chi squared	248	347
N	5224	5061

and tenure-track and non-tenure-track faculty. The estimated percentage changes that occur in both types of faculty employment in response to any given change in revenue per student are much smaller in panels A and B, than the comparable estimates in Table 3.4. The demand for tenured and tenure-track faculty is now relatively unresponsive to changes in the group's average salary – every one percentage point change in the group's average salary leads to a smaller change in the opposite direction in employment of the group – while percentage changes in non-tenure-track faculty members' average salary now lead to equal but opposite changes in their employment levels. Increases in tenure-track faculty salaries, holding constant non-tenure-track faculty salaries, are associated with higher non-tenure-track faculty employment in these models.

Panels C and D of the table again introduce the possibility of lagged adjustment. Again, adjustment of tenured and tenure-track faculty to changes in equilibrium levels is faster than the adjustment of non-tenure-track faculty members. As in the first two panels of the table, non-tenure-track faculty members' employment levels are more sensitive to their average salaries than are tenure-track faculty members' employment levels to their average salaries. Again, non-tenure-track faculty members' employment levels are positively related to tenure-track faculty members' salaries.

3.4   NEW HIRE EQUATIONS

Each year the American Association of University Professors (AAUP) collects (but does not publish) information on the number of continuing full-time faculty members (by rank) employed at each academic institution that responds to the AAUP's annual salary survey.[14] Continuing faculty members in a rank are defined as full-time faculty members who were employed at the university in the rank in the previous year and who are still employed at the university in the current year, regardless of their current ranks.

If one subtracts the number of continuing faculty members at an institution in a rank in a year from the number of faculty members in the rank in the previous year and sums the differences across ranks, one obtains an estimate of the number of full-time vacant faculty positions that potentially could have been filled by new faculty hires at the institution. That is, ignoring changes in the institution's desired faculty employment level caused by changes in enrollments, changes in revenues, or changes in average salaries of faculty members, this vacancy estimate tells us the number of full-time faculty new hires that are required in the year to keep full-time faculty employment at the institution constant.

While the AAUP data does not distinguish between 'vacancies' that are due to the departure of tenured and tenure-track faculty members and those that are due to the departure of non-tenure-track faculty members, it is possible to construct an estimate of each type of vacancy by assuming that the departures of all professorial ranked faculty members are departures of tenure and tenure-track faculty members and that the departures of all instructors are departures of non-tenure-track faculty members.[15] Data on the new hires of full-time faculty members for each institution by tenure and tenure-track status, but not rank, are available every other year from 1989 in the Fall Staff Survey. As noted above, full-time faculty members are defined differently in this survey than they are in the AAUP Survey or the Faculty Salary Survey because visiting faculty members and faculty members without instructional responsibilities are included in the Fall Staff Survey.

With this proviso in mind, we use the new full-time faculty hire data from the Fall Staff Survey for 1989 to 1997 to estimate equations in which the number of newly hired faculty members at an institution, who are on tenure or tenure-tracks on the one hand and on non-tenure-tracks on the other hand, are each assumed to depend upon the number of tenure-track faculty vacancies at the institution over the period, the increase in revenue per full-time equivalent student received by the institution, the change in its full-time equivalent student body, the logarithm of the average salary of its tenured and tenure-track faculty, and the logarithm of the average salary of its non-tenure-track faculty, members. Models are estimated that both include and exclude year dichotomous variables.[16]

The estimated coefficients from these models appear in Table 3.6. Turning first to the results for new hires of tenured and tenure-track faculty members, the models that use either the number of professorial vacancies at the institution (panels A and B) or those that use the total number of faculty vacancies (including instructors) (panels C and D) perform very similarly. Only about 3 to 4 per cent of all vacancies for full-time faculty members in a year were filled by new hires of tenure and tenure-track faculty members during the year. Increased revenue per student leads to increased full-time tenured and tenure-track new hires, as do increases in the number of full-time equivalent students. However, these variables' coefficients are not always statistically significantly different from zero and, at the margin, each increase of 100 full-time equivalent students leads to the hiring of only about 0.2 more full-time tenured and tenure-track faculty members. Higher average salaries for professorial faculty are associated with fewer tenured and tenure-track faculty new hires, but this relationship is statistical significant only in the models that exclude year effects.[17]

*Table 3.6   Number of new hire faculty, institutional fixed effects
(t statistics in parentheses)*

	New hire tenure and tenure-track faculty	New hire non-tenure-track faculty
(A) Without year effects		
Professorial vacancies	0.0440 (2.32)	
Instructor vacancies		−0.2814 (−2.6)
Revenue change per FTE in 1000	0.2322 (1.35)	0.4921 (2.06)
FTE change in 100	0.2126 (2.13)	0.0523 (0.38)
Log (ave. ten. and ten.-track fac. sal.)	−14.6044 (−2.75)	6.4247 (0.87)
Log (ave. non-tenure-track fac. sal.)	2.1517 (0.58)	−2.1235 (−0.41)
R^2	0.8436	0.8365
N	1868	1868
(B) With year effects		
Professorial vacancies	0.0403 (2.11)	
Instructor vacancies		−0.2923 (−2.7)
Revenue change per FTE in 1000	0.1901 (1.09)	0.5162 (2.14)
FTE change in 100	0.1744 (1.72)	0.0461 (0.33)
Log (ave. ten. and ten.-track fac. sal.)	−1.3842 (−0.14)	32.8974 (2.42)
Log (ave. non-tenure-track fac. sal.)	2.6754 (0.72)	−1.3754 (−0.27)
R^2	0.8443	0.8375
N	1868	1868
(C) Without year effects		
Total vacancies	0.0315 (1.8)	−0.0098 (−0.4)
Revenue change per FTE in 1000	0.2242 (1.3)	0.4744 (1.98)
FTE change in 100	0.2155 (2.16)	0.0722 (0.52)
Log (ave. ten. and ten.-track fac. sal.)	−14.4818 (−2.73)	7.8810 (1.07)
Log (ave. non-tenure-track fac. sal.)	2.2026 (0.6)	−2.0518 (−0.4)
R^2	0.8432	0.8354
N	1868	1868
(D) With year effects		
Total vacancies	0.0275 (1.57)	−0.0091 (−0.37)
Revenue change per FTE in 1000	0.1808 (1.04)	0.5025 (2.08)
FTE change in 100	0.1762 (1.73)	0.0712 (0.5)
Log (ave. ten. and ten.-track fac. sal.)	−1.3129 (−0.13)	32.5641 (2.39)
Log (ave. non-tenure-track fac. sal.)	2.7293 (0.74)	−1.3725 (−0.27)
R^2	0.8440	0.8363
N	1868	1868

Turning to the results for full-time non-tenure-track new hires, non-tenure-track new hires are negatively associated with the number of instructor vacancies at an institution and unrelated to the total number of full-time vacancies. The former result may reflect that 'vacancies' for instructors are often involuntary in nature, when the demand for them declines, academic institutions fail to reappoint faculty members in the role, which creates 'vacancies'. Other factors held constant, the greater the number of such vacancies the fewer the number of non-tenure-track faculty appointments. Increases in revenues per student are associated with increases in non-tenure-track new hires, but changes in full-time equivalent student employment are not. In the models that include year effects, increases in the average salaries of tenured and tenure-track faculty members are positively and statistically significantly associated with increases in the hiring of non-tenure-track faculty. Increases in the average salaries of non-tenure-track faculty are negatively associated with fewer full-time non-tenure-track faculty hires, however this latter relationship is never statistically significantly different from zero.

3.5   CONCLUDING REMARKS

Our chapter has presented evidence from a variety of sources that show that, during the decade of the 1990s, the usage of full-time non-tenure-track faculty and part-time faculty continued to grow at four-year colleges and universities in the United States. Lacking data on the salaries of part-time faculty, we could not estimate demand functions for them. However, models of the demand for full-time faculty and for full-time faculty new hires that we did estimate suggest, in the main, that as the salaries of full-time non-tenure-track faculty decline relative to the salaries of full-time tenure and tenure-track faculty, the relative usage of full-time non-tenure-track faculty will increase.

Between 1989 and 1997, the ratio of the average salary of lecturers to the average salary of all professorial faculty members at four-year colleges and universities in the United States declined from 0.642 to 0.607 in the Faculty Salary Survey data. This suggests that declining relative salaries of full-time non-tenure-track faculty members played a role in their increasing relative usage during the period.[18] Four-year American colleges and universities have been able to attract lecturers at salaries that have been falling relative to their tenure-track colleagues' salaries because of the large number of PhDs available to fill such positions in many fields. However, this does not imply that lecturers and other full-time non-tenure-track faculty members are happy in their roles and the growing salary gap between them and their tenured and tenure-track counterparts is undoubtedly one of the main forces leading to efforts by various unions to unionize full-time non-tenure-track faculty members.[19] Hence, the relative cost advantage of full-time non-tenure-track faculty members may diminish in the future.

Of course parents of college-age students, taxpayers more generally, state legislators and governors, and the trustees of private colleges and universities may reasonably ask why they should be concerned about the growing use of part-time and full-time non-tenure-track faculty members. Surprisingly, very few studies have addressed whether the increased substitution of part-time and full-time non-tenure-track faculty for tenure-track faculty at higher education institutions leads to adverse academic outcomes for undergraduate students, such as less learning in any class, longer times to degree, lower graduation rates, or a lower proportion of graduates going on to post-graduate study. Analyses of these issues will be essential if public institutions want to make the case to their state legislators and governors, and private academic institutions want to make the case to their trustees, that better funding would enable them to increase their usage of tenure-track faculty members and that this would enhance undergraduate students' educational outcomes.[20] Our own preliminary research[21] that uses institutional-level panel data provided by the College Board, suggests that when an institution increases the share of its full-time faculty that is non-tenure-track, or increases the share of its faculty that is employed part-time, it is associated with reductions in the six-year graduation rate of the institution's undergraduate students.

Finally, it is well known that the proportion of PhDs granted by US universities that go to US citizens has been falling over a long period of time. In some science and engineering fields, and in economics, the proportion of PhDs granted to US citizens is now well under 50 per cent (see, for example, Siegfried and Stock 2001). Universities and public policymakers would do well to contemplate what the likely affect of their increased usage of part-time and full-time non-tenure-track faculty is on the desire of US college graduates to go on to PhD study. Put more starkly, by increasing their reliance on non-tenure-track faculty, American colleges and universities may be making PhD study a less attractive option than would otherwise by the case.

ACKNOWLEDGEMENTS

Without implicating them for what remains, we are grateful to the Andrew W. Mellon Foundation and the Atlantic Philanthropies (USA) Inc. for their financial support of CHERI.

An earlier version was presented at the TIAA-CREF Institute conference on 'Retirement, Retention and Recruitment' in April 2004 and we are grateful to our discussant Richard Freeman and other participants at the conference for their comments on that version.

NOTES

1. Ronald G. Ehrenberg and Daniel B. Klaff (2002) provide some preliminary evidence using data from the State University of New York (SUNY) system.
2. Both surveys are components of Integrated Postsecondary Education Data System (IPEDS), released by the National Center for Educational Statistics, accessed at www.nces.ed.gov/ipeds/.
3. The one exception is the Doctoral II category in which the public share is slightly higher than the private share.
4. Data for 2001 are currently not available for the Faculty Salary Survey.
5. The latter restriction is necessary because it is impossible to determine whether a blank represents zero or missing data in a year. As a result, the shares of full-time faculty members that are part-time may be overstated in these data.
6. The Fall Staff Survey also contains information on the usage of graduate teaching *and* research assistants. From 1989 to 2001, the usage of graduate assistants, relative to total full-time faculty, increased by about 20 per cent at both private and public research and doctoral universities.
7. Elastic demand curves are ones in which the percentage change in employment that occurs in response to a given percentage change in the average salary for the group is larger than the percentage change in salary.
8. We exclude instructors initially because nationally over 15 per cent of them at Research I and Research II institutions, and 25 to 30 per cent of them at other institutions, are tenured or on tenure-track lines.
9. The latter is computed as the total institutional revenue (including tuition and fees, appropriation, grants and contracts, sales and services, and other sources) minus the funding for Pell grants that the institution receives from the federal government.
10. Let $(F_T/E)^*$ be the equilibrium level of tenured and tenure-track faculty per student for an institution in year t that results from equation (3.2) in the text. The partial adjustment model specifies that $(F_T/E) - (F_T/E)_{t-1} = k((F_T/E)_t - (F_T/E)_{t-1})$, where k is the adjustment coefficient. If k equals one, then full adjustment occurs in one year. If k is less than one, adjustment to equilibrium is only partial in a year. This model leads to an equation similar to (3.2), save that the lagged value of tenured and tenure-track employment per student also appears on the right-hand side and this variable's coefficient is equal to one minus k. A similar equation is specified for non-tenure-track faculty.
11. For example, the coefficient of about 0.15 on the lagged value of lecturer employment implies that about 85 per cent of the adjustment to the new equilibrium level of lecturer's employment occurs within the one-year period.
12. We experimented with allowing more complex adjustment processes, such as including lagged values of both faculty employment levels in each faculty employment equation or allowing the speed of adjustment to equilibrium to depend upon the fraction of faculty with tenure or on tenure tracks. However, these extensions did not improve the fits of our models.
13. Appendix B provides details of how the average salaries of tenured and tenure-track faculty, on the one hand, and non-tenure-track faculty, on the other hand, are computed by us.
14. The AAUP salary survey builds on the IPEDs *Faculty Salary Survey* and faculty members are thus defined in the AAUP survey as faculty members with at least some instructional responsibility.

15. Sadly the AAUP began collecting continuing faculty data for lecturers only in 1996, so lecturers 'vacancies' must be excluded from these analyses.
16. Institutional dichotomous variables are included in these equations for the reason discussed in Appendix A.
17. As Appendix A makes clear, excluding year effects imposes the restriction that the ratio of the average salary of tenured and tenure-track faculty in a rank to the average salary of non-tenure-track faculty in a rank at an institution does not vary over time. So this is a very restrictive assumption.
18. As we have discussed above, not all lecturers are non-tenure-track, not all professorial faculty are on tenured or tenure-track lines and instructors (left out of the computation of the ratio) are employed on all three types of appointments. However, we cannot estimate more accurately how the average salary of full-time non-tenure-track faculty members has changed vis-à-vis the average salary of their tenured and tenure-track counterparts, because the method we used to compute relative salaries of the two groups to conduct the estimation that led to Table 3.5 required us to assume that in a given year the ratio of salaries of the two groups at an institution were constant across ranks, but varied across institutions. These ratios were treated as unobserved institutional dichotomous variables that were subsumed in the more general institutional dichotomous variables that are included in our model.
19. By way of an example, in May 2003 non-tenure-track faculty members at the University of Michigan voted to create a union to represent the 1300 full-time and part-time non-tenure-track faculty at the university (Smallwood, 2003).
20. One study of community college students that randomly assigned them to sections of a remedial mathematics course that were taught by part-time and tenure-track full-time faculty found no differences in the amounts that students learned (Bolge, 1995). Another study of a Midwestern comprehensive institution found, using four years of data on fall entering freshmen, that the greater the proportion of part-time faculty that students had during their first semester in college, the lower the probability that they would return for their second semester (Harrington and Schibik, 2001). Studies by economists have tended to focus on how instructor type (including graduate students) influences the amount that students learn in first-year classes (Finegan and Siegfried, 1998; Watts and Lynch, 1989) and the results vary across studies. Bettinger and Long (2004) use data from Ohio public four-year colleges to study the impact of adjunct faculty and graduate students (as compared to full-time faculty regardless of tenure or tenure-track status) on student enrollment and success in subsequent courses in a subject. They find that adjuncts and graduate students tend to reduce student interest in taking subsequent courses, but that the effects are small and vary across disciplines.
21. See Ehrenberg and Zhang (2004).

REFERENCES

Anderson, Eugene L. (2002), *The New Professoriate: Characteristics, Contributions and Compensation*, Washington DC: American Council on Education.

Arellano, Manuel and Stephen Bond (1991), 'Some tests of specification for panel data: Monte Carol evidence and an application to employment equations', *Review of Economic Studies*, **58** (April), 277–97.

Baldwin, Roger G. and Jay L. Chronister (2001), *Teaching Without Tenure: Policies and Practices for a New Era*, Baltimore, MD: Johns Hopkins University Press.

Bettinger, Eric and Bridget Terry Long (2004), 'Do college instructors matter? The effects of adjuncts and graduate assistants on students' interest and success', National Bureau of Economic Research working paper no W10370, Cambridge, MA: National Bureau of Economic Research, March.

Bolge, Robert D. (1995), 'Examination of student learning as a function of instructor status (full-time vs. part-time) at Mercer County Community College', unpublished paper, Mercer County Community College, available from ERIC (ED382241).

Conley, Valerie M., David W. Leslie and Linda J. Zimbler (2002), *Part-Time Instructional Faculty and Staff: Who They Are, What They Do, and What They Think*, Washington DC: US Department of Education, National Center for Educational Statistics (NCES 2002–163); see also *Education Statistics Quarterly*, **4** (2) (Summer).

Ehrenberg, Ronald G. and Daniel B. Klaff (2002), 'Changes in faculty composition within the State University of New York system: 1985–2001', Cornell Higher Education Research Institute working paper WP38, accessed at www.ilr. cornell.edu/cheri/wp/cheri_wp 38.pdf.

Ehrenberg, Ronald G. and Liang Zhang (2004), 'Do tenure and tenure-track faculty matter?', NBER working paper no. 10695, Cambridge, MA.

Ehrenberg, Ronald G., Michael J. Rizzo and George H. Jakubson (2003), 'Who bears the growing cost of science at universities?', *National Bureau of Economic Research working paper 9627*, Cambridge, MA, April.

Finegan, T. Aldrich and John J. Siegfried (1998), 'Do introductory economics students learn more if their instructor has a PhD?', *American Economist*, **42**, Fall, 34–46.

Harrington, Charles and Timothy Schibik (2001), 'Caveat emptor: Is there a relationship between part-time faculty utilization and student learning outcomes and retention', paper presented at the 41st Annual Meeting of the Association for Institutional Research, Long Beach CA, June.

Siegfried, John J. and Wendy A. Stock (2004), 'The market for new PhD economists in 2002', paper presented at the Allied Social Science Associations Meeting, San Diego, CA, January.

Smallwood, Scott (2003), 'Non-tenure-track faculty members vote to unionize at U. of Michigan', *Chronicle of Higher Education*, **49** (May), A15.

Watts, Michael and Gerald J. Lynch (1989), 'The principles courses revisited', *American Economic Review*, **79**, (May), 236–41.

APPENDIX A

Table 3A.1   Full-time non-tenure-track faculty/total full-time faculty

	1989	1991	1993	1995	1997	1999*	2001*
Public (sample size)							
Research I (53)	0.245	0.253	0.263	0.286	0.332	0.356	0.375
Research II (25)	0.183	0.171	0.179	0.192	0.233	0.244	0.274
Doctoral I (27)	0.160	0.193	0.191	0.202	0.213	0.235	0.237
Doctoral II (34)	0.176	0.176	0.200	0.206	0.212	0.226	0.240
Comprehensive I (229)	0.133	0.133	0.132	0.129	0.141	0.153	0.179
Comprehensive II (21)	0.181	0.141	0.132	0.119	0.146	0.182	0.199
Liberal arts I (4)	0.134	0.110	0.140	0.125	0.117	0.109	0.121
Liberal arts II (61)	0.213	0.211	0.187	0.202	0.195	0.223	0.242
Total	0.191	0.194	0.201	0.212	0.241	0.260	0.281
Private (sample size)							
Research I (26)	0.312	0.358	0.344	0.335	0.410	0.432	0.434
Research II (11)	0.173	0.165	0.186	0.180	0.196	0.222	0.230
Doctoral I (19)	0.233	0.193	0.231	0.212	0.234	0.256	0.274
Doctoral II (15)	0.132	0.122	0.153	0.137	0.144	0.159	0.191
Comprehensive I (164)	0.188	0.197	0.195	0.207	0.212	0.242	0.254
Comprehensive II (58)	0.207	0.199	0.216	0.227	0.220	0.239	0.230
Liberal arts I (149)	0.155	0.158	0.149	0.149	0.154	0.173	0.183
Liberal arts II (319)	0.287	0.294	0.297	0.292	0.286	0.321	0.328
Total	0.235	0.248	0.250	0.248	0.275	0.301	0.309

Note: *The numbers for 1999 and 2001 are from the preliminary data released by NCES

Source: National Center for Education Statistics, Fall Staff Survey (2004)

APPENDIX B

Let F_{ijt} be the number of faculty members of rank i at institution j in year t. Let f_{ijt} be the fraction of faculty members of rank i at institution j in year t that have tenured or tenure-track appointments. Finally, let S_{ijt} be the average salary of faculty members of rank i at institution j in year t. Then the number of faculty members at institution j with tenured or tenure-track appointments in year t is simply the sum over all ranks (i) of $F_{ijt}f_{ijt}$ and the number of faculty members on non-tenure-track appointments is simply the sum over all ranks (i) of $F_{ijt}(1 - f_{ijt})$. Each of these sums can be directly calculated from the *Faculty Salary Survey* data. Put another way, we know from the data the number of tenured and tenure-track and the number of non-tenure-track faculty members at each institution in each year.

We know the average salary of faculty members of each rank at each institution in each year. We do not have information on the average salary of faculty members at each rank in each year by tenure-track status. However, an estimate of these numbers can be obtained if one is willing to assume that the average salary of tenured and tenure-track faculty at a rank is a constant multiple of the average salary of non-tenure-track faculty at the rank. This multiple is assumed to be constant across ranks at a given institution over time but is allowed to vary over time. That is, letting the subscript T represent tenured and tenure-track faculty and the subscript N non-tenure-track faculty, we assume

$$S_{ijtT} = m_{jt} S_{itjN} \qquad \text{(B.1)}$$

and

$$m_{jt} = b_i d_t. \qquad \text{(B.2)}$$

It immediately follows that the average salary of tenure and tenure-track faculty members across all ranks at institution i at time t (S_{itT}) is given by the sum across all ranks of $S_{ijt} b_i d_t F_{ijt} f_{ijt}$ divided by total tenured and tenure-track faculty employment at the institution. The average salary of non-tenure-track faculty members at the institution is similarly calculated by replacing the f_{ijt} by $(1 - f_{ijt})$ in the expression above. All the variables in each of these two expressions are known numbers save for b_i and d_t which are treated as parameters that vary across institutions and over years. When one takes the logarithm of each average salary expression, as is done when we estimate logarithmic demand equations (Table 3.5) and new hire equations (Table 3.6), the logarithm of each average salary is equal to the sum of the logarithm of a known number and the logarithms of an institutional and a year effect. Hence the b_i and d_t are subsumed in the institutional and time fixed effects.

4. The growing postdoctorate population at US research universities

Jennifer Ma and Paula E. Stephan

4.1 INTRODUCTION

US research universities are heavily populated by postdoctoral fellows. Indeed, by the National Science Foundation (NSF)'s count there were approximately 30 000 postdoctoral appointees in science and engineering at US universities in the fall of 2001.[1] Only ten years earlier the number of post-docs stood at slightly less than 23 000.

Eleven universities currently have 500 or more postdoctorates on campus, working in the fields of science and engineering. Harvard University heads the list with 1596, followed by The University of California, Berkeley (819); The Massachusetts Institute of Technology (808); and The University of Colorado (796). In terms of the distribution, the top ten universities host almost 25 per cent of all postdoctorates in science and engineering, and the top 20 host almost 40 per cent.[2]

Because post-docs are usually recruited by research faculty and funded through research grants going directly to the faculty principal investigator, university administrators have traditionally paid little attention to their presence and, when asked, often have had difficulty in identifying the post-doctoral population working on their campus.[3] However, as the number of post-docs has increased and their job prospects for an independent research career have declined, the level of their professional dissatisfaction has grown and universities have begun to realize that the complex set of issues related to post-docs can no longer be ignored. A statistic that communicates in part the emerging tension on campuses surrounding post-docs is that there are currently 50 known active post-doc associations on campuses, including those of Stanford, Yale, Johns Hopkins, the University of Illinois and the University of Chicago.

The post-doc position has a long tradition in the United States, especially for certain science and engineering fields. In such fields, for new PhDs with an interest in pursuing an academic career at a research university, the post-doctoral position has become almost a necessary condition given that departments, when making tenure-track hires at the rank of assistant professor, generally direct their searches to the postdoctoral pool instead of those who have just received their doctoral degree. For example, for decades the typical career path of a research life scientist in the United States has involved obtaining a postdoctoral position upon the receipt of a PhD. As of April 1995, approximately two-thirds of the tenured or tenure-track faculty in biology who have received their doctoral training in the USA have held at least one postdoctoral position after obtaining their doctoral degree.[4]

Two dimensions of postdoctoral training have changed over the years, however, leading to a dramatic increase in the number of post-docs populating university campuses. One involves the increasing number of new PhDs taking a first post-doc position, including individuals who received their doctoral training abroad as well as individuals from fields that traditionally did not include post-doc work as a component of training. The other involves a lengthening of the duration of individuals' post-doc experience. In earlier years, individuals typically stayed in a postdoctoral position for only two years. This no longer is the case. For example, 35 per cent of life science PhDs observed in 1999 were in postdoctoral positions three to four years after graduation, compared to 12 per cent in 1977; 20 per cent held postdoctoral positions five to six years later, compared to 5 per cent in 1977.[5]

In this chapter, we examine factors contributing to both of these trends. In section 4.2 we present some summary data collected by the NSF on all postdoctoral appointments in science and engineering fields. These data are for all postdoctorates in these fields including those who received their doctoral degrees abroad.

In section 4.3 we estimate the propensity of new PhDs to take a post-doctoral position. In section 4.4 we examine factors that affect the duration of postdoctoral experience by estimating a model of postdoctoral duration for individuals who have held one or more postdoctoral positions. We are particularly interested in how these outcomes relate to the academic labour market for scientists and engineers, as well as the availability of research funding. Due to data availability, the analysis in sections 4.3 and 4.4 is limited to individuals who received their PhDs in the United States.

4.2   THE US POSTDOCTORATE POPULATION

In this section, we present some summary statistics on the postdoctorate population in the USA from the Survey of Graduate Students and Post-doctorates in Science and Engineering, also called the Graduate Student

Survey (GSS), conducted by the NSF and the National Institutes of Health. The GSS survey has been conducted annually since 1966. In earlier years, data were collected from a limited number of doctorate-granting institutions. Starting in 1975, data have been collected from all institutions offering graduate programs in any science, engineering or health field. The 2001 GSS survey covered 11 967 graduate departments at 606 institutions (including 242 master's-granting and 364 doctorate-granting institutions) in the USA and outlying areas.

The purpose of the GSS survey is to obtain the number and characteristics of graduate science and engineering students and postdoctorates in US institutions. Data items for the survey are collected at the academic-department level. For post-docs, the survey collects information on postdoctoral trainees regardless of where their degree was awarded. Table 4.1 presents the number of post-docs from 1987 to 2001 by broad field category.[6] We see that the number of post-doc positions in science has grown dramatically in the period 1987 to 2001, increasing by almost 60 per cent. During this period, the number of post-docs in engineering has more than

Table 4.1   *Postdoctorate population in science and engineering at US universities, 1987–2001*

	Total post-docs	Biological sciences	Engineering	Physical sciences	Other
1987	18 771	10 358	1443	4945	2025
1988	19 687	10 667	1685	5185	2150
1989	20 864	11 425	1912	5385	2142
1990	21 770	11 930	1939	5565	2336
1991	22 811	12 478	2243	5693	2397
1992	23 825	13 172	2351	5757	2545
1993	24 611	13 779	2434	5648	2750
1994	25 786	14 469	2589	5810	2918
1995	26 060	14 661	2635	5814	2950
1996	26 489	14 907	2665	5791	3126
1997	27 155	15 096	2964	5897	3198
1998	27 765	15 781	2847	5925	3212
1999	28 874	16 123	3187	6092	3472
2000	30 155	16 764	3309	6202	3880
2001	29 971	16 913	3113	6152	3793

Source: Authors' calculations based on data drawn from various years' Survey of Graduate Students and Postdoctorates in Science and Engineering. Other includes mathematics, computer sciences, agricultural sciences, psychology and social sciences. Health fields are excluded from the counts.

doubled. By contrast, the number of post-docs in the biological sciences, which started the period with a very large base, has grown by slightly more than 60 per cent.

One factor that has contributed to the rise in the post-doc population relates to the increasing propensity to hire post-docs from those who have received their PhD training abroad. Although NSF does not collect data by country of doctorate, in recent years it has collected data by citizenship status. In 2001, 59.7 per cent of all postdoctorate appointees in the USA were temporary visa holders, up from 53.6 per cent in 1998.[7]

4.3   THE PROPENSITY TO TAKE A POSTDOCTORAL POSITION

We draw on data from the annual Survey of Earned Doctorates (SED) to estimate the propensity of a newly-minted PhD from a US institution to accept a postdoctoral position upon graduation. The SED is the census of all PhDs awarded in the United States and is conducted by the NSF and administered by academic institutions at or near the time individuals receive their PhDs. The purpose of the survey is to collect information on the number of individuals receiving PhDs in the US and their demographic and educational background. The survey includes several questions on an individual's postgraduate plans such as:

- How definite are your immediate (within the next year) postgraduate plans?
- What best describes your immediate (within the next year) postgraduate plans?
- For what types of employer will you be working within the next year?

The response rate of the SED is high, with more than 90 per cent replying to the survey instrument each year. For the 2001 survey, the response rate was approximately 92 per cent.

We limit our study to those trained in one of ten broad fields in science and engineering for the period 1981 to 1999 who indicate that they do not plan to be in a foreign country after graduation. These ten broad fields are agriculture, physics, astronomy, chemistry, computer science, earth science/oceanography, engineering, mathematics, health/medicine and biology. In our sample, approximately 64 per cent of the respondents indicate that they have made definite plans for work or future study at the time they complete the questionnaire. Another 26 per cent indicate that they are negotiating with a specific organization, or more than one; seeking appointment but have no specific organization in mind at this time; and other. Together these activities are referred to as 'seeking.' The plans of the remaining 9 per cent are not known.

We distinguish, where possible, between those taking a postdoctoral appointment at an academic institution and those taking a postdoctoral position in another sector, such as industry or government. The distinction can be made clearly only for those with definite plans since many of those 'seeking' do not indicate the sector where they are looking. The distinction is important because a large number of postdoctoral positions are held outside of academe. For example, during the period 1981–95, of the 69 945 new PhDs with definite plans to take a postdoctoral appointment, 70 per cent were headed to academe; the other 30 per cent were headed to another sector.

Here we examine the propensity to take a postdoctoral position for those who have definite plans as well as for the larger group of individuals that includes those seeking a position. We define individuals to have definite plans if they are returning to or continuing in pre-doctoral employment or if they have signed a contract or made a definite commitment. The 'seeking' group includes individuals who are negotiating with a specific organization, or more than one; seeking appointment but have no specific organization in mind at this time; and other. We define a postdoctoral appointment to be a postdoctoral fellowship, a postdoctoral research associateship, a traineeship or 'other study, internship, residency'.

The independent variables in the model are defined in Table 4.2; means and standard deviations are also presented. In the model, we control for demographic characteristics such as age and gender, citizenship status, marital status, number of dependents and field of doctoral study. We also include variables to indicate whether the respondent worked full-time or part-time during the last year in graduate school, and whether the respondent attended a top-ten graduate program in the field.

Table 4.2 shows that, for most variables, the means for the 'definite' group and the combined group of the 'definite' and the 'seeking' are similar. One notable difference is that a higher proportion of those with definite plans are US citizens.

The coefficients for the logit equation, estimating the odds that an individual has definite plans to take a postdoctoral position, are presented in Table 4.3 as well as the standard errors. For ease of exposition we present not only the actual logit coefficients but also the more easily interpreted odds ratio. By way of example, for a dummy variable such as female, a value of 1.0 of the odds ratio indicates that the odds of the event in question occurring are the same for women as for men, the benchmark. An odds ratio greater than 1.0 (for example 1.5), tells us that the odds of the event

Table 4.2   Summary statistics of explanatory variables for the propensity model, 1981–99

Variable name	Definition	Definite group		Definite or seeking group	
		Mean	Standard deviation	Mean	Standard deviation
AGE AT PHD	Age	32.585	5.251	32.787	5.262
USCITZ	Equal 1 if US citizen	0.704	0.456	0.663	0.473
USPERM	Equal 1 if permanent resident	0.071	0.257	0.083	0.276
FEMALE	Equal 1 if female	0.254	0.436	0.255	0.436
MARRIED	Equal 1 if married	0.592	0.491	0.587	0.492
AGRI	Equal 1 if degree in agriculture	0.057	0.232	0.064	0.245
PHYS	Equal 1 if degree in physics	0.069	0.254	0.072	0.259
ASTR	Equal 1 if degree in astronomy	0.009	0.097	0.008	0.092
CHEM	Equal 1 if degree in chemistry	0.134	0.341	0.124	0.330
COMP	Equal 1 if degree in computer science	0.039	0.193	0.038	0.191
EART	Equal 1 if degree in earth science or oceanography	0.036	0.185	0.036	0.187
ENGI	Equal 1 if degree in engineering	0.166	0.372	0.180	0.384
MATH	Equal 1 if degree in mathematics	0.055	0.228	0.057	0.233
MEDI	Equal 1 if degree in health or medical field	0.069	0.254	0.068	0.252
USBA	Equal 1 if bachelor's degree from US institution	0.733	0.442	0.693	0.461
DEPENDS	Number of dependents	0.833	1.191	0.867	1.180
PREFTEMP	Worked full-time last year in graduate school	0.288	0.452	0.246	0.430
PREPTEMP	Worked part-time last year in graduate school	0.061	0.240	0.077	0.266

Table 4.2 (continued)

Variable name	Definition	Definite group		Definite or seeking group	
		Mean	Standard deviation	Mean	Standard deviation
PREFELLOW	Had fellowship last year in graduate school	0.580	0.493	0.582	0.493
PREOTHER	Other support last year in graduate school	0.017	0.130	0.019	0.136
TOPAGRI	Equal 1 if from top ten PhD program, agriculture	0.016	0.126	0.018	0.134
TOPPHYS	Equal 1 if from top ten PhD program, physics	0.018	0.132	0.016	0.126
TOPBIOL	Equal 1 if from top ten PhD program, biology	0.032	0.175	0.028	0.164
TOPASTR	Equal 1 if from top ten PhD program, astronomy	0.003	0.061	0.003	0.057
TOPCHEM	Equal 1 if from top ten PhD program, chemistry	0.026	0.159	0.021	0.145
TOPCOMP	Equal 1 if from top ten PhD program, computer science	0.010	0.097	0.009	0.093
TOPEART	Equal 1 if from top ten PhD program, earth science	0.009	0.095	0.009	0.094
TOPMATH	Equal 1 if from top ten PhD program, mathematics	0.012	0.110	0.011	0.106
TOPMEDI	Equal 1 if from top ten PhD program, health and medical field	0.011	0.106	0.011	0.104
TOPENGI	Equal 1 if from top ten PhD program, engineering	0.172	0.377	0.183	0.387

*Table 4.3   Logit model results for those who received a PhD between 1981
and 1999 (dependent variable: post-doc)*

Variable name	Definite group			Definite & seeking group		
	Logit coefficient (47.0%)	Standard errors	Odds ratio	Logit coefficient (44.7%)	Standard errors	Odds ratio
INTERCEPT	3.705	0.063		2.962	0.050	
AGE AT PHD	−0.061**	0.001	0.941	−0.055**	0.001	0.946
USCITZ	−0.611**	0.032	0.543	−0.536**	0.024	0.585
USPERM	−0.441**	0.027	0.643	−0.467**	0.020	0.628
FEMALE	0.055**	0.015	1.057	0.258*	0.012	1.026
MARRIED	−0.135**	0.014	0.874	−0.108**	0.011	0.898
AGRI	−1.540**	0.029	0.214	−1.349**	0.023	0.260
PHYS	−0.894**	0.026	0.409	−0.818**	0.021	0.441
ASTR	−0.385**	0.073	0.680	−0.248**	0.061	0.780
CHEM	−1.392**	0.019	0.320	−0.951**	0.016	0.386
COMP	−3.369**	0.049	0.034	−3.006**	0.039	0.049
EART	−1.392**	0.035	0.249	−1.111**	0.028	0.329
ENGI	−1.859**	0.022	0.156	−1.656**	0.017	0.191
MATH	−2.735**	0.034	0.065	−2.397**	0.026	0.091
MEDI	−1.800**	0.029	0.165	−1.631**	0.024	0.196
USBA	−0.392**	0.031	0.676	−0.409**	0.024	0.664
DEPENDS	−0.156**	0.007	0.855	−0.109**	0.005	0.897
PREFTEMP	−1.066**	0.028	0.344	−0.576**	0.020	0.562
PREPTEMP	−0.395**	0.034	0.674	−0.135**	0.024	0.874
PREFELLOW	0.079**	0.027	1.082	0.325**	0.018	1.385
PREOTHER	0.004	0.052	1.004	0.274**	0.039	1.315
TOPAGRI	0.057	0.051	1.059	0.040	0.039	1.041
TOPPHYS	0.105*	0.047	1.110	0.148**	0.039	1.160
TOPBIOL	0.652**	0.042	1.919	0.705**	0.034	2.025
TOPASTR	0.600**	0.127	1.814	0.440**	0.106	1.553
TOPCHEM	0.129**	0.035	1.138	0.187**	0.032	1.206
TOPCOMP	0.166*	0.084	1.181	0.181*	0.071	1.199
TOPEART	0.555**	0.063	1.743	0.573**	0.053	1.773
TOPMATH	0.689**	0.058	1.991	0.607**	0.049	1.836
TOPMEDI	−0.006	0.066	0.994	0.007	0.055	1.007
TOPENGI	−1.565**	0.021	0.209	−1.313**	0.017	0.269
1982	0.067	0.041	1.070	0.065**	0.035	1.067
1983	0.219**	0.041	1.245	0.159**	0.035	1.172
1984	0.384**	0.041	1.469	0.305**	0.035	1.356
1985	0.298**	0.041	1.348	0.272**	0.035	1.313
1986	0.486**	0.041	1.626	0.444**	0.034	1.558
1987	0.646**	0.041	1.908	0.540**	0.034	1.717

Table 4.3 (continued)

Variable name	Definite group			Definite & seeking group		
	Logit coefficient (47.0%)	Standard errors	Odds ratio	Logit coefficient (44.7%)	Standard errors	Odds ratio
1988	0.678**	0.040	1.969	0.588**	0.034	1.800
1989	0.601**	0.040	1.825	0.536**	0.033	1.708
1990	0.672**	0.039	1.957	0.623**	0.033	1.865
1991	0.698**	0.039	2.010	0.626**	0.033	1.870
1992	0.827**	0.039	2.286	0.715**	0.033	2.045
1993	0.916**	0.040	2.500	0.802**	0.033	2.229
1994	0.981**	0.039	2.666	0.836**	0.032	2.306
1995	0.964**	0.039	2.623	0.758**	0.032	2.133
1996	0.661**	0.038	1.937	0.505**	0.031	1.656
1997	0.413**	0.038	1.512	0.263**	0.032	1.301
1998	0.412**	0.038	1.510	0.297**	0.032	1.345
1999	0.581**	0.038	1.788	0.461**	0.032	1.586
Likelihood ratio	61 208			66 443		
Number of observations	171 569			240 866		

Notes:
*indicates that the estimate is significant at the 0.05 level.
**indicates that the estimate is significant at the 0.01 level.

in question occurring for women are 1.5 times those for men or 50 per cent higher for women than for men.[8]

The results are presented for the 'definite' group as well as for the 'definite and seeking' group. The findings are fairly straightforward. We see that relative to biologists (the benchmark), PhDs in all the other nine fields are less likely to take a postdoctoral position. Results for the 'definite and seeking' group show that the field with the lowest likelihood of taking a postdoctoral position, other things being equal, is computer science with an odds ratio of 0.049. This suggests that computer science PhDs are about 5 per cent as likely to take a postdoctoral position as PhDs in biology. Other than biology, the field with the highest likelihood is astronomy with an odds ratio of 0.78, indicating astronomy PhDs are 78 per cent as likely to take a postdoctoral position as biology PhDs.

Where the individual trains matters as well. In seven of the ten fields, those graduating from a top-ten program in their field are more likely to take a postdoctoral position than those who did not train at a top-ten

program.[9] But exceptions occur: for example, graduates from top-ten programs in engineering are significantly less likely to take a postdoctoral position – an indication, no doubt, of the strength of the market in engineering
during this period, especially outside the academic sector.

Personal attributes affect the likelihood of taking a post-doc. Ceteris
paribus, older individuals are less likely to accept postdoctoral positions,[10]
as are married individuals. The probability of being a post-doc is also negatively related to the number of dependents (other than spouse) that the
individual has. These results are consistent with the theory that postdoctoral training is seen as an investment in additional human capital. Thus,
individuals who have shorter horizons or capital constraints are less likely
to opt for the investment.

Our results also indicate that what the individual did during the last
year in graduate school is also important. Not surprisingly, those who
worked full-time are considerably less likely to take a post-doc position;
those who had a fellowship are considerably more likely to take a post-doc
position.

Citizenship status also matters, as does the country of undergraduate
training. We consistently find that US citizens or permanent residents are
less likely to take a postdoctoral position compared to those who have temporary visas (the benchmark). A likely reason that individuals on temporary visas may be more likely to take a postdoctoral position than those who
are not temporary residents is that in many cases postdoctoral positions are
classified as training positions, which allow such individuals to remain in
the United States after receiving their PhD. We also find that those who
received their bachelor's degree in the United States, other things being
equal, are less likely to take a postdoctoral position.

The results also indicate that the odds of taking a postdoctorate position are consistently higher for those who received their PhD degree after
1981, the benchmark year. Beginning in 1983 the year coefficients are
positive and highly significant. The odds ratios show a consistent increase
over time through to 1994, with a significant dip in the years 1996–99. By
way of example, individuals who got their PhD degree in 1994 were 2.3
times as likely to take a postdoctoral position as those who received their
degree in 1981, while those who got their degree in 1998 were only 1.35
times as likely. This could be related to the overall job market boom in the
mid- to late 1990s.

Table 4.4 reports similar results, but this time the period is restricted to
1981–95 so that we can distinguish those taking a post-doc in academe from
the larger group. The sample is restricted to those with definite plans. Prior
to discussing the academic results, we note that when the dependent variable remains indicative of a postdoctoral position regardless of sector, the

Table 4.4   *Logit results for those who received a PhD between 1981 and 1995 (dependent variable: academic post-doc (32.9 per cent))*

Independent variables	Coefficient	Standard error	Odds ratio
INTERCEPT	2.653**	0.073	
AGE AT PHD	−0.051**	0.002	0.950
USCITZ	−0.669**	0.039	0.512
USPERM	−0.677**	0.034	0.508
FEMALE	0.010	0.017	1.010
MARRIED	−0.064**	0.016	0.938
AGRI	−1.218**	0.036	0.296
PHYS	−0.832**	0.030	0.435
ASTR	−0.851**	0.084	0.427
CHEM	−0.864**	0.021	0.422
COMP	−2.856**	0.072	0.058
EART	−1.310**	0.045	0.270
ENGI	−1.583**	0.030	0.205
MATH	−2.268**	0.045	0.104
MEDI	−1.442**	0.037	0.236
USBA	−0.250**	0.038	0.779
DEPENDS	−0.015**	0.008	0.857
PREFTEMP	−0.693**	0.032	0.500
PREPTEMP	−0.262**	0.040	0.770
PREFELLOW	0.114*	0.029	1.121
PREOTHER	−0.128	0.057	0.770
TOPAGRI	0.076	0.064	1.079
TOPPHYS	0.040	0.051	1.040
TOPBIOL	0.351**	0.036	1.421
TOPASTR	0.445**	0.127	1.561
TOPCHEM	0.159**	0.039	1.172
TOPCOMP	0.209	0.119	1.232
TOPEART	0.521**	0.076	1.683
TOPMATH	0.649**	0.075	1.914
TOPMEDI	−0.093	0.090	0.911
TOPENGI	−1.375**	0.028	0.253
1982	0.024	0.041	1.024
1983	0.104**	0.041	1.110
1984	0.217**	0.041	1.243
1985	0.100**	0.041	1.105
1986	0.232**	0.040	1.261
1987	0.300**	0.040	1.349
1988	0.328**	0.039	1.389
1989	0.250**	0.039	1.284
1990	0.011	0.040	1.011

Table 4.4   (continued)

Independent variables	Coefficient	Standard error	Odds ratio
1991	0.030	0.039	1.030
1992	0.152**	0.039	1.164
1993	0.249**	0.039	1.283
1994	0.247**	0.039	1.280
1995	0.290**	0.039	1.336
Likelihood ratio	27 215		
Number of observations	123 497		

Notes:
* indicates that the estimate is significant at the 0.05 level.
** indicates that the estimate is significant at the 0.01 level.

results for this abbreviated period of time (1981–95) remain fairly consistent with the above findings for the extended period of time (1981–99). The only exception is that the fellowship variable is no longer significant.

The results are fairly similar when we focus on those taking a post-doc position in academe rather than those taking a postdoctoral position regardless of sector. The only major difference is that those coming from top physics programs are no longer more likely to take a post-doc than their peers from non-top-ten programs. We also find that there is no significant difference between the probability of taking a post-doc in the years 1990 and 1991 and the benchmark year 1981. We have no clear explanation related to this finding.

One objective of this research is to determine the degree to which the probability of taking a postdoctoral position relates to the job market (especially the job market in academe) for newly minted scientists and engineers. Measures of the strength of the job market are notoriously difficult to construct. For example, information on academic job vacancies is not readily available. Here we use two alternative measures of the job market. One is supply-oriented and controls for the number of PhDs minted each year by field. The other is demand-oriented, and controls for the total current fund revenue for all private and public institutions to proxy the demand for PhDs by academe.

Table 4.5 summarizes results concerning the impact of the size of the PhD's cohort on the probability of individuals taking a postdoctoral position.[11] Generally speaking, we find that the probability of taking a postdoctoral position, either in academe or in any sector, is positively and significantly related to the size of one's PhD cohort. There are but a couple

*Table 4.5   Relationship of taking a postdoctoral position to number of
PhDs in cohort by field, 1981–95*

Field	Post-doc position, any sector	Post-doc position, academe
Biology	+**	−**
Chemistry	−*	−
Physics	+**	+*
Computer science	+**	+**
Engineering, any field	+**	+**
Earth science and oceanography	+**	+**
Mathematics	+**	+**
Agriculture	+**	+
Astronomy	+**	−
Medical fields	+**	+*

Notes:
* indicates that the estimate is significant at the 0.05 level.
** indicates that the estimate is significant at the 0.01 level.
See text for detailed explanation.

of exceptions. First, chemists coming from larger cohorts are less likely to report that they are taking a postdoctoral position. Second, biologists coming from larger cohorts are less likely to report that they are taking a postdoctoral position in academe; they are more likely to report that they are taking a postdoctoral regardless of sector. This result is somewhat curious. It may signify that demand for postdoctoral positions in academe did not keep pace with the supply of applicants, causing individuals to search outside academe for postdoctoral positions.

We use the per cent change in total current fund revenue for private and public institutions as a proxy for demand for PhDs by academe. The data on the total current fund revenues are from the Finance Survey of the Integrated Postsecondary Education Data System (IPEDS), conducted by the National Center for Education Statistics. Because total fund revenue data are available only for the period 1980–95, we estimate the basic post-doc logit equation for this period, substituting the percentage change in current fund revenue for the time variable. (Revenue data for public institutions are available for a longer period of time but are available for private institutions only up to 1995.)

We find the probability of taking a post-doc to be negatively and significantly (at the 1 per cent level) related to the per cent change in current fund revenue. This is true regardless of whether we focus on the population of 'definite and seeking' or simply the population that has definite plans. It also holds when, for the latter group, we examine the probability of holding an academic postdoctoral position, rather than a post-doc regardless of sector.

For the more inclusive time period, 1981 to 1999, we use the per cent change in total current fund revenue for public institutions as a measure of demand for PhDs by academe. Again, we find a negative and highly significant relationship between the demand measure and the probability of taking a postdoctoral position. Both the cohort and current fund revenue results are consistent with the hypothesis that young scientists and engineers seek postdoctoral positions in reaction to unfavorable job prospects in the traditional (academic) sector.

For the more abbreviated period, 1981 to 1995, we also examine the joint impact of the supply and demand variables at the field level. The cohort results for this joint model are fairly comparable to those reported in Table 4.5 for all post-docs; there are fewer instances where the cohort variable is significant in the academic post-doc equations. The demand variable is significant with the expected sign in the fields of earth science and oceanography and agriculture for both the post-doc and academic post-doc equations.

We also examine the impact that changes in the NIH budget have had on the probability of taking a post-doc position for the period 1981 to 1999 for PhDs in biology. We measure changes both in constant and current dollars.[12] We find the probability of taking a postdoctoral position to be negatively and significantly (at the 1 per cent level) related to the percentage change in current dollars. We find the relationship to be insignificant when percentage change is measured in constant dollars. The counter-intuitive result for current dollars may reflect changes occurring at the end of the 1990s when the post-doc frenzy had begun to decline as individuals began to choose alternative career paths, and is consistent with our findings that the odds of taking a post-doc dipped in the years after 1995. When we restrict the period to 1981 to 1995, we find the probability of taking a post-doc to be positively and significantly (at the 1 per cent level) related to the percentage change in the NIH budget, as measured in constant dollars. We find the coefficient on percentage change in current dollars to be insignificant.

By way of summary, our results clearly suggest that several factors contributed to the dramatic increase in postdoctoral positions that occurred in the late 1980s and early 1990s. They include (1) the increasing proportion of temporary residents in the graduate population; (2) the increasing proportion of degrees being awarded in biology; (3) the increasing size of PhD classes, especially in the fields of life sciences and engineering, and (4) declines in the growth of resources (measured in current dollars) available at both public and private institutions.

4.4 THE DURATION OF POSTDOCTORAL EXPERIENCE

As we mentioned earlier, in addition to more PhDs taking a post-doc position, the length of individuals' post-doc experience has also increased over the years. In this section, we first document the trends in the length of individuals' post-doc experience. We then estimate a model to examine various factors that contribute to these trends.

The data used in this section are drawn from the Survey of Doctorate Recipients (SDR). The SDR is a biennial longitudinal survey of doctorate recipients in the USA. The SDR is administered by the Science Resources Statistics (SRS) division of the NSF. The sampling frame for the SDR is the SED, which is the census of all PhDs awarded in the USA.

The longitudinal nature of the SDR survey permits one to study individuals over time, as they move from one position to another. In most survey years, the SDR asks if the respondent's current position is a post-doc position and, if so, the reasons the respondent took the post-doc. The 1995 survey includes a module with retrospective questions on individuals' career histories as well as past postdoctoral positions. Specifically, the 1995 special module ascertains for those who were no longer in a post-doc position the start and stop dates of the most recent post-doc, the second most recent post-doc, and the third most recent post-doc. For those holding a post-doc at the time of the survey, it asks for information on the current position as well as for information on up to two previous post-doc positions.

Based on this information, we calculate the length of an individual's post-doc experience by adding up the total number of months of the individual's current and past (up to three) post-doc appointments. For individuals who report starting a new post-doc position before the previous position has ended, we count the overlapping months only once.

Figure 4.1 plots the median length of individuals' post-doc experience, by the year in which their doctorate degrees were received. We exclude individuals who received their PhDs after 1990 because many were still in a post-doc position at the time of the survey and, therefore, the median lengths for these individuals are incomplete.

Clearly, the median length of individuals' post-doc experience for the ten fields has increased significantly between 1965 and 1990. The median length is 24 months for the 1965 cohort and 34 months for the 1990 cohort, a 42 per cent increase. The median length peaks at 36 months for the 1981 and 1982 cohorts.

Figure 4.2 breaks down the median length of post-doc experience by field for the entire 26-year period. It shows that there are significant differences

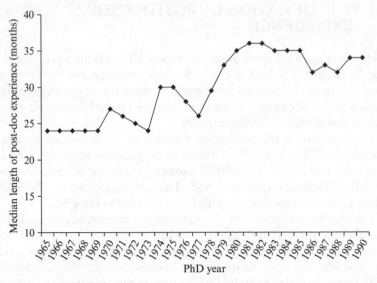

Figure 4.1   Median length (in months) of total post-doc experience for ten fields by PhD year

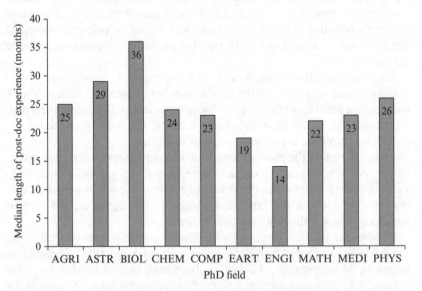

Figure 4.2   Median length (in months) of total post-doc experience by field for those who received a PhD between 1965 and 1990

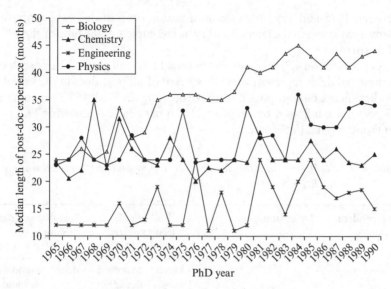

Figure 4.3   Median length (in months) of total post-doc experience for four fields by PhD year

across fields. During this period, biology PhDs stayed in post-doc positions the longest (36 months) followed by astronomy PhDs (29 months). Engineering PhDs stayed in post-doc positions the shortest (14 months).

Figure 4.3 plots the median lengths of post-doc experience for the largest four fields by PhD year. It shows that the median post-doc length has been going up for biology, physics, and engineering; the trend is most pronounced for biology. The median length for chemistry post-docs has stayed fairly flat.

To examine factors that have contributed to this trend in the lengthening of post-doc experience, we estimate a model in which the length of post-doc experience is explained by a variety of variables, including an individual's demographic characteristics such as age, number of dependents other than spouse in the household, marital status, race, gender and citizenship status. The demographic variables are measured at the time individuals received their PhDs. We also include in the model indicators for an individual's PhD year, field, and whether the most recent post-doc position offered pension and health benefits.

We restrict the analysis to those who have held at least one post-doc position and at most three post-doc positions, because the retrospective questions ask information only about the three most recent post-doc positions. Moreover, we restrict our sample to those who received their PhD between 1975 and 1990 because information on post-doc experience for many individuals in the later cohorts was incomplete at the time of the 1995 SDR survey.

As with section 4.3, we focus on ten broad field categories. The post-docs in these ten fields represent over 80 per cent of all post-docs in the sample. Of these fields, biology post-docs make up more than half (55.7 per cent) of all post-docs, followed by chemistry (12.0 per cent), engineering (9.7 per cent) and physics (8.5 per cent).

Table 4.6   Summary statistics for the full sample and postdoctoral sample, SDR 1975–90

Independent variables	Definition	Full sample (Sample size: 11 620)		Post-doc sample (Sample size: 5008)	
		Mean	Standard deviation	Mean	Standard deviation
AGE AT PHD	Respondent's age when received the first PhD	31.434	5.004	30.273	3.810
ASIAN	Respondent is Asian	0.171	0.377	0.167	0.373
BLACK	Respondent is Black	0.044	0.205	0.037	0.188
USTEMP	Temporary US resident	0.111	0.314	0.115	0.319
USPERM	Permanent US resident	0.055	0.227	0.042	0.200
FEMALE	Respondent is female	0.240	0.427	0.264	0.441
MARRIED	Respondent is married	0.616	0.486	0.556	0.497
DEPEND	Number of dependents	0.906	1.185	0.659	0.994
AGRI	Agriculture	0.041	0.199	0.030	0.171
MEDI	Medical or health	0.078	0.268	0.038	0.190
ENGI	Engineering	0.251	0.434	0.097	0.296
COMP	Computer sciences	0.022	0.148	0.004	0.066
MATH	Mathematics	0.051	0.221	0.023	0.149
ASTR	Astronomy	0.008	0.091	0.014	0.117
EART	Earth sciences	0.036	0.187	0.032	0.175
CHEM	Chemistry	0.104	0.306	0.120	0.325
PHYS	Physics	0.070	0.255	0.085	0.280
BIOL	Biology (benchmark)	0.338	0.473	0.557	0.497
PENSION	Most recent post-doc provided pension benefits	–	–	0.281	0.449
HEALTH	Most recent post-doc provided health benefits	–	–	0.817	0.387

Table 4.6   (continued)

Independent variables	Definition	Full sample (Sample size: 11 620)		Post-doc sample (Sample size: 5008)	
		Mean	Standard deviation	Mean	Standard deviation
BADJOBS	Reason for taking most recent post-docs was other jobs not available	–	–	0.124	0.330
ACADEME	Most recent post-doc was in academe (benchmark)	–	–	0.676	0.468
INDUSTRY	Most recent post-doc was in industry	–	–	0.056	0.229
GOVT	Most recent post-doc was in government	–	–	0.218	0.413
OTHER SECTOR	Most recent post-doc was in other sector	–	–	0.051	0.220
1976	Respondent received first PhD in 1966	0.048	0.213	0.054	0.225
1977		0.045	0.208	0.046	0.209
1978		0.047	0.211	0.049	0.215
1979		0.047	0.212	0.053	0.224
1980		0.044	0.206	0.043	0.203
1981		0.049	0.217	0.052	0.222
1982		0.051	0.220	0.057	0.231
1983		0.055	0.227	0.059	0.236
1984		0.063	0.242	0.063	0.243
1985		0.072	0.258	0.068	0.252
1986		0.074	0.261	0.069	0.254
1987		0.083	0.275	0.080	0.272
1988		0.090	0.286	0.079	0.270
1989		0.091	0.288	0.088	0.284
1990		0.091	0.288	0.094	0.292

Table 4.6 provides the summary statistics of these explanatory variables for the post-doc sample as well as for the full sample. Table 4.6 shows that, compared to the full sample, individuals in the post-doc sample received their first PhD degree about a year earlier than those in the full sample. A much higher proportion of the post-doc sample is in biology (55.7 per cent) than in the full sample (33.8 per cent). In addition, a slightly

higher proportion of the post-doc sample consists of temporary visa holders. These statistics are consistent with what we found in the propensity model in section 4.3.

Table 4.6 also shows that in the post-doc sample 67.6 per cent of the individuals held their most recent post-doc in academe (benchmark), 5.6 per cent in industry, 21.8 per cent in government and 5.1 per cent in other sectors. In terms of the fringe benefits, 81.7 per cent of the post-doc sample reported their most recent post-doc positions offered health benefits. However, only 28.1 per cent reported their most recent post-doc positions offered pension benefits.

Table 4.7 reports results from our basic Ordinary Least Square (OLS) model of the total length of an individual's post-doc experience. We include

Table 4.7   OLS regression results of postdoctoral length model, 1975–90 PhD cohorts (dependent variable: post-doc length)

Independent variables	Coefficient	Standard error	$Pr > |t|$
	Column 1	Column 2	Column 3
INTERCEPT	40.303	2.877	<0.0001
AGE AT PHD	−0.104	0.085	0.219
ASIAN	2.093	0.990	0.035
BLACK	−2.450	1.583	0.122
USTEMP	2.423	1.153	0.036
USPERM	−1.357	1.569	0.387
FEMALE	−0.591	0.709	0.404
MARRIED	−1.789	0.708	0.012
DEPEND	−1.176	0.378	0.002
AGRI	−15.108	1.751	<0.0001
MEDI	−14.758	1.580	<0.0001
ENGI	−23.190	1.085	<0.0001
COMP	−23.419	4.410	<0.0001
MATH	−18.407	1.988	<0.0001
ASTR	−8.159	2.515	0.001
EART	−16.993	1.691	<0.0001
CHEM	−14.323	0.946	<0.0001
PHYS	−11.157	1.096	<0.0001
PENSION	9.290	0.676	<0.0001
HEALTH	2.722	0.783	0.001
BADJOBS	2.692	0.907	0.003
INDUSTRY	−2.441	1.288	0.058
GOVT	0.229	0.724	0.752
OTHER SECTOR	1.797	1.342	0.181
1976	−0.662	1.855	0.721

Table 4.7 (continued)

Independent variables	Coefficient	Standard error	Pr > | t |
	Column 1	Column 2	Column 3
1977	−2.112	1.925	0.273
1978	−2.494	1.902	0.190
1979	1.645	1.866	0.378
1980	9.402	3.232	0.171
1981	11.233	3.158	0.005
1982	11.082	3.150	0.029
1983	8.204	3.138	0.223
1984	10.008	3.116	0.014
1985	9.817	3.077	0.045
1986	7.382	3.056	0.021
1987	7.849	3.022	0.093
1988	6.390	3.025	0.179
1989	6.448	2.997	0.122
1990	3.553	2.988	0.795
Dependent mean (months)	35.8		
Number of observations	5008		
R-square	0.190		

all individuals who received a PhD between 1975 and 1990 and held at least one, but at most three post-doc positions. The dependent variable in this model is the total length of an individual's post-doc experience. The results suggest that the length of an individual's post-doc experience is negatively associated with the age at which an individual received his/her PhD. However, the estimate is not statistically significant. This indicates that while younger PhDs are more likely to take a post-doc position (as suggested by the results from section 4.3), age does not play a significant role in how long individuals spend in post-doc positions after they take a post-doc position.

Personal characteristics play an important role. The results show that those on temporary US visas spend on average 2.4 months more in post-doc positions than US citizens and the estimate is significant. Asians tend to stay in post-doc positions longer than whites (benchmark) and the estimate is statistically significant. Everything else equal, Asians spend about 2.1 months longer in post-doc positions than whites. Blacks on average spend about 2.5 months shorter in post-doc positions than whites. (Note that other races are excluded from the analysis due to their small sample sizes.)

Married individuals on average spend 1.8 months shorter in post-doc than others and the estimate is statistically significant. Post-doc length is negatively associated with the number of dependents (other than spouse) and the estimate is significant. These results are consistent with the theory that post-doc training is considered an investment in additional human capital and individuals with capital constraints are less likely to opt for the investment.

Results also show that field of training matters a great deal. Compared to biology post-docs (benchmark), individuals in other fields spend between 8 to 23 fewer months in post-doc positions, depending on the field. For example, engineers and computer scientists on average spend 23 fewer months in post-doc than biologists; astronomers on average spend about 8 fewer months in post-doc than biologists. The estimates of all field variables are statistically significant at the 0.1 per cent level. These results show that not only are biology PhDs more likely to take a post-doc position (as suggested by results from section 4.3), they also tend to spend more time in post-doc positions.

The sector in which the most recent post-doc position is held seems to matter somewhat. Compared to those whose most recent post-doc is in academe (benchmark), those whose most recent post-doc is in industry spend 2.4 fewer months in post-doc and the estimate is significant.

The fringe benefits provided by the most recent post-doc position play an important role in the length of an individual's post-doc experience. Everything being equal, those who receive pension benefits stay on a post-doc position 9.3 more months than those who do not have pension benefits. Those who receive health insurance stay on 2.7 more months than those who do not receive health insurance.

The results also show that most PhD year dummy variables (1979 to 1990) are positive and statistically significant (the benchmark is 1975). This suggests that the length of post-doc experience has been rising during the period between 1979 and 1990.

The 1995 SDR post-doc module includes questions on the reasons for taking the post-doc positions. One in eight respondents state that they took the most recent post-doc because other jobs were not available. Although this is clearly a highly subjective measure of labor market conditions, in the absence of other measures we include it in the analysis. We find that those who report 'bad jobs' as the reason for having taken the most post-doc position hold the position 2.7 months longer than those who do not report this as the reason.

We also estimate a duration model of post-doc length.[13] The duration model allows us to include all post-docs in the analysis while taking into account the fact that some individuals were still on a post-doc position at the time of the 1995 survey (right-censored). In the duration model, the dependent variable is the log of the post-doc length. Results are reported in columns 1 and 2 in Table 4.8. To put these results in perspective, we also estimate our OLS model using the log of post-doc length as the dependent variable for the time period 1975–90 and report the results in columns 3 and 4. These results show that estimates from the duration model are very similar to those from the OLS model, further confirming that our OLS results are robust.

Table 4.8   *Duration and OLS regression results (dependent variable: log of post-doc length)*

Independent variables	Duration model 1975–90 PhD cohorts		OLS model 1975–90 PhD cohorts	
	Coefficient Column 1	Standard error Column 2	Coefficient Column 3	Standard error Column 4
INTERCEPT	3.713	0.085	3.561	0.090
AGE AT PHD	0.000	0.003	−0.006	0.003
ASIAN	0.086	0.029	0.039	0.031
BLACK	−0.079	0.046	−0.134	0.050
USTEMP	0.069	0.034	0.104	0.036
USPERM	−0.050	0.045	−0.032	0.049
FEMALE	−0.008	0.020	−0.022	0.022
MARRIED	−0.059	0.020	−0.037	0.022
DEPEND	−0.032	0.011	−0.040	0.012
AGRI	−0.405	0.051	−0.507	0.055
MEDI	−0.419	0.045	−0.458	0.049
ENGI	−0.762	0.031	−0.861	0.034
COMP	−0.840	0.125	−0.934	0.138
MATH	−0.527	0.057	−0.618	0.062
ASTR	−0.266	0.071	−0.180	0.079
EART	−0.478	0.049	−0.603	0.053
CHEM	−0.405	0.027	−0.448	0.030
PHYS	−0.314	0.032	−0.345	0.034
PENSION	0.283	0.020	0.239	0.021
HEALTH	0.080	0.022	0.174	0.024
BADJOBS	0.140	0.027	0.003	0.028
INDUSTRY	−0.035	0.037	−0.063	0.040
GOVT	0.008	0.021	0.009	0.023
OTHER SECTOR	0.030	0.039	0.024	0.042
1976	−0.029	0.052	−0.030	0.058
1977	−0.022	0.054	−0.092	0.060
1978	−0.100	0.053	−0.091	0.060
1979	0.064	0.052	0.006	0.058
1980	0.076	0.055	0.050	0.061

Table 4.8   (continued)

Independent variables	Duration model 1975–90 PhD cohorts		OLS model 1975–90 PhD cohorts	
	Coefficient Column 1	Standard error Column 2	Coefficient Column 3	Standard error Column 4
1981	0.137	0.053	0.118	0.059
1982	0.081	0.051	0.094	0.058
1983	0.012	0.051	0.050	0.057
1984	0.131	0.051	0.108	0.057
1985	0.081	0.050	0.078	0.056
1986	0.107	0.050	0.122	0.056
1987	0.100	0.049	0.090	0.054
1988	0.084	0.049	0.071	0.054
1989	0.127	0.049	0.106	0.053
1990	0.084	0.049	0.018	0.053

Notes:
For the duration model, the total number of observations is 5006 (4698 non-censored).
For the OLS model, the number of observation is 5008.

4.5   CONCLUDING REMARKS

US research universities have become increasingly populated by postdoctoral fellows. During the 1990s, for example, the proportion of PhDs on US campuses who were post-docs increased by over 16 per cent. This increase is a mixed blessing for research universities. On the one hand, post-docs receive training and contribute to the research productivity of the university. On the other hand, the growing number of post-docs on campuses, coupled with their poor job prospects, has led to considerable dissatisfaction among them. This in turn creates morale problems for laboratories. It can also have negative spillover effects for undergraduates pondering a career in science or engineering.

Here we have examined factors contributing to this increase, paying particular attention to the propensity of individuals to take a post-doc and the amount of time individuals spend in post-doc positions. We find that the increased propensity to take a postdoctoral position can be attributed to a change in the mix of doctoral students, particularly to the increased proportion of PhDs being awarded in the life sciences and the increased proportion of temporary residents in the graduate population. The increased propensity to take a post-doc position also relates to adverse job market conditions experienced by PhDs during the period.

We find that increased duration can be explained by some of the same factors. These include the increasing proportion of temporary residents in the graduate population and the increased number of degrees being awarded in the life sciences. Adverse job market conditions also appear to play a role, although we have a subjective measure of the state of the market. We also find the duration of the post-doc experience to be positively related to the provision of pension and health benefits.

In recent years, as the proportion of the campus community who are post-docs has grown, university administrators have begun to address many of the complex issues related to post-docs. These include length of tenure in position, pay and fringe benefits. It is now becoming somewhat common, for example, for universities to limit tenure in a postdoctoral position to five years, and many universities now provide the fringe benefits that historically were not provided to post-docs. These are fixes that can be made at the university level. The major issue of job market prospects, however, is outside the scope of the local university. Our work suggests that during the late 1990s, when the economy heated up, the propensity to take a post-doc declined. Universities have little direct impact on short-term economic growth. But, they do have the ability to influence the way in which national research funds are distributed and committed. One possible 'fix' to the post-doc situation is to use federal funds increasingly to support career positions of research scientists. Gerbi and Garrison (2004) recommend that universities 'look beyond the current scheme of graduate students and postdoctorals to staff the academic research laboratory,' recognizing the importance of the research scientist's position and rewarding research scientists with salaries that make the position an 'honorable career.'

ACKNOWLEDGEMENT

We would like to thank Grant Black of Indiana University South Bend and Jake Rugh (formerly of the TIAA-CREF Institute) for their assistance. We also thank Science Resources Statistics, National Science Foundation for providing access to the Survey of Doctorate Recipients and the Survey of Earned Doctorates. We have benefited from the comments of Robert Clark, Richard Freeman and Bill Amis. Stephan would like to acknowledge the financial support provided by the TIAA-CREF Institute for this project, and from the Andrew W. Mellon Foundation for support of work with the Survey of Earned Doctorates.

NOTES

1. Source: National Science Foundation, Graduate Students and Postdoctorates in Science and Engineering: Fall 2001, Table 46.

2. Source: National Science Foundation, Graduate Students and Postdoctorates in Science and Engineering: Fall 2001, Table 48, accessed at www.nsf.gov/sbe/srs/nsf03320/pdf/ nsf03320.pdf. Post-doctoral positions in health fields are excluded because many of these positions are held by MDs working in clinical fields.
3. Sixty-nine per cent of all postdoctoral appointees in 2001 were supported by federal funds. Among those on federal support, 80 per cent were supported by research grants. Source: National Science Foundation, Graduate Students and Postdoctorates in Science and Engineering: Fall 2001, Table 47.
4. Source: Authors' calculations based on data from the 1995 Survey of Doctorate Recipients.
5. Source: Authors' calculations based on data from various years' Survey of Doctorate Recipients.
6. The GSS survey includes the following fields: physical sciences, earth, atmosphere, and ocean sciences, mathematical sciences, computer sciences, agricultural sciences, biological sciences, psychology, social sciences, engineering, and other health fields. Health fields are excluded from the calculations.
7. Sources: National Science Foundation, Graduate Students and Postdoctorates in Science and Engineering: Fall 2001, Table 47 and National Science Foundation, Graduate Students and Postdoctorates in Science and Engineering: Fall 1998, Table 48. Postdoctoral positions in health fields are excluded from the calculations.
8. For a quantitative variable, if we subtract 1.0 from the odds ratio and multiply by 100, the resulting number can be interpreted as the percentage change in the odds for each unit increase in the independent variable.
9. A top program in a given field is defined as one ranked in the top ten based on the National Research Council's 1993 ranking of scholarly quality for all fields except agriculture and medicine. A top program in these two fields is defined as being among the top ten institutions for federally funded R&D expenditures in the given field. For our fields that are more broadly defined than the NRC program definitions, such as biology, our rankings are based on the mean of all NRC-rated programs at an institution that fall under our field definition.
10. We consistently found the non-linear term 'age-squared' to be insignificant and thus use only the variable 'age.'
11. The sample is restricted to those with definite plans.
12. Data are taken from www.aaas.org/spp/rd/hist04c.pdf, accessed February 2004.
13. Our duration model is estimated using the Lifereg procedure in SAS.

REFERENCES

Cox, D.R. (1972), 'Regression models and life tables (with discussion)', *Journal of the Royal Statistical Society*, Series B 34, 187–220.
Cox, D.R. (1975), 'Partial likelihood', *Biometrika*, **72**, 269–76.
Gerbi, Susan A. and Howard H. Garrison (2004), 'The workforce for biomedical research – who will do the work', in Ronald Ehrenberg and Paula Stephan (eds), *Science and the University*, Madison: University of Wisconsin Press.
Levin, Sharon, Paula Stephan and Mary Beth Walker (1995), 'Planck's principle', *Social Studies of Science*, **25** (2), 275–84.
Maresi, Nerad and Joseph Cerny (1999), 'Postdoctoral patterns, career advancement, and problems', *Science*, **295** (5433), 1533–5.
Mervis, Jeffrey (1999), 'Cheap labor is key to the US research productivity', *Science*, **295** (5433), 1519–21.
National Research Council: Committee on Dimensions, Causes, and Implications

of Recent Trends in the Careers of Life Scientists (1998), *Trends in the Early Careers of Life Scientists*, Washington, DC: National Academy Press.

Schmidt, Karen (1999), 'Will the job market ever get better?', *Science*, **285** (5433), 1517–19.

Stephan, Paula and Sharon Levin (2000), 'Career stage, benchmarking and collective research', *International Journal of Technology Management*, **22** (7/8), 676–87.

Stephan, Paula and Sharon Levin (2002), 'Implicit contracts in collaborative scientific research', in Philip Mirowski and Ester-Mirjam Sent (eds), *Science Bought and Sold*, Chicago: University of Chicago Press, pp. 412–30.

5. Planning for the generational turnover of the faculty: faculty perceptions and institutional practices

Jerry Berberet, Betsy E. Brown, Carole J. Bland, Kelly R. Risbey and Carroll-Ann Trotman

5.1 OVERVIEW

Perhaps no challenge is more critical to the future of higher education than the ability of colleges and universities to plan for and effectively manage concurrent mass retirements and mass hirings. Over the coming decade an entire generation of faculty, hired during the higher education expansion of the 1960s and early 1970s, will retire and a new generation of faculty will be hired to educate an increasingly diverse student body and carry higher education forward into the twenty-first century. This chapter addresses the overarching concerns about what will be lost and what will be gained as the academy navigates this transition. Our theory is that institutions and their faculty must act as partners to minimize the loss of intellectual capital and cultural traditions during this generational turnover. Two faculty surveys – one focused on late-career faculty and the other on early-career faculty – were designed to probe this theory and provide insights into the work patterns, values, and perceptions of faculty during this time of change. The chapter presents results of the late-career faculty survey and the development of the early-career survey; together they will offer a holistic analysis of the challenges and opportunities facing academia during this time of 'generational change.' Our findings will help colleges and universities to plan strategically for policies and practices that deal effectively with faculty retirement, recruitment and retention, and assist institutions, pension providers, and faculty members with planning for retirement.

5.2 THE LATE FACULTY CAREER AND GENERATIONAL TURNOVER

Our survey of senior faculty grew out of the recognition that approximately one-half of all faculty in American higher education are aged 50 and older, that colleges and universities have as much as two-thirds of their faculty payrolls invested in these faculty, and that a 'generational turnover' of the American professoriate will occur over the first decade of the 21st century, as the late-career faculty cohort retires in large numbers. The need to understand faculty planning for retirement and its impact on institutions, as well as the values, work patterns, and sources of motivation and satisfaction that influence senior faculty behavior, provided the foundation for our survey.

The survey was conducted for the following purposes:

1. To learn about faculty work patterns, professional interests, and institutional relationships in the late career;
2. To solicit faculty plans regarding retirement, including what might cause them to retire early or delay retirement;
3. To gain insights into ways faculty members and their institutions might cooperate for mutual benefit during the late career and, possibly, in retirement; and
4. To identify ways in which late-career and retiring faculty might serve as resources as institutions find and retain new faculty members who will replace them.

Furthermore, the survey tests an adult development theory that the late career is a time of narrowing interests, more focused commitments, and a desire to make contributions that 'leave a legacy,' in the process making meaning of a person's life and career (Bland and Bergquist 1997). This survey complements earlier work on senior faculty retirement, including the 2000 AAUP survey of colleges and university retirement policies (Cool 2002) and the 1999–2000 Mellon College Retirement Project survey of senior faculty at liberal arts colleges, the results of which were presented at the TIAA–CREF Institute 'Dialogue on Faculty Retirement Incentives' in November 2002.

With the support of the TIAA–CREF Institute and active participation of the American Association of Higher Education, three sectors of higher education – the Associated New American Colleges (comprising 19 independent comprehensive colleges), the 16-campus University of North Carolina, and the five-campus University of Minnesota – collaborated in fall 2003 on a comprehensive online survey of faculty aged 50 and older at large public research universities and public and private comprehensive and liberal arts colleges and universities. Faculty as young as age 50 were included in the cohort both to develop a longitudinal view of faculty in the late career and to facilitate faculty–institutional collaboration in late-career planning.

Nearly 2000 valid responses were received, a response rate that ranged from a high as 38.8 per cent at the University of Minnesota to 15.6 per cent at the University of North Carolina. (Although a somewhat low response rate, UNC respondents and non-respondents are demographically similar.) Creative Analytics, Inc., a survey and assessment firm in Indianapolis, collaborated in survey design, managed the website where the survey questionnaire was posted, and provided summaries of the data and data files for additional analysis of responses.

5.2.1 Preliminary Findings

A profile of highly productive, generally satisfied senior faculty who plan to retire well past age 65 and are anxious to play meaningful roles at their institutions emerged from our study. Survey findings also suggest that there is significant potential for senior faculty and their institutions to work together in planning for the faculty generational turnover, especially if institutions recognize what motivates faculty and are sensitive to institutional governance and management issues that have historically caused divisions between faculty members and administrators. The data tables and interpretations that follow highlight the demographic, financial, and attitudinal profiles and work patterns of senior faculty. Tables 5.1–5.4, 5.6 and 5.7 present mean responses to survey items. Percentages in Tables 5.5, 5.8, and 5.9 are derived from summing the two highest responses on a four-point scale asking respondents to rate agreement, significance, or importance on survey statements asking for an opinion; thus, percentages reflect the per cent of 'agree/strongly agree,' 'significant/very significant,' or 'important/very important' responses.

5.2.2 Demographic and Professional Profile of Respondents

Demographic analysis of survey responses in Table 5.1 reveals great similarity across the three survey sectors, including such variables as age, gender, racial/ethnic identity, and marital status. The professional profile that emerges from the survey is of a senior faculty cohort, overwhelmingly full-time, of largely tenured, white, male full professors. What at first sight may appear to be a somewhat surprising consistency may simply be the result of similar hiring patterns and practices during a period of higher education

Table 5.1   Demographic characteristics of respondents (September 2003)

	ANAC	UNC	UM	All
Respondents (number)	554	835	560	1949
Response rate (%)	28.4	15.6	38.8	21.8
Mean age (yrs)	57	58	58	58
Gender (% women)	36	33	25	32
Racial/ethnic identity (% white)	94	91	94	93
Marital status (% married)	79	79	83	80
Women faculty married (%)	59	59	62	59

expansion in both public and private sectors, when both sectors filled faculty positions from a common pool of candidates being turned out in increasing numbers as doctoral programs expanded. Although the numbers of women and minorities in graduate school were growing, their numbers were not large, and the major impacts of affirmative action in admissions and faculty hiring lay in the future. The higher percentage of responses by minority faculty members at the University of North Carolina probably reflects the presence of five historically black institutions in the UNC system.

A striking feature of the demographic profile is the significant difference, consistently across the three sectors, in marital status between men (90 per cent married) and women faculty (60 per cent married). (While it is not our intention in this essay to analyse gender differences in detail, important statistical differences will be noted. A full-fledged gender analysis of survey results is underway.)

Survey findings in Table 5.2 support the view that senior faculty have not been a highly mobile cohort, in part because of the tight job market by the time they had built a professional resumé that might have given them job mobility. The similar longevity in higher education and at their current institutions across the sectors is consistent with other demographic similarities in the data. At the University of Minnesota the cohort is overwhelmingly tenured, and the percentage of female tenured professors is much higher than at ANAC and UNC, although the percentage of female respondents is somewhat lower at UM. Also at UM, virtually all senior faculty are on the tenure track, compared with the 14 per cent of the respondents who do not hold tenure-track appointments at ANAC and UNC institutions.

Perhaps the most unexpected result in the professional profile data is the significant percentage of respondents (35 per cent) who hold administrative assignments and the amount of work time that is devoted to these assignments. The administrative workload data may be slightly inflated because 5 per cent of the respondents hold dual faculty and administrative

Table 5.2   Professional profile of respondents

	ANAC	UNC	UM	All
Mean years in higher education	24	25	28	26
Mean years at current institution	18	19	23	20
Full-time (%)	97	96	96	96
Tenured (%)	77	87	96	84
Women tenured (%)	65	67	93	74
Not on tenure track (%)	14	14	2	11
Professor (%)	53	61	74	62
Women professors (%)	32	42	58	42
With administrative appointments (%)	38	35	32	35
Time allocated to administration (%)	41	57	44	49

appointments that are largely full-time administration. Still, the survey cohort as a whole carries a significant burden of their institutions' administration, and it is tempting to speculate that there is a correlation with their feeling (84 per cent agree/strongly agree) that their institutional service is insufficiently rewarded.

5.2.3   Work Patterns

Our survey elicited a highly positive profile of the late-career faculty member as a productive professional and responsible citizen of an academic institutional community. Indeed, the data in Table 5.3 suggest that senior faculty members in research universities as well as liberal arts and comprehensive institutions spend significant time teaching and that faculty members in the latter two types of institutions are active scholars. The survey provides empirical evidence to rebuff the stereotypes, caricatures, and myths regarding what amount and type of work faculty conduct. Table 5.3 presents self-reported evidence that senior faculty work hard – a mean of 57 hours per week, consistent across the three sectors and nearly identical among men and women. Our analysis of responses by age cohort reveals that this pattern of work holds up even into the very late career where age 60 and older respondents reported working a mean of 56 hours per week.

The survey also asked faculty members to assess the extent that their work patterns are aligned with how they believe their institutions expect them to allocate their work time (Table 5.4). In the main, there is high correlation within the ANAC cohort, although respondents say they spend slightly less time in research and creative activities than they believe their

Table 5.3   Faculty work patterns

	ANAC	UNC	UM	All
Hours worked per week	54	57	57	57
Hours teaching	31	24	22	26
Hours research/creative activities	7	13	17	12
Hours institutional and community service	11	14	12	13
Hours professional development	3	3	2	3
Other	2	3	4	3
Papers and publications last three years	3	6	9	6

Table 5.4   Work allocation vs. perception of institutional expectations

	ANAC		UNC		UM	
	Actual (%)	Exp. (%)	Actual (%)	Exp. (%)	Actual (%)	Exp. (%)
Hours teaching	59	56	46	42	40	34
Hours research/ creative activities	13	17	20	29	29	39
Hours institutional and community service	20	18	26	19	24	19
Hours professional development	5	6	5	5	4	4

Note: Percentage totals equal less than 100 per cent because only primary categories of faculty work are included in the table. As such, the category of 'other' was excluded.

institutions expect. Faculty members at the Universities of North Carolina and Minnesota spend a larger number of hours teaching and in institutional and community service than their perceptions of institutional expectations and a smaller number of hours in research and creative activities. In fact, the number of papers and publications faculty report in all three sectors reveals a record of substantial scholarly productivity, perhaps supporting a conclusion that faculty, on balance, appear to allocate their time well among all three of their primary endeavors.

While late-career faculty members appear to welcome institutional engagement and service, survey results suggest that they feel lukewarm encouragement at best from their institutions for such involvement. Survey results also suggest that institutions provide inadequate encouragement for time spent on service initiatives. For example, in addition to the high percentage noted earlier who feel that their institutions inadequately reward institutional service, 48 per cent feel that their expertise and leadership abilities are underutilized.

These findings may suggest that actual faculty work patterns and perceptions are more alike in various types of institutions than is commonly believed. It is tempting to ask whether there may be some stereotyping among faculty members in their perceptions of institutional expectations. Considering that all respondents work more teaching and service hours than they believe their institutions expect, and feel their service work is inadequately rewarded, it would be interesting to determine if institutions do in fact have larger research expectations and smaller teaching and service expectations than senior faculty members report working.

It seems apparent that this faculty work ethic comes at a cost – 52 per cent of respondents indicate that their job 'is a source of considerable personal strain' and 54 per cent agree that the 'low level of appreciation' they feel that they receive from their institution is stressful. Moreover, 86 per cent complain of not having time 'to give a piece of work the attention it deserves' and 73 per cent say that feeling 'burned out' would cause them to retire earlier. The burden of balancing work and other responsibilities appears to fall heaviest on women, 92 per cent of whom report time pressures as a source of stress.

5.2.4   Sources of Motivation and Satisfaction

Higher education employs a variety of *extrinsic* incentives to encourage the faculty's hard work and productivity, among them salary increases, publication expectations, tenure, promotion, and sabbaticals. Table 5.5 indicates the powerful role *intrinsic* factors play as well as sources of faculty motivation and satisfaction. Indeed, the responses to intellectual stimulation of one's field, and the opportunity to have institutional impact, reflect among the highest rates of agreement to items in the entire survey, with favorable student evaluations close behind. Interestingly, the influence of merit pay for performance receives sector responses that are among the most divergent

Table 5.5   Sources of motivation and satisfaction

	ANAC (%)	UNC (%)	UM (%)	All (%)
Intellectual stimulation of my field	98	98	99	98
My contributions have a positive impact at my institution	93	95	93	94
Favorable student evaluations	90	87	88	88
Merit pay based on performance	74	92	88	86

in the survey; although still high, merit pay ranks only seventh among possible incentives among ANAC respondents. (The higher UNC response on this item may reflect the absence of significant salary increases from the state in the last three years.) Overall, these survey results are consistent with other studies of faculty motivation and satisfaction which rank intellectual inquiry at the top, followed by desire for membership in a meaningful academic community, to have institutional impact, and to be recognized for one's work (Wergin 2001).

This review of the demographic and professional profile of senior faculty respondents, and their work patterns and motivations, provides an essential prelude for exploration of the late-career transition to retirement – the variables influencing the decision to retire, what institutions must seek to replace in hiring the faculty of the future, roles senior faculty might play in the faculty generational turnover, and the aspirations of late-career faculty for their retirement years.

5.3   TRANSITION TO RETIREMENT: PERSPECTIVES AND PLANS

Survey questions regarding retirement plans resulted in an almost uniform mean of 66 as the planned retirement age (men age 66, women age 65), and an equally uniform one-third in each sector indicated they 'did not know' when they would retire. Notably, the mean planned retirement age increases to 68 in the age 60 and older respondent cohort, and only 13 per cent (250 respondents) said they were likely to retire in the next three years. Early and phased retirement programs are more widely in place at the Universities of North Carolina and Minnesota than at ANAC member institutions, but they are popular in all three sectors and may have significant influence in the timing of faculty retirements. For example, 53 per cent of ANAC respondents would like their institutions to develop phased retirement. Table 5.6 reveals that nearly one-third of respondents plan to take advantage of phased retirement programs where they are available. Table 5.6 also suggests that a significant percentage of faculty members at the Universities of North Carolina and Minnesota are unaware that their institutions offer phased retirement (18 and 31 per cent respectively, desiring its availability when it is already available), a response that emphasizes the importance of effective communication of retirement options and benefits to faculty.

Financial circumstances, of course, play a key role in retirement decisions. Our survey results (Table 5.7) yield the intriguing finding, in spite of a fairly wide disparity in income levels across the three sectors, that

Table 5.6   Retirement plans

	ANAC	UNC	UM	All
Mean planned retirement age (yrs)	66	66	67	66
Planned retirement age (age 60 and older cohort)	67	68	68	68
Don't know when they will retire (%)	31	33	33	32
Mean years to planned retirement (yrs)	9	8	9	9
Likely to retire in next three years (%)	13	15	10	13
Institution offers phases retirement plan (%)	40	95	83	76
If not, would like phased retirement availability (%)	53	18	31	32
Plan to enter phased retirement program (%)	16	32	38	29

Table 5.7   Financial profile of respondents

	ANAC	UNC	UM	All
Base salary ($)	64 514	84 362	95 465	81 767
Other institutional income ($)	3 077	5 041	9 677	5 790
Income from other sources ($)	7 527	10 143	12 311	10 001
Total income from above sources ($)	76 922	98 688	116 944	97 712
Current income needed to retire (%)	76	76	77	76
Income needed for retirement ($)	60 724	74 940	89 732	75 114
Don't know income needed for retirement (%)	25	24	24	24

respondents uniformly believe they will need 76–77 per cent of their current income for life in retirement. This consistency may result from respondents' heeding the advice of the sponsors of some faculty retirement programs that they will need at least 75–80 per cent of their working income in retirement to maintain their purchasing power before retirement. Obviously, such a consistent percentage relates to a wide variance in projected retirement incomes. The faculty financial profile makes clear that faculty in all three sectors receive significant income, ranging from 15 to 25 per cent of their income total, from institutional and other sources beyond their base salaries. The availability of such income should not be ignored in projecting financial circumstances leading faculty to retire. It should also be noted that a quarter of respondents profess not to know how much income they will need in retirement.

As they may appear to be a kind of anomaly, it should be explained that the higher income levels of University of Minnesota respondents appear to be influenced by the fact that nearly a quarter of these faculty are in medical and health science fields. Moreover, many of these and other UM faculty members are on eleven-month rather than nine-month appointments.

Table 5.8   Retirement planning issues

	ANAC (%)	UNC (%)	UM (%)	All (%)
Reasons to delay retirement				
High work satisfaction	88	90	89	90
Financial/other incentives (e.g., phased retirement plan)	88	80	83	83
Rising cost of health care	87	80	83	83
Anxieties about state of the economy	76	74	74	75
Institutional support for professional development	69	66	63	66
Opportunity to assist institution in planning to replace me	65	64	66	65
New institutional opportunities	40	46	42	43
Reasons to retire earlier				
Having sufficient income to retire	84	84	84	84
Feeling 'burned out'	75	75	68	73
Work environment dissatisfaction	64	74	67	69
Not performing job to my expectations	65	64	72	66
Availability of an early retirement program	70	61	70	66
Financial pressures facing institution	29	29	25	28

A major aim of the survey was to discover circumstances that could trigger faculty members' decisions to retire earlier than planned or to delay retirement. The findings in Table 5.8 are not startling, but they do suggest personal and professional circumstances that institutions can influence to their benefit. High work satisfaction, health care considerations, and financial incentives stand out as powerful drivers of faculty behavior regarding decisions to retire. It seems particularly noteworthy that approximately two-thirds of respondents indicate that opportunities for new institutional roles, faculty development support geared to the late career, and opportunities to assist their institution to achieve institutionally-beneficial retirement transitions could influence them to delay retirement. Acting on such possibilities could prove to be invaluable to colleges and universities in retaining the services of senior faculty who will continue to make critical institutional contributions. Where accelerated retirement seems a preferred course of action, it is helpful to know that two-thirds of respondents would find early retirement programs attractive.

In weighing faculty views when developing retirement policies, it seems instructive that only 28 per cent of respondents agree that financial pressures facing their institution might cause them to retire earlier. At the same time, survey responses also suggest a kind of 'self-regulation' among late-career faculty, many of whom respond that they would retire earlier than planned if their performance fell below their expectations or they felt 'burned out.'

Concerns noted earlier about health and health care carry over as the highest priority of late-career faculty members in thinking about the relationship they would like to have with their institutions in retirement. Indeed, health care benefits in retirement and motivation received from the intellectual stimulation of their disciplines received the strongest positive responses of the entire survey. Faculty concerns about health issues, however, simply reflect one of the most important concerns of our time and should not overshadow the equally significant faculty desire to remain part of the academic community they cherished during their professional careers (Table 5.9). Survey findings strongly suggest a desire to continue a mutually-beneficial connection with their institution in retirement, whether through opportunities for part-time teaching or maintaining library, office, and computer access. An area potentially significant to institutions seems evident in a full one-third of respondents who express interest in various institutional volunteer roles, and the 18 per cent even willing to volunteer for institutional fundraising roles.

As Americans increasingly retire in good health and with life expectancies 15–30 years beyond their retirement date, we have begun to look at

Table 5.9   Institutional relationships in retirement

	ANAC (%)	UNC (%)	UM (%)	All (%)
Health care benefits from institution	97	99	98	98
Library privileges	79	82	86	82
Opportunities for part-time teaching or other paid activities	72	72	69	71
Access to office space, computers, photocopying, etc.	68	72	83	74
Parking privileges	53	68	55	60
Retired faculty association amenities, e.g., campus space to meet	40	38	38	38
Volunteer in areas such as student recruitment, tutoring, mentoring	35	35	35	35
Volunteer as speaker/liaison to alumni/community groups	34	30	30	31
Volunteer in institutional fundraising roles	18	15	21	18

quality of life and the potential civic and community contributions of these years in new and vibrant ways. Higher education may have an unparalleled opportunity to provide the farsighted leadership society expects and which higher education can model, with possibilities for direct and perhaps critical institutional benefits as a new generation of faculty comes on board.

5.3.1 Summary Comments on the Senior Faculty Survey

Our survey results portray a senior faculty cohort that has much in common – demographically, attitudinally, and professionally – across different institutional types and the public and private sectors of higher education. Respondents as a group plan to retire at about age 66, until they reach age 60 when their mean projected retirement age becomes 67 or 68. This tendency to delay retirement as faculty members age appears related to continuing high levels of work satisfaction and concerns about the need for sufficient retirement income and the rising costs of health care. In pinpointing the important role that health benefits will play in faculty retirement decisions and during retirement, our survey results parallel those of the Mellon College Retirement Project survey of private liberal arts college faculty, which found that the availability or lack of health benefits is the single most important variable in faculty decisions to retire (Cool 2002). Indeed, 98 per cent of respondents in our survey agreed or strongly agreed that health benefits are important in the relationship they want to have with their institution during retirement, the highest positive response in our entire survey. In light of this response, the predictions by Sylvester S. Schieber and John Rust elsewhere in this volume (Chapters 6 and 7) are particularly relevant: both cite changes in the costs and long-term funding of retiree health care benefits that may lead colleges and universities to decrease benefits or increase eligibility requirements for such benefits. This trend is already widespread among for-profit employers and some higher education institutions. In the future, the disappearance or reduction of retiree health care benefits is likely to significantly affect retirement rates of faculty under 65 years of age (i.e., not eligible for Medicare benefits).

Our survey responses also suggest that the availability of early and phased retirement programs influence faculty retirement decisions and that most faculty members desire these options: 29 per cent of all respondents plan to enter phased retirement, although it is not widely offered at ANAC member institutions. Analyses of satisfaction with phased retirement programs by David W. Leslie and Natasha Janson (Chapter 11) and Steven G. Allen (Chapter 9) included in this volume indicate that such programs are attractive to faculty members who are generally satisfied with their jobs and want to continue their relationship with their institutions as they transition from full-time employment into retirement. Both authors report that phased retirees express very positive views of their experience in the programs. Allen's study is particularly relevant to the findings of our senior faculty survey, since he reports on a survey of participants in the UNC Phased Retirement Program. The percentage of UNC respondents to the senior faculty survey who intend to enter phased retirement (32 per cent) is within the percentages of retiring tenured faculty members at UNC campuses who have entered the program each year since its inception, suggesting that the program may continue to attract 25–35 per cent of retiring tenured faculty members.

In addition, our survey results provide a glimpse of faculty aspirations for life during retirement. It seems clear that most faculty want to maintain contact with the academic community they experienced (and enjoyed) during their professional careers, and that retired faculty and their institutions might 'have their cake and eat it, too' through continued involvement of retired faculty in institutional life. Not only are late-career faculty interested in retirement perks such as library and parking privileges and access to office space and computers, but they are also interested in opportunities for part-time teaching or other paid activities. One-third would volunteer for roles involving students (e.g., admissions, tutoring, mentoring, student organization advisor), or as speaker or liaison to alumni and community groups. Perhaps strikingly, nearly one in five would volunteer for institutional fundraising roles. The reality that most respondents are in the driver's seat regarding their retirement age decisions (since 84 per cent of respondents are tenured) and that only 13 per cent of survey respondents plan to retire in the next three years, underscores the case for collaboration.

Our profile of highly productive senior faculty contradicts the generalized mythology about older faculty as 'deadwood' – an inflexible 'old guard' with whom productive collaboration is dubious, if not impossible. Our findings also support the hypothesis that policies regarding such variables as workload flexibility, institutional roles and rewards, late-career professional development, health care, and early and phased retirement will influence the retirement decisions of faculty members, either toward earlier or delayed retirement, including many who may plan to retire well past age 65.

These findings underscore a number of provocative senior faculty issues, providing one lens through which the generational turnover of faculty can be analysed. A holistic view of this period of transition, however, also requires that these findings be buttressed with research on the incoming early-career faculty cohort. Due to downward student demographic patterns and constricted higher education finances, a tight academic job market between the late-1970s and mid-1990s resulted in the hiring of many fewer new faculty than earlier. This not only resulted in a smaller cohort of mid-career faculty in their late thirties to early fifties to carry the faculty leadership torch in the near future, but the depressed academic job market resulted in a cutting back of some PhD programs and declining attractiveness of academic careers among doctoral students. Consequently, in addition to ambivalence about the value of older faculty to their institutions and limited recognition of what may be lost as the senior faculty generation retires, there is uncertainty about whether replacement candidates will be available in sufficient quantity (and perhaps quality) to meet higher education's needs during the generational turnover. Moreover, the growing practice of replacing retiring faculty with contract (non-tenure-track) and part-time new faculty hires may exacerbate this uncertainty. As Schuster and Finkelstein have documented, more than half of all new faculty positions are off the tenure track (Rice 2004, p. 31). Taken together, the circumstances facing institutions as they hire the next generation of faculty members may be as challenging, if not more challenging, than those they face in responding to a large cohort of late-career faculty members contemplating retirement.

5.4 THE EARLY FACULTY CAREER AND THE GENERATIONAL TURNOVER

For the 16-campus University of North Carolina, as for other higher education institutions, recruitment and retention of faculty is a major concern. In fact, in 2001 the University of North Carolina Office of the President projected that its campuses will need to hire approximately 10 000 FTE faculty members by 2010 to replace retiring faculty and meet projected enrollment growth. While effective strategies to recruit faculty will continue to be important, those strategies that are crucial to the retention of faculty will assume equal, if not greater, importance. It is vital for the system that campuses are able to recruit qualified and capable junior faculty who want to be teachers and academics, and that these faculty can move successfully through the university ranks. In light of this challenge, the university is developing strategies for faculty recruitment and retention. To ensure that these strategies reflect the realities of campuses in hiring and retaining faculty, the Office of the President is undertaking research, supported by the TIAA–CREF Institute, to explore the expectations, perceptions, and concerns of recently hired tenure-track and non-tenure-track faculty and recently tenured faculty on issues related to faculty recruitment and retention.

The specific aims of the project are the following:

1. To identify the broad range of factors perceived as supportive of the recruitment and retention of faculty at the 16 UNC campuses;

2. To identify the broad range of factors perceived as barriers to the recruitment and retention of faculty at the 16 UNC campuses;
3. To develop a targeted survey that will be distributed to recently hired and recently tenured faculty members;
4. To identify similarities and differences in the expectations, perceptions, and concerns among individuals from different types of campuses at different stages in their careers and with different types of appointments: that is, among senior and early or mid-career faculty, tenure-track/ tenured and full-time non-tenure-track faculty, and faculty from institutions representing six different Carnegie classifications (including five historically Black universities and one historically Native American-serving university);
5. To use this information to guide the development of university policies and legislative agenda.

Unfortunately, the factors that promote the recruitment and retention of young faculty are not well understood on many campuses, and recent research addressing these issues suggests that faculty expectations are not being met. For example, Rice et al. (2000) found three concerns for tenure-track early-career faculty: a lack of a comprehensible tenure system, particularly in regard to feedback, evaluation, and the tenure process; a lack of community or a culture of collegiality – faculty feel isolated in a competitive environment; and a lack of an integrated life. These concerns vary dramatically from those of late-career faculty as reflected in the survey data reported above. However, as with their late-career colleagues, what early-career faculty believe they need to succeed may not be matched by the resources and support that they receive from their institutions. In order to develop strategies to address faculty recruitment and retention, it is important to understand how the needs and perceptions of early and mid-career faculty may differ from those of senior faculty and how policies and interventions can be balanced to meet the needs of faculty in different age cohorts.

The UNC survey of early and mid-career faculty members will complement the survey of senior faculty and provide for comparisons between the perceptions and needs of these two faculty cohorts. While sources of satisfaction among early and mid-career faculty members may resemble those of their more senior colleagues, their sources of stress, both personal and professional, will likely be very different – including balancing work and family responsibilities, navigating the tenure track, and adjusting to the realities of faculty work. While UNC institutions can use the results of the senior faculty survey to refine practices and policies in order to retain and support older faculty as they approach retirement, at the same time they may need to focus on another set of policies and practices to address issues of concern to early- and mid-career faculty in the current academic climate. This project is designed to elucidate these issues and guide campuses in developing strategies to attract and retain a cadre of newer and younger faculty members whose needs and expectations are likely to vary dramatically from those of their more senior colleagues.

The research project, which began in January 2004 and is expected to take eight months to complete, has two parts with complementary research methodologies. In Part I, in-depth telephone interviews are being conducted with representative faculty from UNC campuses. For the purpose of these interviews, the 16 campuses have been divided into six groups according to the Carnegie classification system: specialized institutions (1 campus), general baccalaureate institutions (2 campuses), liberal arts baccalaureate institutions (1 campus), master's comprehensive institutions (7 campuses), doctoral/research intensive institutions (3 campuses), and doctoral/research extensive institutions (2 campuses). Additionally, the health-related professional schools at UNC campuses such as medicine, dentistry, veterinary medicine, and nursing have been placed in a separate category termed 'medically related professions,' reflecting an assumption that the challenges for faculty new to these disciplines may differ from those of faculty in other fields.

Interviews are being conducted with individuals in the following career tracks: (1) early-career full-time tenure-track faculty employed at their institution for fewer than seven years; (2) early-career full-time non-tenure-track faculty employed at their institutions for fewer than five years; (3) mid-career full-time tenured faculty who have been tenured for fewer than five years; and (4) mid-career full-time non-tenure-track faculty who have been employed for fewer than ten years. Tracks 1 and 2, the early-career full-time tenure-track and non-tenure-track faculty, will provide information germane mainly to recruitment factors. Tracks 3 and 4, the mid-career tenured and full-time non-tenure-track faculty, will clarify current factors related mainly to faculty retention and success. The limit on employment to 'fewer than ten years' was deemed necessary to ensure that the issues raised will be relevant to current employment practices. (Part-time non-tenure-track faculty were surveyed or participated in focus groups with members of the Non-Tenure-Track Faculty Committee as part of a comprehensive study of non-tenure-track faculty in the UNC system in 2001.[1])

The interviews have been scripted to elicit open-ended discussion. Ten interviews will be conducted within each of the seven groups. Interview subjects are roughly equally distributed by gender and race. Each will be taped for transcription, and the content and topics of the interviews will be collated and assembled for further analysis. The areas to be explored are modeled on those identified by Rice et al. (2000), and will include, but will not be limited to, the following:

The faculty recruitment and retention process

- Reasons for choosing an academic career;
- Reasons for choosing a position at the faculty member's current institution;
- The institution's interest in and support for teaching, research, and public service;
- Required time-commitment to meet expectations;
- Economic benefits and hurdles;
- Benefits (health, retirement, other);
- Quality of life, job location, and family support;
- Observations on diversity and the importance of diversity to education.

Faculty retention and success

- Tenure and promotion processes;
- Economic benefits and hurdles;
- Required time-commitment to meet expectations;
- Quality of institutional support;
- Role of colleagues and senior administrators.

The information gleaned from the sessions will allow important hypotheses to be generated and tested in a survey planned for Part II of the project. From the interviews, master lists of issues and concerns will be compiled, and the similarities and differences among the career tracks and different campuses will be identified.

In Part II of the research, issues identified in the interviews will be compiled in a survey that will be administered to early and mid-career faculty within the UNC system. Cognitive interviews will be conducted with a small but representative number of potential survey respondents to obtain comments and responses to survey items, ensure agreement on the meaning of key words used in the survey, and identify how items will likely be interpreted by survey respondents. The final version of the survey items will be developed into a web-based survey to be administered by the UNC Office of the President in conjunction with UNC campuses. Several UNC campuses are already undertaking research related to the current project, including a campus climate survey at UNC Charlotte and a study of faculty retention at UNC Chapel Hill. Questions from the Office of the President survey will be incorporated into these efforts as pilot tests for the proposed UNC-wide survey.

Results of the survey will be analysed at the campus and system level to determine those factors having the most influence on decisions made by early and mid-career faculty to accept positions at UNC campuses and remain in those positions through the tenure process and beyond. The identification of these factors is particularly timely for the University of North Carolina, where debate is taking place over ways to maintain academic quality and retain excellent faculty members in the face of increasing enrollment and essentially flat state revenues. For example, faculty recruitment and retention was a major issue as the University's Board of Governors discussed possible tuition increases for UNC campuses for 2004–05. In the argument over the need for increased campus revenues, board members questioned how many prospective faculty members turn down offers to work at UNC campuses and how many current faculty offered positions at other institutions accept or turn down counter-offers from UNC campuses because of non-competitive salaries and benefits. While non-competitive salaries and benefits are clearly important influences on faculty recruitment and retention, our belief is that there are additional, non-revenue issues that influence the career decisions of early-career faculty. Research by Rice et al. (2000), Austin (2002), Trotman et al. (2002), and Trower (2002), among others, suggests that other factors may be equally important influences on whether faculty choose to accept and remain in academic positions, including the perceived level of support from colleagues and the institution, geographic location, and the balance between teaching and research in work assignments.

Preliminary analysis of the transcripts of interviews conducted so far suggests that for UNC junior faculty members, such issues as the clarity of expectations for tenure and support for achieving it, the important role (for better or worse) of the department chair or head, the importance of supportive senior colleagues, competitive employee benefits (even more than salary), and campus commitment to such values as collegiality and diversity affect faculty members' satisfaction and may influence their decisions to remain at UNC campuses or pursue other positions. While many of these issues differ from those identified as important to late-career faculty members in the survey of senior faculty members, several of them parallel the findings of the senior survey, including collegiality, campus values, senior faculty support for junior faculty, and employees benefits such as health insurance. If these preliminary results are borne out in additional interviews and in the university-wide survey, UNC institutions may be able to leverage the interests and values of senior faculty to provide the support and mentoring essential to recruiting and retaining junior faculty members.

Combined with campus-based research, the project will enable UNC to assess the importance of a number of factors in faculty recruitment and retention and develop a multifaceted approach balancing fiscal and non-fiscal responses to these factors. The UNC survey results will be of interest to university campuses across the country as well as to other researchers who study the factors that influence potential faculty to accept academic positions and remain at their institutions. We hope that the results will also constitute an important contribution to knowledge about the faculty workforce across age cohorts, types of institutions, and faculty appointment types.

5.5   CONCLUSIONS

Our preliminary analysis of results of the senior faculty survey suggests positive opportunities, as well as areas of caution, for colleges and universities as they approach a period in which faculty will retire in large numbers. The profile from the survey of a hard-working, institutionally-motivated, and flexible professoriate suggests that institutions could benefit from taking advantage of faculty interests in new roles and their seeming willingness to cooperate in retirement transitions beneficial both to institutions and to faculty members. This senior faculty work ethic and well of goodwill may be invaluable if concerns about the size of the new faculty replacement pool materialize. Senior faculty members who continue their involvement with their institutions – by delaying retirement, entering phased retirement programs, or maintaining relationships with their institutions in retirement – can assist with the recruitment and retention or augment the pool of replacement faculty members.

Survey results suggest that institutions might be well-advised to pay particular attention to influences on senior faculty perceptions and behavior as they consider their policies and practices regarding the late faculty career and retirement:

- Sources of faculty motivation and frustration in the late career;
- Need to stay engaged with late-career faculty members and their interests, or risk losing their engagement with the institution;
- Potential new roles to safeguard senior faculty productivity and satisfaction and provide new institutional benefits;
- Role of health benefits in influencing faculty to retire or delay retirement;
- Potential of phased retirement as a hedge against uncertainties regarding the new faculty replacement pool;
- Potential institutional roles faculty might play in retirement.

When completed, the survey of early-career faculty by the University of North Carolina should add to institutions' knowledge about what motivates faculty members to accept and remain in the positions for which they are recruited. In particular, the results promise to add to our understanding of differences in satisfaction and retention rates among different groups of early-career faculty, including tenure-track/tenured compared to non-tenure-track faculty, faculty in research extensive and intensive institutions compared to those in masters and baccalaureate institutions, and faculty at historically minority-serving institutions compared to those at majority institutions. This more detailed understanding should also inform policies about such issues as health care benefits, dependent care and work–family provisions, faculty compensation, and expectations for performance, all of which may influence the longevity of the new generation of faculty members in our institutions. This new generation promises to be a large but considerably less homogeneous cohort than the generation reflected in the results of the senior survey. In the short run, the challenge for institutions will be to develop policies and establish relationships that will meet the needs of both generations of faculty, while effectively serving their multifaceted missions.

NOTE

1. The results of this study are included in 'Report and Recommendations of the Non-Tenure-Track Faculty Committee,' available at the UNC Office of the President website: www.northcarolina.edu/content.php/aa/reports/ntt_faculty/index.htm. Relevant data from this report will inform the current research, but part-time faculty members will not be included as subjects.

REFERENCES

Austin, Anne E. (2002), 'Creating a bridge to the future: Preparing new faculty to face changing expectations in a shifting context,' *Review of Higher Education*, **26** (2): 119–44.

Berberet, Jerry and Linda McMillin (2002), 'The American professoriate in transition,' *Priorities*, no. 18, Spring, Association of Governing Boards quarterly report.

Bland, Carole J. and William H. Bergquist (1997), *The Vitality of Senior Faculty Members: Snow on the Roof – Fire in the Furnace*. ASHE-ERIC Higher Education report, volume 25, no. 7, Washington, DC: George Washington University Graduate School of Education and Human Development.

Clark, Robert L. and P. Brett Hammond (2001), *To Retire or Not? Retirement Policy and Practice in Higher Education*, Philadelphia: University of Pennsylvania Press.

Cool, Kenneth E. (2002), 'Retirement patterns at liberal arts colleges,' paper on the Mellon Faculty Retirement Project presented at TIAA-CREF Dialogue on Faculty Retirement Incentives,New York, 19 November.

Finkelstein, Martin J. and Jack H. Schuster (1998), *The New Academic Generation: A Profession in Transformation*, Baltimore, MD: Johns Hopkins University Press.

McMillin, Linda A. and William G. (Jerry) Berberet (2002), *A New Academic Compact: Revisioning the Relationship of Faculty and Their Institutions*, Bolten, MA: Anker Press.

Rice, R. Eugene (2004), 'The future of the American faculty: An interview with Martin J. Finkelstein and Jack H. Schuster,' *Change*, March/April, 26–35.

Rice, R. Eugene, Mary Deane Sorcinelli and Anne E. Austin (2000), *Heeding New Voices: Academic Careers for a New Generation*, New Pathways: Faculty Careers and Employment for the 21st Century working paper series, inquiry no. 7, Washington, DC: American Association of Higher Education.

Trotman, Carroll-Ann, M. Elizabeth Bennett, Nicole Scheffler and J.F. Camilla Tulloch (2002), 'Faculty recruitment, retention, and success in dental Academia,' *American Journal of Orthodontics and Dentofacial Orthopedics*, **122**, 2–8.

Trower, Cathy A. (2002), 'Can colleges competitively recruit faculty without the prospect of tenure?' in Richard P. Chait (ed.), *The Questions of Tenure*, Cambridge, MA: Harvard University Press, pp. 182–220.

Wergin, Jon F. (2001), 'Beyond carrots and sticks: What really motivates faculty,' *Liberal Education*, Winter, 50–3.

6. The future of retiree health benefits in higher education in the United States

Sylvester J. Schieber

6.1 INTRODUCTION

Many employers in the United States today are grappling with what to do about the retiree health benefit plans they have been sponsoring. In some cases this matter has arisen because the character of these benefits and the regulatory environment in which they operate has raised concerns about the rationale for employer sponsorship of retiree health insurance. Cost inflation for health benefits generally, and particularly for prescription drug benefits that are a major part of retiree health benefit costs, has accentuated the concerns that some employers have about sponsoring these programs. The demographic composition of the workforce and the prospect of burgeoning retiree populations is another consideration that employers are taking into account. Finally, the recent adoption of legislation expanding Medicare's coverage to include drug benefits for eligible retirees after 2006 naturally raises questions about what employers now sponsoring their own retiree health insurance programs ought to do relative to the new coverage.

This chapter explores the myriad issues that employers are now considering as they decide their future role in providing retiree health insurance. The ultimate focus of the chapter is on what is happening in the world of higher education and how employers in this sector of the economy are currently treating retired faculty and how the health insurance now being provided might change in the future. For a variety of reasons, however, many employers in the private sector are substantially ahead of those in the public and non-profit sectors in considering what they should do with their retiree health benefit programs. Because of this, the initial discussion presented here is in broader context than just focusing on the situation in higher education.

In some regards, the employer sponsorship of retiree health benefits in the United States may seem entirely irrational. The initial part of the discussion in the next section briefly describes the role that employer-sponsorship of these benefits has played and why we find ourselves in the situation that we do at this time. In the third section of this chapter, the general trends in retiree health benefits are explored. In the fourth section, the analysis turns specifically to the situation in higher education in the provision of retiree health benefits for faculty members. The final section provides some general conclusions.

6.2   BACKGROUND

The United States is unique in the developed world in the way in which it finances the delivery of health care goods and services. The majority of the US population receives health insurance coverage through a patchwork of public and private programs with varying levels of benefits. In other countries, private individuals receive their health goods and services through comprehensive mandated health insurance coverage or national health service delivery systems.

In 2002, total health expenditures in the United States were $1553 billion, representing 14.9 per cent of gross domestic product (GDP) in the US economy that year. Of all health care expenditures in the United States that year, 50.4 per cent were privately financed (CMS 2004). By comparison, among the other G-7, about 76 per cent of their annual expenditures on health care are financed through public mechanisms (OECD 2001).

While a larger share of health expenditures in the United States tends to come from private sources than in most countries, the direct outlay of cash at the point of consumption in the United States only amounted to 13.7 per cent of total outlays in 2002. The rest of the private expenditures on health care goods and services was paid through insurance programs or other third-party payment mechanisms. Of the public expenditures, 70.7 per cent were financed by the federal government. Of federal expenditures, 52.9 per cent was through Medicare. Medicaid accounted for 29.2 per cent of federal health expenditures and 49.3 per cent of state and local expenditures (CMS 2004).

Medicare and Medicaid were established during the 1960s because many of the elderly were not covered by private health insurance of any sort and they were believed to be in poorer health and had significant unmet medical needs because of their lack of such insurance (Rice 1964). The enabling legislation creating Medicare was established in 1965 covering only people who had attained the age of 65 and who qualified for benefits based on periods of coverage under the national Social Security program. Coverage was expanded in 1972 to include the disabled. During

1999, 85.4 per cent of Medicare payments to program beneficiaries went to people 65 years of age and older (CMS 2001, Table 14). That year 97.2 per cent of the non-institutionalized population over the age of 65 in the United States was covered by Medicare (DHHS 1999). Some of those not covered by Medicare never worked in covered employment long enough to qualify for the benefits, or did not qualify for spousal coverage because they were never married long enough to someone who earned coverage.

While Medicare was structured to provide a broad base of health care protection for the elderly and disabled, it did not cover a substantial portion of their health care expenditures. In 1999 Medicare paid for 53 per cent of the medical care consumed by program beneficiaries (CMS 2002). Mindful of the share of medical care consumption that would be covered under Medicare, and of the implications this would have for low-income people qualifying for program benefits, federal law provided Medicaid supplemental benefits to provide a more comprehensive level of coverage to such individuals. In addition to being covered by Medicare, 13 per cent of all people over the age of 65 in 2000 were also covered by Medicaid (CMS 2000). In 1999, total Medicaid payments were $153.5 billion. Of these, $42.5 billion was for persons age 65 and above (CMS 2001, Tables 101 and 104). During 1999 Medicaid covered 12 per cent of the Medicare beneficiaries' total cost of medical care consumption (CMS 2002).

For the elderly who did not qualify for Medicaid coverage as a supplement to Medicare, the voids in the package of benefits provided through Medicare resulted in the provision of overlapping coverage by private insurance. In 2000, 22 per cent of the elderly covered by Medicare purchased medigap insurance on their own. Another 29 per cent were covered by employer-sponsored retiree health benefit plans that provided supplemental coverage. Four per cent of the elderly under Medicare had a medigap plan that they purchased on their own plus employer-sponsored coverage. An additional 18 per cent were in Medicare health maintenance organizations (HMOs), which cover many services in full, thereby making supplemental policies unnecessary. Two per cent were covered by some sort of other public health insurance program. This left only 12 per cent of all Medicare-covered elderly who had no supplemental coverage at all (CMS 2000).

During 1999, private insurance covered 12 per cent of total health consumption for those covered by Medicare. In addition, Medicare enrollees paid for 19 per cent of their medical care consumption directly out-of-pocket. The latter amount does not include their premiums for Medicare Part B, supplemental private insurance, or HMO premiums (CMS 2002). The implications of having supplemental health insurance to augment

Medicare coverage will vary somewhat from plan to plan. For a typical retiree covered by an employer-sponsored health plan today and eligible for Medicare, an average of about 65 per cent of medical care costs will be covered by Medicare, 25 per cent by the employer plan and 10 per cent out of pocket.

6.3   EVOLVING WORLD OF EMPLOYER-SPONSORED HEALTH INSURANCE

Part of the reason to be concerned about the future of employer-sponsored retiree health benefits is related to a larger context in which employers find themselves sponsoring any sort of health benefit programs. US employers stumbled into the role they play in financing these benefits somewhat by accident. During World War II, wage controls limited employers' ability to compete for workers on the basis of higher pay, but employers were allowed to add benefits that had not been previously provided. Among other things, employers offered workers attractive health insurance coverage to attract and keep them during this period. Health benefits that employers offered as a way to beat wage controls in the 1940s had grown to be 6 per cent of total compensation by the end of the 20th century and for some employers were two or three times that level. Early in the 21st century, the cost of these benefits has grown rapidly.

Over the years there has been some debate over who pays for employer-sponsored health benefits – whether it is the employer through higher compensation costs or the worker through reductions to cash wages or some other elements of compensation. Since the end of World War II, total compensation of US workers, including the self-employed, has hovered around two-thirds of our annual gross domestic product (GDP). This was the case during periods when health costs were very small at the beginning of the period, and when they have been many times higher in recent years. It has been the case when health benefit costs were growing much more rapidly than total compensation costs and when they grew slower than total compensation. As employer-sponsored health benefits have increased over the decades relative to total output produced by workers, the relative share paid in other forms of compensation has declined. Until now, health benefits have likely not played a major role in affecting total compensation of workers or its broad distribution. The evolution of health benefits over the years, the magnitude of their costs, and who benefits from them may change that in the future.

6.4 CHANGING CHARACTERISTICS OF BENEFITS

In the 1950s the nature of the health benefits that employers provided was very different than what most people are familiar with today. Consumption of medical goods or services under the typical employer-sponsored benefit plans was reimbursed on the basis of defined schedules of payments for specific services covered. In the early 1950s, private health insurance benefits were typically limited to inpatient care. A common plan might reimburse hospital room and board charges between $3 and $10 per day (roughly $25 to $75 per day in current terms) for a limit of up to one month per year. Surgical procedures were reimbursed on a fixed schedule of payments and it was not uncommon that the maximum reimbursement for any surgical procedure would be $150 (roughly $1150 in current terms). Ancillary benefits such as anesthesia, laboratory services, operating or delivery room services were generally limited to $1000 or less (roughly $6225 in current terms). Doctor's visits for a single illness might be limited to $50 to $75 (roughly $400 to $600 in current terms) (Strong 1951, pp. 175–85).

By the late 1950s or early 1960s, employers began to add major medical coverage to their basic hospital plans. Under these plans, expenses not covered under the basic plan beyond some threshold of out-of-pocket expenditure by the covered individual would be reimbursed. These plans covered practically all types of necessary medical expenses both in and outside of hospital care, although the plans typically included maximum benefit limits of $10 000 to $20 000. The combination of basic insurance and major medical plans underwent further metamorphosis into single comprehensive plans (Pickrell 1961, pp. 36–44).

As Congress developed the Medicare and Medicaid programs in the 1960s, both the medical community and the general public expressed grave concern about the intrusion of the government into the doctor–patient relationship. Section 1801 of the Social Security Amendments that set up the Medicare program was quite explicit that the government would not exercise 'any supervision or control over the practice of medicine or the manner in which medical services are provided'. The implementation of the legislation followed the practice then prevalent among Blue Cross plans and reimbursed hospitals on the basis of their costs, including capital costs. Under Medicare, physicians were reimbursed on the basis of 'reasonable and customary' charges for the costs of services that were provided under the program. Many employer-provided health programs followed the lead of the government in paying for services provided under their plans on the basis of reasonable and customary charges.

By the end of the 1970s, a survey of slightly more than 800 employer-sponsored benefit programs found that 69 per cent of them ran a combined basic plan supplemented with a major medical plan. The remainder all provided comprehensive major medical coverage. Among the basic medical plans, the survey found that 85 per cent of plans paid the full cost of a semi-private room while a patient was in the hospital and more than 95 per cent of the plans covered stays of longer than a month in the hospital. Charges for services delivered under these plans were covered on the basis of reasonable and customary rates for ancillary benefits in the hospital by 77 per cent of the plans. Fifty-two per cent covered surgical charges, 44 per cent covered in-hospital physician fees, and 35 per cent covered outpatient diagnostic expenses on a reasonable and customary basis. For major medical and comprehensive coverage, the typical deductible in the plans was $100 or less for a covered individual and the plan typically covered up to 80 per cent of costs of services provided under the plan. In 86 per cent of the plans, retirees under the age of 65 were provided some continued coverage under the plan for active workers and 71 per cent provided some level of coverage for retirees beyond the age of 65 (Watson Wyatt Worldwide 1984).

During the 1980s, employers began to adopt a number of plan provisions aimed at controlling costs of their health benefit programs. Among other things, many of them began to offer flexible benefit plans with several different options of health coverage from which people eligible for their benefit programs could choose. Typically, the options would include a couple of choices of indemnity plans plus an HMO option. The differences in the indemnity plans offered would be in the levels of copayments and deductibles covered members would face and in the share of the premium that the members would pay out of their own funds. The typical HMO plan at this juncture provided a relatively comprehensive package of benefits and generally provided coverage of services delivered on a first-dollar basis. In terms of the package of benefits offered, on paper at least, the HMO offering generally looked superior to what was offered in the other choices provided under employer plans. Employers managed the share of people who took the HMO options through alternative pricing of the choices. Higher pricing of the HMO options, and the perception that HMOs restricted physician choice and the delivery of services, encouraged many of those covered by employer plans to stay with their traditional coverage.

As the efforts to control health costs continued to evolve during the late 1980s and into the 1990s, there was a growing sense that many of the characteristics of HMOs were desirable. Employers re-engineered their traditional plans with benefit provisions that mimicked HMOs, but where the services were delivered through networks of independent providers organized by third-party vendors. These new systems of managed care attempted to control the price of services delivered to covered populations through negotiated price schedules with the providers within the networks. They tried to control the volume of services delivered using gatekeepers to direct consumers to use appropriate care within the networks. There was a considerable backlash on the part of consumers to being limited in choice of providers and in the levels of services delivered under this version of managed care. The providers helped to fan this dissatisfaction because they disliked the limits that the system was attempting to impose upon the delivery and pricing of services.

By the end of the 1990s, in response to the overall dissatisfaction with managed care, the sponsors of health insurance plans began to relax many of the controlling features in the managed care systems. Covered members of plans were being given options to utilize services delivered by providers outside of the networks and the gate keeping elements of plans were largely eliminated. In the whole process, however, the package of benefits that was provided from the shift out of the traditional indemnity plan environment to the post-managed care point-of-service environment had become much more generous. The cost of benefits provided under this new generation of plans far outstripped the share of costs paid by participants in the plans through copayments and coinsurance contributions.

6.5   THE COST OF HEALTH CARE SERVICES

In the early 1950s about 40 per cent of the civilian population was covered by some sort of health insurance (Strong 1951, p. 175). Twenty years later, an estimated 80 per cent of the civilian population under the age of 65 and 51 per cent of that 65 and above were covered by some form of private health insurance (Mueller 1973, p. 4). By 2000, 84 per cent of the non-elderly population was covered by public or private insurance and nearly all of the post-65 population had at least one source of third-party coverage (Fronstin 2001). This expansion of health insurance coverage meant that millions of health care consumers faced much lower price barriers to medical care consumption than they would have without such insurance.

In 1960, total health care expenditures in the United States were about 5.1 per cent of GDP and the delivery of health goods and services at the personal level consumed about 4.5 per cent of GDP. At that time, individual patients and their families paid 55.2 per cent of personal health care spending out-of-pocket. From that baseline, two distinctive patterns emerged that are reflected in Figure 6.1.

The growth in insurance coverage and the changing characteristics of the benefits provided by it led to a substantial decline in out-of-pocket spending for personal health care consumption, from 55.2 per cent to

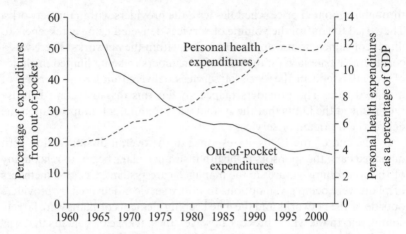

Note: * out-of-pocket expenditures do not include personal premium contributions for insurance coverage.

Source: Center for Medicare and Medicaid Services, Office of the Actuary (2004)

Figure 6.1   Percentage of total personal health care expenditures paid out-of-pocket and percentage of GDP spent on personal health care, 1960 to 2002*

15.9 per cent of all spending on personal health care goods and services over the 43 years covered in Figure 6.1. For consumers, out-of-pocket expenditures on personal health care consumption fell from 2.5 per cent of GDP in 1960 to 2.0 per cent in 2002. Over the same period, total personal health care spending grew from 4.4 per cent to 12.8 per cent of GDP. Total health care expenditures in the United States grew from 5.1 per cent of GDP in 1960 to 14.9 per cent in 2002.

There were several factors behind this extraordinary growth in health care spending. Figure 6.2 shows the annualized rates of growth in GDP per capita and personal health expenditures per capita for each of the decades from 1960 through 2000, and separately for the period 2000 through 2002. The growth rate for per capita personal health care expenditures has consistently exceeded the growth in per capita GDP over each of the periods shown in the figure. In Figure 6.2, the personal medical inflation rates for each of the periods have been decomposed into three components: general price inflation, medical price inflation in excess of general inflation, and growth attributable to more intensive delivery of services due to either changing practice patterns or technology. General inflation and medical care inflation are calculated from the price indices

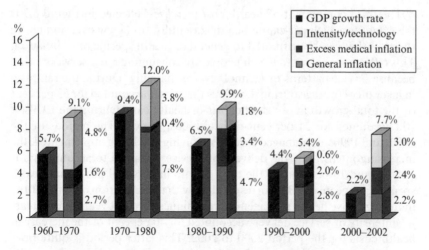

Source: Watson Wyatt calculations based on data from 2001 OASDI Trustees report, national health expenditures data from www.hcfa.gov, and inflation indices from www.bls.gov.

Figure 6.2   *Compound annual growth rates by decade in GDP per capita and medical expenditures per capita for the US population, 1960 to 2002*

published by the Bureau of Labor Statistics. The intensity/technology component is the residual that remains after the two elements of price inflation are removed.[1]

Price inflation reflected in Figure 6.2 is broken into two components. The first of these is general price inflation in the overall economy as calculated from the Bureau of Labor Statistics' consumer price index for all urban consumers (CPI-U). General price inflation accounted for about half of all the rate of growth in per capita health costs during the 1980s and 1990s, but dropped to less than 30 per cent for the period 2000–02. The second component of health cost increases reflected in Figure 6.2 is the extent to which health care prices, as reported as a subcomponent of the larger index, exceed the CPI-U. The health care sector of the US economy by the CPI measures developed by the BLS has historically been prone to excessive price inflation. The extent of this excessive inflation was minor during the 1970s, a period of generally high inflation in the overall econ-omy, but has been significant over most of the remaining period reflected in Figure 6.2. Since the beginning of the 1980s, excessive price inflation in the health sector accounts for about a third of all the rate of growth in per capita health costs.

The third component of health cost increases reflected in Figure 6.2 is the extent to which per capita health care utilization grew over and above the rates that can be attributed to general or health specific price inflation. This reflects the extent to which people are consuming more services either because service patterns or technology are changing. During the ramp-up in insurance coverage during the 1960s this factor accounted for 53 per cent of the total growth in per capita costs of health care. During the 1970s, it still accounted for 31 per cent of health cost growth. The periods of the 1980s and 1990s, as managed care was evolving and being implemented, the increasing intensity of the delivery of services dropped to accounting for only 19 and 10 per cent of the total run up in personal per capita health spending respectively. But corresponding with the relaxation of some of the more aggressive health management techniques in recent years, the increasing intensity of service delivery accounted for 40 per cent of the increase in health costs for the period 2000 to 2002. This latter period is quite brief compared to the other periods reflected in the table and one has to be careful about making comparisons with such a short period to the earlier decade-long rates. However, many of the sponsors of health insurance programs have continued to see the costs of their plans grow significantly more rapidly throughout 2003 and into 2004 than inflation or other underlying economic growth rates. Many plan sponsors are quite concerned that we may be entering a period when both the intensity of services and excess health inflation are exploding uncontrollably. For employers sponsoring health benefits this is becoming particularly worrisome.

6.6   HEALTH BENEFITS AS COMPENSATION

Many economists look at the employer sponsorship of health benefits and conclude that employers should be relatively indifferent as to whether workers want more or less health care or how it is financed. Health care is part of the compensation package, and as long as total compensation paid to a worker does not exceed his or her marginal contribution to the enterprise, it should make little difference to the employer how the compensation is split. This may have been the case at some earlier times but is likely becoming less so.

Figure 6.3 shows the historical levels of employer contributions to private health insurance plans stated as a percentage of cash wages paid to employed workers in the United States. The historical data run through 2001. In that year, the Social Security Administration estimates that the average cash wage level in the United States was $32 922 (SSA 2004). In that year, employer contributions for health insurance equaled 6.6 per cent of

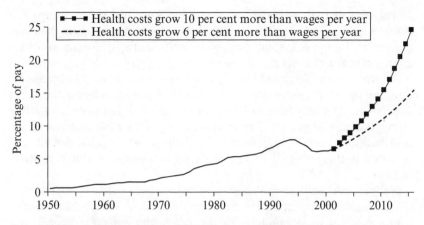

Sources: Historical data were derived from the Bureau of Economic Affairs, US Department of Commerce, *National Income and Product Account* series. The projections were derived by the author as outlined in the text.

Figure 6.3   *Employer contributions to private health benefit plans as a percentage of cash wages paid to employed workers for selected years*

cash wages according to the National Income and Product Accounts data reflected in Figure 6.3. In 2001, premiums for employer-sponsored health benefit plans in a sample of firms studied by the Kaiser Family Foundation increased 10.9 per cent. In 2002, they increased by 12.9 per cent and in 2003, 13.9 per cent. In this sample of firms, health premiums increased by 6.8 percentage points more than workers' earnings increased in 2001, by 9.7 percentage points more in 2002, and by 10.8 percentage points more than wages grew in 2002 (Kaiser 2003, Exhibits 1.1 and 1.2).

Based on the recent history, Figure 6.3 shows the implications of health premiums continuing to increase more rapidly than wages through 2015 under two alternative scenarios. In both scenarios, we assumed that average wages grow at a rate of 4 per cent per year. In the lower of the two health premium increase scenarios, reflected by the dashed line beyond 2001 in the figure, we assumed that health premiums would increase at a rate of 10 per cent per year, or 6 percentage points per year faster than wages were assumed to grow. In the higher of the two, we assumed employer health costs would increase at a rate of 14 per cent per year, 10 percentage points more than the rate of increase in assumed wages.

The point of Figure 6.3 is that employers have gone through health cost increases over the last two or three years that, if played out over the next decade or so, could drive total health costs to equal between 15 and

25 per cent of cash wages paid to workers. Since this is an average and many employers are already starting at a base somewhat higher than that implied by Figure 6.3, some employers are potentially looking at a situation where health costs stated as a percentage of their cash wages are even higher than those suggested here. If employer-provided health benefits do not drive up total compensation costs, but are becoming a larger and larger share of it, then they have to be driving down the relative share of other elements of compensation. This has potentially serious implications for the distribution of total compensation, and this is why health benefit cost growth has the potential to become a serious problem if it persists at recent rates.

Just because health insurance premiums have been outstripping wages or other components of compensation recently does not mean that they can continue to do so indefinitely. To this point, the venerable Washington economist, Herb Stein, used to say, 'If something cannot go on forever, it will stop.' But a lesser known observation of this same wise man was that, 'Economists are very good at saying that something cannot go on forever, but not so good at saying when it will stop' (Fischer 2001). Given the recent history of developments in the provision of health insurance many employers are concerned that we might be in for another stretch of high increases in the costs of health services delivered under their plans. If that happens, it could have significant implications on employers' ability to compensate workers based on their productivity.

6.7 LINKING HEALTH BENEFIT COSTS AND INDIVIDUAL WORKER PRODUCTIVITY

Health care consumption patterns fall along a continuum of need, repetition, and intensity with varying cost implications at the respective points in the continuum. To help in explaining this, consider Figure 6.4. The solid horizontal line in the box represents the utilization continuum. The two vertical lines cutting across the continuum represent conceptual boundaries that distinguish between utilization patterns consumers present to a typical health benefit plan sponsored by an employer. In the figure, people are grouped into one of three categories by the nature of health care services that they use in a typical year. Of course, it is possible that a single individual might fall into more than one category in a year, but most will fall into only one. The first category includes people who can be characterized as occasional users of health care services. The second category captures people who are chronic users of health care services including people who are treated for such ongoing diseases as hypertension, diabetes, and the like.

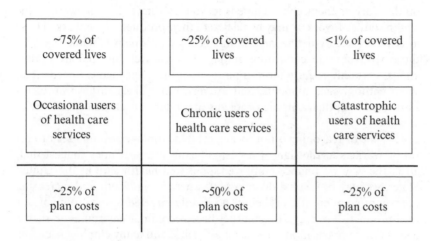

~75% of covered lives	~25% of covered lives	<1% of covered lives
Occasional users of health care services	Chronic users of health care services	Catastrophic users of health care services
~25% of plan costs	~50% of plan costs	~25% of plan costs

Source: Developed by the author

Figure 6.4   Rough characterization of health care utilization under a typical employer-sponsored health plan in the United States in 2003

The final category includes people who incur a catastrophic event that requires intensive care over a variable duration.

Most people covered under a typical employer plan are generally healthy and only occasional users of the plan during any given year. This group may encompass as many as 75 or 80 per cent of all people covered under the plan, although the plan outlays for them are probably less than 25 per cent of total outlays in most cases. The segment of the health utilization spectrum that includes chronic conditions suggests that this segment of the covered population encompasses roughly 25 per cent of covered lives under a typical plan and accounts for as much as 50 per cent of total plan costs. The third segment of the health care utilization spectrum relates to consumption of health care services in catastrophic cases. While the portion of the covered population that might fall into this category of care in any given year might be less than 0.5 per cent of the total covered population, this group can easily account for up to 25 to 35 per cent of total plan costs in any given year.

In an environment where health care costs are expected to increase more rapidly than wages and are expected to become an increasingly larger share of compensation, the pattern of health utilization under employer-sponsored plans takes on increased significance. Within the typical employee population, some share of the benefits delivered under a health benefit plan goes to dependents of workers, but much of the benefit is concentrated on the workers themselves. There is reason to believe that, on average, the health status of workers may be related to their productivity at work. Those in critical care, by definition, cannot be very productive. While many of those with chronic conditions might lead relatively normal lives, they almost certainly require more time to attend to their medical needs than those without such ailments, and are also more likely to have problems associated with their chronic problems that might affect their productivity at work.

This line of reasoning is not to suggest that employers should seek to get rid of workers at the sign of any significant illness. It does suggest that, given the way we finance employer-sponsored health care in the United States, we may be headed down a path where a significant and increasing portion of compensation is being specifically targeted toward some of our least productive workers. In a market-based economic environment, such a pattern of compensation does not make sense and many employers can be expected to attempt to prevent this situation from coming to fruition. For many retirees covered under employer-sponsored health benefit plans this has particular implications.

One other piece of evidence is important before turning specifically to the situation that retirees face; this is the pattern of health care consumption reflected in Figure 6.5 based on analysis of utilization patterns under employer-sponsored medical plans and Medicare and Medicaid. On average, older people consume considerably more health care than younger

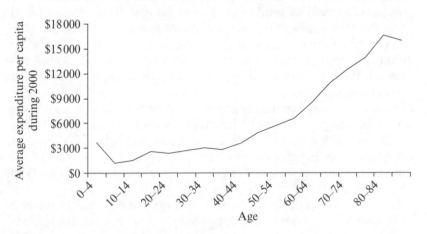

Source: Watson Wyatt Worldwide (1984)

Figure 6.5   Age profile of average expenditures on health care in the United States during 2000

ones. The pattern reflected here is not unique to the United States but reflects the patterns across many developed societies with a variety of organizational structures for financing and delivering health care services (Costello and Bains 2001, p. 24). From the perspective of health plan sponsors, retirees not yet eligible to receive Medicare pose a significant cost risk to their health plans. Even those covered by Medicare would often present higher cost risks than younger workers if he/she is covered by a relatively generous retiree health benefit plan.

The actual relative costs of retiree health benefits compared to those provided to active workers will depend on the characteristics of benefits being provided under the plan and the premium sharing between the employer and the insured person. Many firms include pre-65 retirees in the same plan as active employees. In a typical preferred provider plan offered by larger employers today, an average retiree in this group would typically consume health goods or services worth about twice that provided to the average individual worker covered under the plan. These two average individuals are typically at least 20 years apart in age. Retirees who are ages 65 and older, and who are covered by Medicare but receive supplemental employer health insurance, would typically receive benefits from the employer plan worth something in the range of two-thirds to three-quarters the value of benefits provided to the average working-age individual covered under the plan. The relative share of total benefits provided to retirees under any specific plan will be dependent on the relative size of the retiree population compared to the active workforce, the age distribution of retirees, and the relative sharing of premiums between the employer and beneficiaries within each of the covered groups.

6.8 TRENDS IN RETIREE HEALTH BENEFIT PROVISION

Lawrence Atkins (1994, p. 108) suggests that employer-provided health benefits for retirees evolved mostly without 'design or intent' as a result of collective bargaining over benefits during the 1950s and 1960s. Relatively few retirees were receiving benefits from these plans, and the low cost of providing the benefits on a pay-as-you-go basis made them virtually a 'throwaway' in negotiations. By 1962, 21 per cent of the post-65 population were enrolled in an employer-sponsored plan and another 31 per cent purchased some level of coverage privately (Rice 1964, p. 9).

The enactment of Medicare in 1965 produced savings for these employer-sponsored plans, because Medicare became the primary payer for retirees once they reached age 65. Employer-sponsored plans paid only for the costs not reimbursed by Medicare, and more employers began to offer these plans. Atkins argues that employers adopted these benefits 'because they needed them to make their retirement packages work, because they helped in collective bargaining, because they were attractive to labor in competitive labor markets, and because the costs were rarely significant.' He notes that there were so few retirees at the time that often they were simply kept on the active employee plan. The supplemental packages furnished by employers produced insurance coverage with very low out-of-pocket costs for retirees. From these humble beginnings, retiree health benefits have been buffeted by the same design and cost considerations as employer-sponsored health benefits for active workers, in addition to other problems.

Retiree health benefits are different from health benefits that employers provide to active employers in that they are provided to people who no longer work for the entity providing them. In this regard, they are like a defined benefit pension which raises a set of issues beyond the cost and incidence issues associated with health benefits provided to active workers. In the case of active workers' benefits, they are earned at the time the workers perform their duties for the employer. In the case of retirees' benefits, they are earned long before they are actually provided.

The implications of accruing obligations for employer-sponsored retirement plans and how to deal with them have been understood for many decades. Steven Sass, who has written a history of the evolution of employer pensions in the United States, has written about the 'science of reform' that swept the pension movement in this country in the 1920s. He says the scientific experts of the time understood the importance of eliminating the uncertainty of risk for both employee and plan sponsors. They concluded that the benefits paid under retirement plans had to be expensed 'in conjunction with the employer's receipt of productive labor services'. But the second condition for the soundness of a plan was that monies have to be laid aside to cover obligations as they are earned (Sass 1997, p. 62).

6.9   ACCOUNTING AND PAYING FOR RETIREMENT BENEFITS IN THE CORPORATE WORLD

In 1984, the Financial Accounting Standards Board (FASB) issued Financial Accounting Standard 81 (FAS 81) requiring employers to report on their financial statements either the current cost of retiree welfare benefits or the unfunded liability if the amounts were distinguishable from the benefit costs for active employees. FAS 81 raised employer awareness about unfunded liabilities associated with their retiree health benefit plans and their magnitude was illuminated by a number of well-publicized studies. In 1988, the General Accounting Office (GAO) estimated that retiree health benefit liabilities represented 8 per cent of the value of companies' stock (Thompson 1988). Another study estimated that the annual costs of amortizing these retiree medical liabilities might run as high as 12 per cent of payroll, or 10 times the current rate of pay-as-you-go spending (*Investor's Daily* 1988). By this time, many corporate employers were aware that unfunded retiree medical liabilities had the potential to be quite large relative to the value of assets in their companies or the market values of their stock. While non-corporate entities were not required to comply with the FASB standards, many non-corporate sponsors of retiree health benefit plans became more fully aware of the obligations they faced because of the publicity that was raised in regard to corporate obligations.

With the subsequent promulgation of FAS 106, FASB required that employers estimate and report future obligations associated with retiree health benefit programs on their financial statements for fiscal years beginning after 15 December 1992. The rationale was that retiree medical benefits are a form of deferred compensation for current employees, and the future benefits should be reported as they are earned. The underlying theory was that if an employer is going to hold out these benefits to employees in trade for their work, the obligation of paying for them down the line has to be recognized at the time the work earning the benefit is done and the obligation incurred.

As the FASB moved to require accounting for retiree health obligations, they put in place the first principle underlying secure retirement benefits that Sass tells us has been well known since at least the 1920s. But while the accounting rules for retiree health plans were being tightened, the US Congress enacted significant restrictions on employers' ability to fund welfare benefit plans. The funding restrictions in the Deficit Reduction Act of 1984 (DEFRA) were prompted by concerns that funded plans could be used to shelter significant income from taxation. The legislative history published after passage of the act also noted articles that discussed potential abuses that might occur in the use of welfare plan assets, such as the acquisition of ski chalets or yachts.

DEFRA prohibited employers from taking medical cost inflation and utilization trends into account when funding retiree medical benefits, and limited funding to current retirees. At the time, health care inflation was nearly double the rate of general inflation and utilization rates were trending upwards. FAS 106, on the other hand, required plan sponsors to account for all their future liabilities, including those associated with future medical inflation, increased utilization, and future retirees. DEFRA also limited the employer's deductible contribution, and imposed a 100 per cent excise tax on any assets reverting to the employer from a funded welfare benefit plan.[2] The first condition for securing retiree health benefits was put in place by accounting regulations but the second condition, funding them as they were being earned, was trumped by legal restrictions on the funding of benefits as they were accrued during a covered person's active work life.

The Omnibus Budget and Reconciliation Act of 1989 (OBRA 89) further restricted retiree medical funding opportunities. Prior to OBRA 89 the Internal Revenue Service had allowed 401(h) contributions up to 25 per cent of the pension plan's cost, including the normal or actuarial cost of providing pension benefits to participants.[3] OBRA 89 limited employer 401(h) contributions to 25 per cent of all employer contributions to the pension plan. This meant that employers with well-funded pension plans could no longer contribute to the 401(h) account.

OBRA 90 Section 420 permitted limited transfers of excess defined benefit plan assets into 401(h) accounts. The transferred assets must be used only to pay qualified current retiree health liabilities for the tax year of the transfer. The effect of these legal restrictions has been to eliminate any tax-preferred means to fund health care liabilities of future retirees. The vehicles that do exist are largely for current retirees, and they limit contributions and do not account for growing utilization and medical inflation.[4]

FAS 106 accounting for retiree medical benefits has provided better information to corporate investors and other interested parties concerning the extent of future obligations. More importantly, it prompted corporate executives to closely examine the magnitude of their commitments in sponsoring retiree health benefit plans. For many employers, it became clear that the generous plan designs and premium subsidies offered in an earlier era were now producing unacceptable financial obligations. This was particularly true in view of the high rates of medical inflation in the 1980s and the fact that plan sponsors were limited in their ability to fund these obligations as they accrued.

In a survey of medium and large firms in 1980, 85.6 per cent of them reported that they provided some form of retiree health benefits. By 2000, the percentage reporting these benefits had dropped to 37.1 percent. For the most part, the larger employers continued to sponsor plans, but even there, substantial curtailments in what was offered were the general rule (McDevitt et al. 2002, p. 14). There are a number of common ways that plans have been curtailed without being eliminated by larger employers in the for-profit sector. These include increasing periods of service under the plan in order to qualify for benefits at retirement age, implementing a sliding schedule of premium payments based on service under the plan, capping the dollar amount the employer will contribute for retiree health premiums, and shifting to a notional defined contribution plan where a balance is accumulated over the period of work for an employer and that balance can be used to pay part of the premium for retiree health insurance during retirement. All of these methods are being used extensively to curtail retiree health liabilities in the private sector today.

One 1984 survey of employer plans found that 43 per cent of plans had no service requirement in order for people aged 65 and above to qualify for retiree health benefits, and that another 46 per cent required five years of service or less to qualify (Dopkeen 1987). By 2001, 72 per cent of plans were requiring 10 or more years of service to qualify for benefits for people then eligible to retire, and 87 per cent would require 10 or more years of service for young workers to qualify for such benefits in the future (McDevitt et al. 2002, p. 17). For people eligible to retire prior to age 65 in 2001, 80 per cent of plans had service requirements of 10 years or more in order to qualify for benefits, and 91 per cent had such requirements for younger workers (McDevitt et al. 2002, p. 18). For workers retiring in 2001, the average employer contribution for a pre-65 retiree with 10 years of service was 43 per cent of the total premium for coverage, 53 per cent for a retiree with 15 years of service, 63 per cent for a retiree with 20 years of service, and 71 per cent for a retiree with 25 years of service (McDevitt et al. 2002, p. 19).

Another common device for limiting retiree health obligations is to implement a dollar cap on the annual premium contribution that employers will make for retiree health benefits. In 2001, 26 per cent of large plans had such caps in place for current retirees, 39 per cent had them in place for people nearing retirement, and 45 per cent had them in place for new hires. For pre-65 retirees in 2001, the average cap for current retirees was $4450 and $3900 for future retirees. The average employer contribution at that time was $3074. For post-65 retirees, the average employer contribution caps were $2000 for current retirees and $1740 for future retirees with current average employer contributions at $1304 (McDevitt et al. 2002, p. 20).

Given the recent premium hikes that employers are reporting for their health benefit plans, this suggests that retirees in the average plan will be hitting the employer-contribution caps within the next year or so. It is important to keep in mind that once these premium caps are hit, all additional premium increases fall onto the retiree. If an employer has a plan with a $3000 cap where the employee has been paying 40 per cent of the premium, when the total premium hits $5000 the cost sharing will change dramatically. If the cost of this plan increases by 10 per cent in the year after reaching the cap, in the next year the total cost of the plan will rise to $5500 but the cap will mean the retiree will have to pay a premium of $2500, an increase of 25 per cent over the prior year and the retiree's share of the total premium will rise to 45 per cent.

The establishment of notional retiree medical accounts is a relatively recent development in the private sector employer community. In 2001, among large employers still sponsoring retiree health benefit plans, only 2 per cent had such accounts for current retirees. Seven per cent had set up such accounts for current workers close to retirement eligibility and 13 per cent had established such accounts for new hires (McDevitt et al. 2002, p. 24).

6.10   RETIREE HEALTH BENEFITS FOR FACULTY IN HIGHER EDUCATION

The rules that apply to corporate sponsors of retiree health benefits in regard to how they account for the financial obligations or fund the benefits in these plans do not apply in the same way to most employers in the higher education sector. Virtually all the institutions of higher learning in the United States are either public sector or non-profit entities. In the case of corporations, Securities and Exchange Commission disclosure requirements mean that any firm sponsoring a retiree health benefit program has to comply with the FAS 106 standard. Privately held for-profit organizations and private non-profit entities are not subject to SEC disclosure but are required by ERISA to have an annual audit if they sponsor a defined benefit plan. Theoretically, this would not have to be done in accordance with the Generally Accepted Accounting Principles (GAAP) but it would likely be rare that any normal accountant would use an alternative standard. In addition, any entity that ever goes to banks or other financial institutions for loans would almost certainly have to provide an audit report in compliance with GAAP standards in order to secure any loans. While many private universities may have substantial endowments, it is likely that even they periodically apply for loans, even if only temporary ones, for building projects or other capital investments. Even in cases where the institution might never go to the credit markets, it is likely that their boards of directors would require some sort of standard accounting. Thus, it appears that most private institutions of higher learning are in compliance with at least the FASB's reduced disclosure requirements for non-public entities. These require the estimation of benefit obligations, value of plan assets, and funded status for retirement plans. John Palmer, Michael Flusche and Myra Johnson note in their discussion included in this volume (Chapter 8) that Syracuse University develops FAS 106 estimates of its retiree health liabilities and that these estimates have played a role in their plan design.

In the case of public entities, FASB does not have domain but they are covered by standards set by the Governmental Accounting Standards

Board (GASB) which historically has not had the same requirements as FASB in this area. It is likely that the requirements for public institutions will change in the relatively near future. But in June 2004, GASB issued Statement No. 45, Accounting and Financial Reporting by Employers for Postemployment Benefits Other Than Pensions, which includes accounting standards for retiree health benefits and other nonpension benefits. These new standards require that public employers recognize the cost of accruing benefits in periods when the related services are rendered by workers, that they calculate and report actuarial accrued liabilities for promised benefits associated with past service of workers and the extent to which such benefits have been funded, and that they indicate future cash flows required to meet these obligations. Large employers (those with total annual revenues of $100 million or more) are required to implement these standards for periods beginning after December 15, 2006, while medium-sized employers (those with total annual revenues of $10 million or more but less than $100 million) have an additional year to implement the standards, and small-sized employers (those with total annual revenues of less than $10 million) have two additional years (GASB 2004).

Even if institutions of higher learning are accounting for their retiree health benefits in a fashion similar to that required of corporate entities, the market pressures relative to continuing sponsorship of these benefits may be quite different. For a corporate sponsor, the accounting expense associated with large liabilities drives down profits and potentially depresses the stock price. The liabilities themselves affect the balance sheet of the sponsoring organization in a way that can affect the perceived value of an organization and cause public or financial market pressure to be brought to bear to significantly reduce or eliminate the liabilities. These pressures encourage boards and senior management to modify plans to improve economic performance for the firm and its stockholders. In the case of non-profit institutions, donors may not often know about these obligations even though they have been calculated and there is less of a sense of ownership. Non-profit organizations, by their very essence, are not driven by the same economic motivations as corporate entities. Thus, it is quite possible that characteristics of retiree health benefits in higher education are evolving along a different path than in the for-profit sector.

The imposition of disclosure requirements regarding the financial obligations posed by retiree health plans may have raised the awareness about unfunded obligations and expenses related to these plans in the for-profit sector, but it did not change the fundamental economics underlying them. The provision of a retiree benefit on a pay-as-you-go basis is not economically rational for single employers or workers in the for-profit sector. To put the viability of an unfunded retirement benefit promised to an employee in perspective, we went back to the 1972 Fortune 50 list of industrial companies in the United States. Of the 50 largest companies on that list, 21 of them remained intact and operating under the same corporate structure in 2002 as they did 30 years earlier. Another 21 of them had been purchased or subsumed into some other corporate organization, four had been split into multiple parts, and four had gone through at least one bankruptcy but were still operating. At least three of the 21 that were acquired by another entity had also undergone bankruptcy in the subsequent 30 years since being on the Fortune top 50 list in 1972. No matter how well intentioned the management of a company might be in committing to provide future retirees with health insurance, it is impossible to guarantee that benefit over a normal working career and retirement on a pay-as-you-go basis.

It is not just the survival probabilities of the entities sponsoring these benefits that put them at risk. In some cases where employers might be able to provide retiree health benefits on a pay-as-you-go basis across a period of several decades, they may not be willing to do so because of the pressures imposed upon them by the financial markets. In many regards, private sector employers are like people. Some people insist on paying for things when they buy them. Others are willing to buy things on credit and pay for them later. Just like individuals, employers have different limits on their ability or willingness to take on debt. Some employers with very stable, predictable cash flows may have higher debt capacity than others where revenues and profits are highly cyclical. For plan sponsors, accumulating retiree health liabilities that cannot be funded until later is the equivalent of buying on credit. For employers that are able to handle heavy debt obligations, unfunded retiree benefits may not be a problem as long as they remain economically viable and under relatively consistent management. But the track record of the Fortune top 50 industrial companies from 1972 suggests that is a dicey proposition.

Since virtually all colleges and universities are non-profit institutions, the funding limitations imposed on corporate employers sponsoring retiree health benefits did not apply, so there would have been a greater opportunity to match the securing of retiree health benefits with the accrual of liabilities during workers' careers. For most colleges and universities, the vagaries of market demand for specific goods and services that can lead to the rise and fall of corporate employers also are not applicable.

In order to see what colleges and universities have been doing in providing health benefits for retired faculty members, Watson Wyatt undertook a survey on the subject in February 2004. The survey questionnaire was sent to 263 institutions and garnered complete responses from 67 of them. Of the responding institutions, 18 per cent reported they did not provide retiree health benefits. There were 46 private schools who responded to the survey, of which 12 did not have a plan. Among the latter, the average enrollment was approximately 2300 undergraduate students. Among those reporting a health benefits plan for retired faculty, the average enrollment was around 4300 undergraduate students. There were 22 public schools that responded to the survey and 21 reported providing health insurance to retired faculty. The average enrollment in the latter group of institutions was 19 300 undergraduates.

Table 6.1 indicates the extent to which health insurance is being offered to retired faculty among the schools that were offering such coverage at the beginning of 2004. Among the 34 private institutions that offered retiree health benefits, all of them offered the benefits to retired faculty under the age of 65 who were already retired or eligible to retire. For new hires, however, only 27 offered the prospect of providing retiree health benefits in the future. A number of the private schools that provided retiree health benefits prior to age 65 did not continue to provide such benefits beyond age 65, when the retirees would typically qualify for Medicare. For new hires, only 62 per cent of all the private institutions that offered some benefits currently would provide them beyond age 65 for faculty members now joining the staff. In the case of the public institutions, there is much less indication so far that the provision of coverage is being curtailed to the same extent as it is in the private schools.

The provision of retiree health insurance to retired faculty across the set of institutions reflected in Table 6.1 is important in that it gives a clear

Table 6.1   *Number of institutions of higher learning in survey sample providing retiree health benefits to retired faculty by indication of coverage*

	Private institutions			Public institutions		
	Current retirees	Eligible to retire	New hires	Current retirees	Eligible to retire	New hires
Pre-65 coverage						
Retiree	34	34	27	21	21	20
Spouse	34	34	27	21	21	19
Post-65 coverage						
Retiree	30	29	21	21	20	19
Spouse	30	29	21	21	20	19

Source: Watson Wyatt Worldwide (2004)

indication that the retired faculty members involved have access to continuing health insurance coverage. The value of what they have access to varies considerably from one institution to the next. Table 6.2 shows the extent of cost sharing of premiums between the retirees and the sponsoring institutions for the faculty members, but not necessarily their spouses, for those who are currently retired or eligible to retire.

The public schools are more likely to require that the retirees pay the full premium for the retiree health insurance coverage than private schools are. But the public schools are also more likely to pay the whole cost of the benefit than the private schools. Where premiums are shared, the private institutions generally share the cost on something approaching a 50–50 basis whereas the public employers typically pick up a significantly larger share of the total premium.

As noted earlier, many private companies that continue to sponsor retiree health benefits have undertaken a variety of measures to limit the liabilities that these benefits pose in the future. A number of colleges and universities have adopted limitations similar to those being utilized in the corporate sector but the pattern of adoption of these methods is much less widespread by the academic employers, at least those in the public sector. In a 2001 survey of corporate sponsors of retiree health benefits, roughly 60 per cent of the respondents indicated they had service requirements of 10 years to qualify for retiree health benefits, plus another 30 per cent required more than 10 years for future retirees (McDevitt et al. 2002, p. 18).

In Table 6.3 around 90 per cent of the private academic employers in the current survey are indicating that they have implemented service requirements of 10 years or more for retiring faculty to qualify for retiree health benefits. For the public institutions, on the other hand, 35 per cent or more still have service requirements of 5 years or less to qualify for benefits.

Among the responding academic institutions to the current survey, only 11 per cent of the private and 19 per cent of the public schools indicated they varied the share of premiums paid by current retirees based on service prior to retirement. For faculty members now eligible to retire but still working, the 16 and 29 per cent of the respondents respectively varied premiums based on service. For new hires still being offered benefits in the future, 18 and 29 per cent of the respondents had such variable premium schedules. By comparison, 63 per cent of private plan sponsors in 2001 reported that they would vary premiums based on service for pre-65 benefits and 72 per cent reported they would do so for post-65 coverage (McDevitt et al. 2002, p. 18).

For the schools responding to the survey in 2004, only 9 per cent of the private institutions and 24 per cent of the public ones indicated they had implemented employer contribution caps for health benefits provided to

Table 6.2   Cost and cost-sharing of retiree health benefits provided by private and public colleges and universities in 2004

Pre-65 plan Total reporting	Current retirees				Now eligible to retire			
	Private institutions 31		Public institutions 18		Private institutions 32		Public institutions 18	
	Per cent of total	Average spending ($)	Per cent of total	Average spending ($)	Per cent of total	Average spending ($)	Per cent of total	Average spending ($)
Retiree pays all	16.1	5030	27.8	5030	18.8	4890	27.8	5030
Share expenses	54.8		38.9		65.6		44.4	
Retiree share		2023		950		1958		1432
Employer share		2717		3480		2574		3345
Employer pays all	29.0	4006	33.3	4134	15.6	4508	27.8	4274

Post-65 plan Total reporting	Current retirees				Now eligible to retire			
	Private institutions 29		Public institutions 20		Private institutions 29		Public institutions 19	
	Per cent of total	Average spending ($)	Per cent of total	Average spending ($)	Per cent of total	Average spending ($)	Per cent of total	Average spending ($)
Retiree pays all	13.8	3725	20.0	3562	13.8	3725	21.1	3562
Share expenses	51.7		45.0		65.5		47.4	
Retiree share		1817		679		1866		679
Employer share		1781		3062		1735		3062
Employer pays all	34.5	3625	35.0	3513	20.7	3625	31.6	3644

Source: Watson Wyatt Worldwide

Table 6.3   Utilization of minimum service requirements to qualify for health benefits provided to retired faculty by institutions of higher learning in 2004

	Private institutions			Public institutions		
	Currently retired	Eligible to retire	New hire	Currently retired	Eligible to retire	New hire
Number reporting	29	29	21	21	21	20
Per cent reporting service requirement of:						
None	4	3	5	5	5	5
5 years or less	7	3	5	33	29	30
10 years	48	48	48	38	29	30
More than 10 years	41	45	43	24	38	35

Source: Watson Wyatt Worldwide

current retirees under age 65. For those already over the age of 65, 13 per cent of private and 24 per cent of the public institutions had adopted such caps. In the case of private employers in 2001, 26 per cent had adopted caps for current retirees under age 65 and 24 per cent had them for retirees aged 65 and over. For those now eligible to retire but still working, 12 per cent of private and 24 per cent of public schools had adopted premium caps for faculty retiring before age 65. For those retiring after age 65, 17 and 24 per cent had such caps. The similar private sector rates in 2001 were 39 per cent for both pre- and post-65 retirees (McDevitt et al. 2002, p. 20). Only a handful of the respondents to the current survey, across both the public and private institutions, had hit their premium caps already. By comparison, among the private firms surveyed in 2001, 42 per cent had already hit their pre-65 caps and 50 per cent had reached their caps for post-65 retirees (McDevitt et al. 2002, p. 21).

One response that private employers have adopted to limit retiree health liabilities but to continue to provide some level of benefits for future retirees is the adoption of 'retiree medical accounts' that accumulate during a worker's career and can be used to help pay health insurance premiums during retirement. Rather than paying a percentage of the premium for a defined insurance benefit, the employer makes a fixed contribution to an account, and the retiree is able to use the employer contribution in the account to purchase health insurance.

Like traditional retiree medical plans, retiree medical accounts are not taxable to the employee, they are not prefunded, and employees do not necessarily accrue a vested right to the benefit. Employers can retain the right to modify or eliminate the plan altogether as long as this is clearly communicated to employees and retirees. Employers may continue to offer a choice of one or more group-rated medical plans, but the retiree pays the full premium either from the retiree health account or directly.

Most of the employers reporting retiree medical accounts limit participation in these accounts to employees who have met age and service requirements, for example, age 40 and one year of service. This concentrates benefits on older employees and limits the cost of the benefits. Contribution formulas differ, but participants are typically credited a fixed dollar amount for each year of participation in the plan, and the account may earn interest both before and after retirement. Retiree health accounts are typically 'notional accounts,' meaning that funds are not deposited into these accounts as credits are earned. Rather, these accounts are simply a bookkeeping device that allows the employer and employee to keep track of the dollar amounts that will be made available for retiree medical benefits sometime in the future.

The retirement incentives associated with a retiree medical account are different from those of a traditional retiree medical plan. Where the traditional plan offers the highest present value to employees who retire early, the retiree health account continues to accumulate credits for each additional year of service. By working longer, the employee also reduces the number of costly pre-Medicare years for which retiree medical coverage must be funded. Finally, the traditional plan usually makes additional contributions for spousal coverage, but the retiree health account does not.

Although retiree medical accounts typically provide more limited employer contributions than those associated with traditional medical plans, they represent one way for employers to offer a benefit that is predictable, manageable, and consistent with prevailing strategies to attract and retain employees. Much like savings plans and cash balance plans designed to provide retirement income, retiree health accounts clearly communicate the dollar value of the benefit and encourage the employee to take on greater individual responsibility for retirement planning. In the 2001 survey of private employers, 13 per cent had set up these accounts as a way to control retiree health liabilities but still maintain a plan. In the 2004 survey of academic institutions, only one private school had established such a plan.

Among the respondents to the current survey, 47 per cent of the private institutions and 71 per cent of the public ones indicated that they were at least partially funding retiree health obligations. These response rates were surprisingly high and we asked many follow-up questions of respondents to verify this information. We found a variety of things the schools were doing.

For example, one university reported that they allow retiring employees to convert unused sick leave into an account at retirement to help pay the retiree's premiums which they considered to be partial funding. In almost every case, we concluded there was very little funding taking place. At least in the case of public colleges and universities, our conclusion is consistent with the GASB's assessment of how most public employers have been operating their retiree health benefit plans.

6.11   FUTURE PROVISION OF HEALTH BENEFITS FOR RETIRED FACULTY

To a considerable degree, faculty members retired from institutions of higher learning who have been covered by employer-sponsored retiree health benefits have fared somewhat better than their retired counterparts from the for-profit sector. For many of the latter, the companies that have sponsored retiree health benefits and continue to do so are in the manufacturing, utilities, and financial services sectors of the economy. The employment experience in these sectors has been remarkably different than in the higher education sector over the period since the baby boom generation has entered the workforce. Figure 6.6 shows employment levels compared to 1968 for firms in the manufacturing, utilities and financial services sector

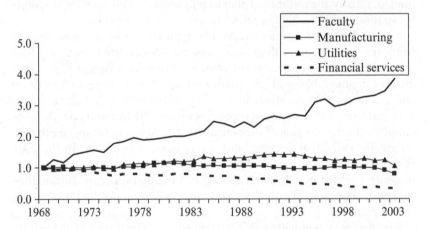

Source: Author's tabulations of the *Current Population Survey*, various years

Figure 6.6   Ratio of current employees to number of employees in 1968 for selected industries, compared to faculty in higher education, by year

from 1968 through to 2003. It also shows the employment of faculty in higher education over the same period. Labor force growth in the three industrial sectors has been relatively flat or declining over most of the period but the employment of faculty in higher education has shown steady growth over most of the period. Where there is little or no employment growth over time, sponsors of retirement plans invariably find that their retiree dependency levels rise, driving up costs of retirement plans, especially those financed on a pay-as-you-go basis.

As we look to the future, there are some indications that employers in the higher education sector may have built up a larger reservoir of future retirees, in relative terms, than many private industrial firms. Partly this is the result of different work and retirement characteristics in the various sectors. Many of the private employers have traditionally had defined benefit plans and have utilized early retirement incentives that encourage workers to retire when they reached their late 50s or early 60s. Academic institutions, which have more generally relied on defined contribution plans, especially for faculty members, have not had similar retirement incentives built into their retirement packages. The incentives built into retirement plans have been shown to affect the timing of retirement by the workers who participate in them (McGill et al. 2004). John Rust's simulations on retirement patterns under alternative levels of retiree health benefit provisions suggest this same phenomena will potentially modify faculty retirement patterns in schools that are now modifying their existing plans or that might do so in the future (see Chapter 7, this volume).

In any event, Figure 6.7 shows that the percentage of faculty over the age of 50 during the late 1960s in institutions of higher learning tended to be below that of workers of similar ages in the private sector industries where retirement plans have been most prevalent. In the last 20 years, however, the situation has completely reversed and higher education now has a much larger concentration of faculty over 50 than among those employed in the major industries where retirement plans prevail.

The combination of domestic economic reorganization, changing regulations and transferring various sorts of activities to foreign countries has resulted in remarkable increases in the ratio of retirees to active workers in virtually all of firms in the manufacturing, utility and financial services industries. Retiree health benefits have become a particular problem in this environment because they have been operated on a pay-as-you-go basis from a funding perspective. The costs of any retirement plan operated on this basis are directly proportional to the ratio of retirees benefiting from it compared to the workers who have to support it. In the case of retiree health benefits, the problem has been greatly exacerbated by the abnormally high rates of inflation in the health sector.

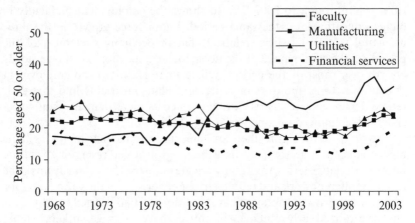

Source: Author's tabulations of the *Current Population Survey*, various years

Figure 6.7   Percentage of faculty in higher education and employees in selected industries aged 50 or over, by year

Despite the fact that employment patterns in higher education have evolved differently from those in many of the industries already troubled by the retiree health obligations they face, the same issues apply in this case as in the others. Retirement may come somewhat later in higher education than in other industries, but the larger share of current workers that are now at advanced ages suggests that retiree dependency ratios among faculty could rise fairly quickly in future years. A disproportionate share of existing faculty are members of the baby boom generation or older. This generation of workers is now approaching the age at which they will begin to retire either because of health considerations or because of normal expectations to do so. Even if they are all replaced by young faculty members, the future ratio of retirees to active workers will increase in the vast majority of cases. The pressures on health costs that apply to other sponsors of health insurance will continue to apply to academic institutions although the burden may continue to be relatively less than in many other cases.

Since faculty members tend to work somewhat later into life than many workers in the for-profit sector, especially those covered by defined benefit plans, many will be eligible for Medicare by the time they receive their employer-sponsored retiree health insurance. The cost of supplementing Medicare is virtually always less than the cost of providing full coverage. With the recent changes adopted in Medicare, this may be even more the case in the future. Still, the prospect of a growing retiree population suggests these costs may become more expensive for institutions still sponsoring the benefits in the future.

Of course, there is always the prospect that the higher education sector will continue to grow more rapidly than the remainder of the economy and that the added employment will allow employers in this sector to continue to escape the aged dependency problems that have plagued other sectors. Much of the growth in the education sector over the past 40 years has been demand driven, and it is not clear that the fundamental market factors that have persisted over this history will continue in coming decades. The baby boom generation and even its echo with subsequent birth cohorts have been accentuated with increasing demand for a college education. This growing demand has been supported by public and private funds that may be constrained by alternative claims in the future. The baby boomer generation's retirement will likely place an unprecedented claim on public budgets unless there are remarkable changes to public pensions and medical programs. To the extent there is retrenching on these programs, it may be concentrated on the middle and upper middle classes, including older workers and retirees who have been major contributors to higher education in the past.

In the case of public institutions of higher learning, the new GASB accounting standard is going to introduce some of the same sorts of pressures on retiree health benefits that they have introduced in the private sector. Given that changes that will be adopted to respond to these pressures will be undertaken in a public policy environment, the changes may not be as rapid as those taken in the private sector, or as radical. But even in the public sector, the recognition of costs associated with retirement plans often leads to changes. If nothing else, the recognition of costs associated with these sorts of programs can lead to reallocation of budgets within organizations and may ultimately result in actual reallocation of resources.

For institutions of higher learning in both the private and public sectors, it appears that most of them have not funded retiree health benefit obligations as they have accrued historically. This raises the prospect that future management of institutions that continue to sponsor these benefits will become hamstrung with obligations that are not properly anticipated and that have the potential to become so large that they pose a threat to the long-term viability of the institutions. Whether an academic institution is in the public or the private sector there are fundamental cross-generational issues that the provision of these benefits raise. The basic principles on which GASB is basing its new standard for accounting for retiree health benefits are the same as those that Steven Sass, the pension historian, has told us plan sponsors learned more than 80 years ago. To secure a retiree benefit over time, the obligation it poses must be accrued as it is being earned and must be funded at the time it is accrued.

It is likely that full accounting and a shift toward funding of retiree health benefits will lead many academic sponsors to reconsider the benefits that they have provided up until the present time. It is clear that some of this reassessment is now underway and that the net result is that benefits are being curtailed or costs shifted to retirees. The implementation of the pre-scription drug benefit recently adopted under Medicare may allow some sponsors to go further in terms of reducing retiree health obligations than they would have gone in the past. This opportunity arises for several reasons.

First, a typical employer-sponsored plan covering retirees also eligible for Medicare now spends something approaching two-thirds of its outlays on prescription drugs. The lack of drug coverage in Medicare has been its major inadequacy as a stand-alone insurance plan. Second, for a substantial number of plans documented in this analysis, 14 per cent of the private school plans and 20 per cent of the public plans, retirees are already paying the full premiums for their retiree health insurance, and the Medicare cov-erage may be no more costly than the existing coverage and may be nearly as comprehensive as current plans up to and including the catastrophic cover-age levels. Third, in many cases the employer cost of the current benefits is roughly as expensive as the Medicare coverage will be up to and including the catastrophic coverage levels. If employers want to continue to provide this level of benefits on a defined benefit basis, they would be better off estab-lishing an actual defined benefit pension plan to provide future retirees a stream of income to cover their Medicare costs for prescription coverage. For the remaining employers that are in a cost-sharing relationship with their retirees the financial picture may not be as clear, but the logic that applies to cashing out current health obligations for the other employers applies here as well. Defining a limited commitment and funding it as it is accrued will be a much sounder guarantee over the long term than what is being provided today.

It is clear that many current employers in this sector have a strong aver-sion to defined benefit pensions. Yet, in sponsoring retiree health benefits it is clear these same institutions have committed themselves to an alternative form of defined benefit plan where they have virtually no control over the escalation of costs over time, where inflation has historically been extremely high and persistent, and where there is little precedent for funding the oblig-ations as they accrue. This is not a logical situation for either the sponsor-ing organizations or the potential beneficiaries of current plans to sustain.

NOTES

1. This latter measure actually understates the role of technology because some portion of excess medical price inflation reflects technology enhancements to existing products and

services provided in the health sector. While the Bureau of Labor Statistics attempts to measure the price changes for a fixed market basket of goods over time, it is not uncommon for elements of the market basket to experience technological improvements, much as new automobiles are improved over time. To the extent that technology enhances the quality of a product in a way that increases its price, the price increase for the product reflects the imbedded improvement rather than price inflation.

2. The contribution limits had a slightly delayed effective date, applying to contributions after 1985, with a special four-year transition rule for plans with excess reserves. Special rules did allow additional contributions for plans covering collectively bargained employees or plans sponsored by tax-exempt employers.

3. A 401(h) account is an account in a pension plan, and is used to provide retiree medical benefits.

4. In addition to the use of 401(h) accounts, there has been increased use of life insurance products such as corporate owned life insurance (COLI) and trust owned life insurance (TOLI). These are more informal vehicles for funding and allow firms to invest in cash-value life insurance on a relatively large group of active and retired employees. The proceeds from these polices are used to pay post-retirement medical benefits. But because COLI is not held in a trust for the purpose of providing post-retirement medical benefits and the proceeds can be used for any purpose, it is not a plan asset for FAS 106 purposes and cannot be used to directly offset FAS 106 liabilities. TOLI proceeds, however, are in a trust and can be considered as an offset to the FAS 106 liabilities. But once again, TOLI only covers funding for current retirees.

REFERENCES

Atkins, G. Lawrence (1994), 'The employer role in financing health care for retirees,' in Judith F. Mazo, Anna M. Rappaport and Sylvester J. Schieber (eds), *Providing Health Care Benefits in Retirement*, Philadelphia: University of Pennsylvania Press and the Pension Research Council, pp. 100–24.

Centers for Medicare and Medicaid Services (CMS) (2000), Medicare Current Beneficiary Survey, 2000 accessed at: www.cms.hhs.gov/mcbs/CMSsrc/2000/Summary1.pdf.

Centers for Medicare and Medicaid Services (CMS) (2001), The 2001 Medicare and Medicaid Statistical Supplement to the Health Care Financing Review, accessed at www.cms.hhs.gov/review/supp/.

Centers for Medicare and Medicaid Services (CMS), Office of Research (2002), data from the Medicare Current Beneficiary Survey 1999, Cost and Use File, accessed at www.cms.hhs.gov/charts/series/sec3-65.ppt.

Centers for Medicare and Medicaid Services (CMS) (2004), Office of the Actuary, National Health Statistics Group, http://www.cms.hhs.gov/statistics/nhe/#download.

Costello, Declan and Mandeep Bains (2001), *Budgetary Challenges Posed by Aging Populations*, Brussels: Economic Policy Committee, European Economic Commission.

Department of Health and Human Services (DHHS) (1999), Agency for Health Care Research and Quality, 1999 Medical Expenditure Panel Survey tabulations by Watson Wyatt Worldwide.

Dopkeen, Jonathan C. (1987), 'Postretirement health benefits,' *Health Services Research*, vol. 21.

Fischer, Stanley (2001), 'Remembering Herb Stein: his contributions as an economist,' prepared for delivery in a session commemorating Herb Stein, at the American Economic Association meeting, New Orleans, LA, 6 January, accessed at http://www.imf.org/external/np/speeches/2001/010601.htm.

Fronstin, Paul (2001), 'Sources of health insurance and characteristics of the uninsured: analysis of the March 2001 Current Population Survey,' EBRI issue brief no. 240, December 2001.

Governmental Accounting Standards Board (GASB) (2004), *Accounting and Financial Reporting by Employers for Postemployment Benefits Other Than Pensions*.

Investor's Daily (1988), 'Retiree health benefits total 12% of payroll', 2 February, p. 9.

Kaiser Family Foundation and Health Research and Education Trust (2003), *Employer Health Benefits: 2003 Annual Survey*, Menlo Park, CA and Chicago.

McDevitt, Roland D., Janemarie Mulvey and Sylvester J. Schieber (2002), *Retiree Health Benefits: Time to Resuscitate?*, Washington, DC: Watson Wyatt Worldwide.

McGill, Dan M., Kyle N. Brown, John J. Haley and Sylvester J. Schieber (2004), *Fundamentals of Private Pensions*, 8th edn, Oxford: Oxford University Press.

Mueller, Marjorie Smith (1973), 'Private health insurance in 1971: Health care services, enrollment, and finances,' *Social Security Bulletin*, **36** (2), pp. 3–22.

Organisation for Economic Co-operation and Development (OECD) (2001) *OECD Health Data 2001*, Paris: OECD.

Pikrell, Jesse F. (1961), Group Health Insurance, revised edition, Homewood, Illinois: Richard D. Irwin.

Rice, Dorothy P. (1964), 'Health insurance of the aged and their hospital utilization in 1962: Findings of the 1963 survey of the aged,' *Social Security Bulletin*, **27** (7), p. 9.

Sass, Steven A. (1997), *The Promise of Private Pensions*, Cambridge, MA: Harvard University Press.

Social Security Administration (SSA) (2004), Office of the Actuary report, accessed at www.ssa.gov/OACT/COLA/awiseries.html.

Strong, Jay V. (1951), *Employee Benefit Plans in Operation*, Washington, DC: BNA Incorporated.

Thompson, Lawrence H. (1988), statement of Assistant Comptroller General, Human Resources Division, before the Subcommittee on Oversight, Committee on Ways and Means, House of Representatives.

Watson Wyatt Worldwide (1984), *1984 Group Benefits Survey*, Washington, DC: Watson Wyatt Worldwide.

7. Impact of retiree health plans on faculty retirement decisions

John Rust

7.1 INTRODUCTION

Tenured faculty members at academic institutions in the US (i.e. colleges and universities) are privileged to hold one of the most secure job contracts available. With essentially no risk of being fired, in a job that offers great working conditions, minimal levels of physical exertion, a high degree of flexibility and personal freedom, in addition to fringe benefit packages that are often far more generous than non-academic jobs, it should not be surprising that many academics have little incentive to retire. Indeed, some academics privately regard their jobs as fully paid 'virtual retirement packages'.

At the same time, colleges and universities are under increasing financial pressure as a result of recent cutbacks in government funding and student financial aid, the decline in the stock market, increased competition for students and research dollars, and rapidly rising costs – including the costs of providing 'fringe' benefits such as health care to their employees. These pressures are especially acute at some of the smaller liberal arts colleges that do not have large endowments and Federal research support, and whose revenues are therefore highly dependent on tuition. Even though tuition at the major public universities has increased rapidly in recent years in order to offset reductions in state and federal funding, these large percentage increases were made from a much smaller base so tuition at most public universities is still generally far less than tuition at private colleges and universities. As a result, many small to medium-sized private liberal arts colleges have much less room to raise their already very high tuition rates without risking significant declines in enrollment. At these schools, the primary focus is on how to reduce costs, given that the possibilities for raising additional revenue (apart from soliciting donations from corporate sponsors and alumni to build endowments) has become far less promising in recent years.

Since faculty salaries and fringe benefits are typically a college or university's biggest single expense, it is not surprising that the focus of most cost-cutting efforts is on either reducing the level or at least constraining the rate of growth in salaries and benefits. In particular, Sylvester Schieber's survey in this volume (Chapter 6) shows that the cost of health insurance benefits is rising at an unsustainable rate of over 10 per cent per year in recent years, and that 'if played out over the next decade or so, could drive total health costs to equal something between 15 and 25 per cent of cash wages paid to workers.' (p. 111–12).

Just as many non-academic businesses have chosen to cut health care benefits and replace full-time workers with lower paid 'temporary workers' for whom they do not have to pay health insurance and other types of benefits (or in the most extreme cases, 'outsourcing' or 'down-sizing' by eliminating the jobs entirely), colleges and universities are under similar pressures to reduce costs by cutting benefits and replacing tenured faculty with lower paid untenured assistant professors, instructors, and lecturers (in many cases saving the costs of the generous fringe benefit packages offered to their 'permanent' employees) and in the extreme, to leave the slots created by retirements unfilled for the indefinite future.

The nature of the tenure contract imposes a huge 'rigidity' on colleges and universities that most regular firms do not face: tenured faculty cannot generally be 'fired' but must be persuaded to leave (i.e. retire) voluntarily. Further, anti-age discrimination legislation such as the 1967 Age Discrimination in Employment Act and its 1986 amendment banned the use of mandatory retirement and a 2003 ruling by the Internal Revenue Service further reduces a college or university's flexibility in how they can structure financial incentives to encourage older tenured faculty to retire. The 2003 IRS ruling makes it illegal to use actuarially unfair payout formulas in 'defined benefit' pension schemes to create incentives for early retirement. Furthermore, due to tax, regulatory and accounting advantages, more and more academic institutions are switching to 'defined contribution' pension plans that are basically neutral in terms of the incentives they create for early versus late retirement.

Even though a university or college may be bound by its tenure contract, there is typically nothing beyond ordinary competitive pressure and a sense of moral obligation to provide generous fringe benefit packages to its staff. In addition to typically generous health insurance and retiree health insurance packages, many academic institutions also provide private supplemental disability benefits and other types of fringe benefits such as college tuition subsidies for children of academic staff. If the tenure contract does not obligate the academic institution to provide these costly fringe benefits, then it should not be surprising that many of these costly 'perks' associated with an academic job are at risk for cutback or even complete elimination.

A 2002 survey of 387 colleges and universities by the College and University Professional Association (CUPA) for Human Resources found that

67 per cent provide some type of retiree health insurance coverage – a rate of provision that is significantly higher than for non-academic employers, although less than the 89 per cent coverage rate provided by US companies with 1000 or more employees reported in the 2003 Kaiser/Hewitt Survey on Retiree Health Benefits. However the financial pressures facing colleges, combined with the unprecedented double-digit rates of increase in health care costs in the US in recent years (with typical health insurance premiums rising at a rate of between 10 to 15 per cent per year), has forced many academic institutions to reconsider their retirement packages, and shift an increasing share of the premiums and costs of health care onto faculty retirees. The CUPA survey found that for two-thirds of the colleges surveyed, health care insurance rates increased by more than 10 per cent, and one in seven colleges reported rates of increase of more than 20 per cent from the previous year.

In the face of rapidly escalating health care costs, over 80 per cent of US companies have been either had to pass on higher premiums to their employees or reduce the generosity of their coverage of health care costs – generally by increasing deductibles and co-insurance rates. Indeed, in 2002 33 per cent of US companies reduced or eliminated their health care coverage entirely. Higher educational institutions have dealt with these problems in much the same way: 'In an effort to preserve coverage for employees without busting their budgets, colleges and universities in recent years have raised premiums, deductibles, and the co-payments for drugs and doctor visits. Some institutions have questioned how long they can continue to take care of retirees' health care' (*Chronicle of Higher Education* June 2004). A 2003 survey by the Henry J. Kaiser Foundation found that 10 per cent of firms with 1000 or more employees had cut or eliminated their retiree health benefits. Although I am not aware of comparable data for educational institutions, it is reasonable to predict that increasing numbers of academic institutions will be forced to reduce or even eliminate their retiree health benefits as part of a series of cost cutting measures in order to make ends meet in increasingly difficult times.

There is no easy solution to the financial pressures facing colleges and universities, and naive efforts to cut costs by reducing or eliminating retiree health insurance benefits could backfire and end up costing more than continuing with the status quo. When a college eliminates or substantially reduces the generosity of its retiree health plan, it also significantly reduces the incentive for its existing faculty to retire. It may be tempting for a college or university to cut retiree health insurance benefits under the hypothesis that retirees are a less powerful group, that is 'unseen and unheard' compared to more visible political opposition to reducing health insurance benefits that could be generated by existing employees. However, if a college attempts to save costs via the 'least painful' strategy of cutting benefits for a group that it perceives to be the least politically troublesome – i.e. retirees – existing faculty are sure to take note of the change in policy and will have even less incentive to retire than they currently have.

Thus, colleges and universities have to balance the cost savings from cutting back on their retiree health plans with the potential cost increases due to delayed retirement by its existing tenured faculty. In general if a college wants to encourage a tenured faculty member to retire, it must be keenly aware of the fact that its faculty members already have a very secure and comfortable position. The risk of uninsured health care costs may well be the biggest single risk facing many tenured faculty members. Since a tenured faculty member has the default option of not retiring, a cost-cutting measure that imposes additional financial risks on faculty during their retirement years must be compensated in some way (i.e. by a higher retirement benefit) otherwise they will delay their retirement as part of an overall strategy for coping with these additional risks. If faculty are risk averse and do not have good alternative private health insurance options prior to their eligibility for Medicare at age 65, it could end up costing a college more in terms of higher retirement benefits to compensate its faculty for the increased risks of health care costs than it saves from the cost-cutting measures. Alternatively, if the college simply cuts retiree health care benefits without an offsetting increase in retirement benefits, then the likely outcome is that its tenured faculty will delay their retirements, and this alternative could also be more costly than the status quo (or even more costly than incurring greater costs to increase the level of generosity of the college's retiree health insurance package). *In general, when a firm has employees that are sufficiently risk averse, it is typically cheaper to pay them with a compensation package that includes insurance against their most pressing risks, than to forgo the insurance and pay them entirely in cash and force them to 'self-insure' their risks.*

The goal of this chapter is provide a conceptual framework that could prove useful in the design of faculty compensation, retirement, health insurance and fringe benefit packages. To my knowledge no previous study has provided such a framework. Instead, the design of retirement 'schemes' chosen by academic institutions and private firms seems to be largely the result of *ad hoc* experimentation, and recommendations of specialized consulting companies, whose advice seems guided more by intuition and previous experience than by an extensive body of scientific research. While I would not discount the importance of intuition, common sense, and practical experience in the design of compensation and retirement packages, I believe that economic methods – both theoretical models and econometric studies – could significantly improve our understanding of the factors influencing faculty retirement decisions and, as a by-product, enable higher educational institutions to design more effective compensation, fringe benefit, and retirement plans.

In this chapter I adapt a version of the classical 'life-cycle model' in economics to the specifics of the academic job contract, accounting for the job security and employment incentives provided by tenure and the types of pension plans and health care coverage that are typically offered at universities and colleges in the US. The life-cycle model assumes that decision makers are rational, forward-looking planners who are risk averse, and choose how much to work and how much to consume and when to retire (i.e. when to give up their tenured teaching appointment and start collecting their pension benefits) in order to maximize their expected discounted utility over their remaining lifetime. Unlike many other occupations, academics are modeled as having a much stronger attachment to their work (i.e. a lower disutility of effort). This is a strong part of the explanation, independent of financial incentives, why academics are more reluctant to retire compared to individuals in most other industries and occupations. Even though they have tenure, faculty members do face risks, including risk of health problems leading to disability, the risk of uninsured or partially insured health care costs wiping out accumulated retirement savings, and uncertainty about their future earnings, both while employed at their academic job and subsequent earnings at a possible post-retirement job.

A major advantage of the life-cycle model is that it generates predictions of how a rational individual's behavior would change in response to changes in the rules governing the payment of their pensions, and the details of their health insurance coverage. Thus, the model allows me to undertake a series of 'computational experiments' to assess how a person's decisions about retirement, consumption and savings, and their overall level of welfare would be affected by increasing or decreasing the level of generosity in their health insurance, either before or after retirement. Confirming previous research by Rust and Phelan (1997) (who modeled retirement decisions of blue-collar workers), I find that even for moderate levels of risk aversion, the concern about low-probability, but potentially 'catastrophic' out of pocket health care costs has a significant impact on retirement decisions. If a university attempts to save costs by eliminating or substantially increasing the co-insurance rates in its retiree health plan without making an equivalent reduction in the degree of generosity of its health insurance plan for current employees, the increased level of risk this imposes on retirement years relative to working years is predicted to lead to significant postponements in retirement ages. There are ranges of parameter values for which such a policy is more costly than the status quo, i.e. maintaining retiree health insurance benefits even though they may be relatively costly.

Even though the life-cycle model developed here is just an illustration that is in many respects an oversimplified caricature of the full complexities of actual retirement decisions, the model is able to capture the main tradeoffs facing faculty members as they approach the end of their academic careers. With access to better data, it is possible that a more elaborate and realistic version of this model could provide a reasonable approximation to actual behavior. If it is able to accurately predict how faculty respond to changes in various aspects of their compensation packages, it could be a useful practical tool to help colleges and universities deal intelligently with the challenging problem of rapidly rising health care costs.

I refer the reader to Chapter 6 by Sylvester Schieber in this volume for a summary of some of the typical features of employer-provided and retiree health insurance coverage offered by colleges and universities. These features motivate the model I develop in section 7.2 – a specialized version of the life-cycle model that can be used to predict the effect of changes in employee and retiree health plan provisions on the retirement decisions of tenured faculty member at a hypothetical college or university in the US. Section 7.3 undertakes several computational experiments designed to illustrate the behavioral and welfare effects of various changes to pension benefits and health insurance coverage, including the impact on retirement ages and the total expected discounted cost of providing these benefits. Section 7.4 offers some concluding remarks.

7.2   A MODEL OF THE ACADEMIC RETIREMENT DECISION

This section develops a specialized version of the life-cycle model, which I refer to as the *academic retirement model* (ARM). The model captures the key features of the tenure contract, and is able to reflect the details of a variety of different academic pension plans (including defined benefit and defined contribution plans such as 403-B plans), and various types of health insurance and retiree health insurance packages. While the focus of this chapter is on the effects of variations in health insurance plans on retirement decisions, ARM can also be used to evaluate a wide array of other faculty retirement incentives such as phased retirement plans (the subject of Steve Allen's analysis in Chapter 9), and various types of 'buy-outs' and 'window plans' (the subject of John Pencavel's analysis in Chapter 10).

ARM generates predictions of an individual faculty member's behavior, starting at some initial age (I assume age 50 here) through the duration of their employment at their university or college until retirement, including any post-retirement work, until their death. Each period (assumed to be one year in length) the faculty member makes decisions about how much to consume and how much to save, whether or not to retire (if not already retired), whether or not to do either full or part-time post-retirement work (if retired), whether to apply for Social Security benefits (if over the Social Security early retirement age), or wait to apply for Social Security at the normal retirement age, or delay their application further to take advantage of the Social Security *delayed retirement credit*. The ARM includes various sources of risk and uncertainty, including uncertainty about future health status and age of death. If a faculty member becomes disabled and finds it prohibitively difficult to continue working, he/she also has the option to apply for Social Security disability benefits (these benefits are payable, if awarded, even if the person is below the Social Security retirement age).

An individual's decisions depend on their current information which includes their current age, wealth, health, and employment status. In addition to health and mortality risks, an individual faces uncertainty about future health care costs (which depend on health status), and future earnings. Earnings are assumed to be relatively predictable prior to retirement, reflecting the relative security of tenure (i.e. nominal wage cuts almost never occur, and the main uncertainty is by how much real wages will increase). However, after a person retires there may be considerably more uncertainty about earnings levels reflecting the lower security level provided by 'ordinary' untenured jobs, temporary positions, consulting opportunities, etc. The faculty member can support him or herself in their retirement years via a combination of post-retirement earnings, defined-benefit pension and Social Security payments, and the decumulation of private savings and defined contribution pension balances. However due to the possibility of uninsured or uncovered health care costs, the individual will want to maintain a significant precautionary or 'buffer stock' of assets to cover these costs. Precautionary savings also help insure against protracted periods of low earnings and the possibility that a person might live longer than expected.

The details of the model and the various assumptions about the faculty member's preferences, their beliefs about whether they will become disabled, when they will die, what types of post-retirement job opportunities they will have, the risks they face for out-of-pocket health care costs (i.e. costs of medical care that are not covered by their employer or retiree health insurance), and other details underlying the solution of the life-cycle model are described in Rust (2004). Using numerical methods (Rust, 1996), I solved the life-cycle model under a 'base case scenario' intended to capture the beliefs of a 'typical academic' at a university with a defined contribution pension plan and a generous employee and retiree health insurance plan. I assumed that at age 50, the person has an average wage (used to calculate Social Security benefits) of $40 000 and current annual earnings of $64 857. I assume that the faculty member is moderately risk averse, and as long as the faculty member is in good health the disutility of doing full-time academic work is very low until age 80 after which it starts to rise at a more rapid rate. If the faculty member becomes disabled, then the disutility of working is significantly higher at all ages, and rises more rapidly with age than for a faculty member who is in good health. My assumptions about the health and mortality of dynamics for academics reflect the fact that most academics are healthier and have lower risk of dying at any given age than in the population at large. I also assume that if a faculty member continues to stay in their tenured job, they expect that their real income will grow at approximately 1.5 per cent per year at age 50, but this rate of increase in earnings declines linearly to slightly more than 0 per cent by age 80. Further, I assume that the faculty member believes there is relatively little uncertainty around this projected growth rate. However if the faculty member retires and chooses to engage in full or part-time post-retirement work, their average wage rate is lower (approximately three-quarters of the wage rate they would earn by remaining at their tenured job) and the variability of their earnings is significantly higher than their earnings in their tenured faculty job. Finally, I assume that faculty discount future utility at a rate of $\beta = 0.92$ per year, and that they can obtain a 4 per cent real rate of return on their savings and pension fund accumulations.

One of the most important assumptions driving the results in the next section is the assumption about health insurance coverage and health care costs. Under the 'base case' scenario, I assume that the faculty member is covered under a generous health insurance plan provided by the University, which pays 100 per cent of the premiums both before and after retirement until their death. I assume the plan is a 'family plan' that covers all members of the household, and the plan has cost and coverage characteristics similar to the coverage offered by Duke University to its faculty and staff (see http:// www.hr.duke.edu/). The annual premium for this plan is $9000, which is about equal to the average premium in the US for a family health insurance plan in 2003 (Kaiser Family Foundation/Hewitt Associates, 2004). I assume that, given the deductibles and coinsurance rates for this plan, the distribution of out of pocket health care costs under this plan can be approximated by a member of a three-parameter family of distributions described in Rust (2004). This family has a 'Pareto upper tail', i.e. it reflects the fact that, due to incomplete coverage of all medical expenses and positive coinsurance rates, there is a small risk that the person could incur 'catastrophic' out-of-pocket health care costs, even though they are covered by a health insurance policy. My assumptions imply a mean and variance of out of pocket health care costs equal to $1253 and

$1641, respectively, for individuals who are in good health, and $1563 and $3927, respectively, for individuals who are disabled.

The current rate of growth in health insurance premiums – both private health insurance and Medicare – is in excess of 10 per cent per year. As Schieber's analysis (Chapter 6, this volume) points out, this rate of increase is not sustainable in the long run since it exceeds the real growth rate of the economy. In the base case analysis, I assume that premiums and overall health care costs will grow at 14 per cent (real) for the next 15 years, after which a major national health care reform occurs that causes health premiums and costs to stop growing entirely, flattening out at the values it reaches 15 years from now and staying fixed at that level thereafter. The 14 per cent figure is the average rate of growth in premiums in the latest Kaiser Family Foundation/Hewitt Associates Survey of employee and retiree health benefits.

Under the base case solutions of the ARM, I assume that the mean of the distribution of out-of-pocket health care costs will increase at 14 per cent per year for the next 15 years (from age 50 to age 65) before levelling off. I consider this to be a *worst-case* scenario, since it seems likely that actions by the government and firms will eventually arrest this high and long-term unsustainable rate of increase. Indeed, recent evidence (Freudenheim 2004) suggests that already 'increases in health care premiums are slowing' to a rate of about 10 per cent in 2004, 'well below the annual increases of 14 to 18 per cent in the last few years but still more than double the overall inflation rate'. However since the purpose of this chapter is to illustrate the predictions of the ARM, I have decided to illustrate it under a worst-case scenario of 15 years of continued increases of 14 per cent per year rather under a more realistic scenario where the rate of increase in health care costs will flatten out much sooner. The reader should keep this in mind when interpreting the results in subsequent sections.

The solution to the ARM consists of four *decision rules* which are functions of the state variables that specify the optimal choices for the four decision variables in the problem:

$$c_t = c_t(w, y, ss, r, h)$$
$$l_t = l_t(w, y, ss, r, h)$$
$$rd_t = rd_t(w, y, ss, r, h)$$
$$ssd_t = ssd_t(w, y, ss, r, h) \qquad (7.1)$$

where c_t denotes consumption at age t, l_t denotes the person's labor supply decision (full-time, part-time or not working), rd_t denotes the retirement decision ($rd_t = 1$ if the person retires, $rd_t = 0$, otherwise), and ssd_t denotes the Social Security decision (apply for old age benefits, or disability benefits (if eligible), or don't apply for benefits). The other variables on the right-hand side of the decision rules given above are the *state variables* describing the state of the faculty member at age t. Thus, w_t denotes the sum of their accumulated net worth and (defined contribution) pension balance. The variable y_t denotes last year's annual earnings (if not retired), or the earnings in the year before the person retired otherwise. The remaining variables denote the person's Social Security status (ss_t), their retirement status (r_t), and their health status h_t, where the t subscript denotes the values of these time-varying variables when the age of the person is t. The Social Security state ss_t can take the values $0, 62, 63, \ldots, 70$, where $ss_t = 0$ denotes not receiving Social Security benefits, and $ss_t = 62$ denotes receiving early retirement benefits at age 62, and so forth. The model also accounts for Social Security disability benefits. The retirement and health state variables are assumed to be simple binary state variables: $r_t = 1$ denotes that the person has already retired, $r_t = 0$ denotes not having retired yet, and $h_t = 0$ denotes good health and $h_t = 1$ denotes being disabled.

The retirement decision can be represented as a threshold rule in wealth:

$$rd = \begin{cases} 1 & \text{if} \quad \omega > \lambda_t(y, ss, h) \\ 0 & \text{otherwise} \end{cases} \tag{7.2}$$

The retirement threshold is an increasing function of pre-retirement earnings y. Optimal consumption is an increasing function of both y and w for any given values of the state variables. Note that at very low levels of wealth w the individual is *liquidity constrained* and the optimal consumption rule is to consume 100 per cent of the person's wealth: $c_t = w_t$ when w_t is sufficiently small. In our simulations in the next section we will be focusing on faculty members whose combined pension accumulations and net worth w_t is sufficiently large that they are unlikely to ever be liquidity constrained (there is a small risk that they could become liquidity constrained if they experience catastrophic health care costs that wipe out their accumulated net worth). When there is no liquidity constraint the marginal propensity to consume out of wealth, i.e. the derivative of C_t with respect to w, is significantly below 1. This low marginal propensity to consume reflects a *precautionary savings motive*, i.e. the individual wishes to save a significant share of their accumulated wealth as a 'buffer stock' against unexpected health care costs o_t, and unexpectedly low post-retirement earnings (which could be partly due to unexpected health problems that make post-retirement work very difficult), and a desire to have enough assets to supplement Social Security benefits in the event that the individual lives longer than expected.

The decision rule for labor supply is similar to the retirement decision, in that the discrete labor supply decision takes the form of a threshold rule, where, for any given income level (where if the person is retired, the y

variable records the last earnings level in their tenured job), there is a threshold value of wealth such that, if the person's wealth is greater than this level, he/she decides not to work at all. Prior to retiring from the university, we assume that the person's only choice is to work full-time. However after retiring, the person can choose whether to work full- or part-time, or not at all. If wealth levels are sufficiently low, the person works full-time, and if wealth levels are sufficiently high the person does not work. Thus, there is an intermediate range of wealth where the individual chooses to work part-time after retiring. Similarly, fixing the person's wealth, w, employment will generally be an increasing function of the person's expected earnings (provided w is not so high, or the person is not too old or disabled that they would choose not to work at all). The state variable y, lagged earnings, is positively related to expected earnings from employment. Thus, for sufficiently low levels of y the individual will choose not to work, and for sufficiently high levels of y the person works full-time. For intermediate values of y part-time work is optimal.

7.3 SIMULATING THE EFFECTS OF CHANGES IN HEALTH INSURANCE

This section presents stochastic simulations of the ARM under a 'base case' scenario, and four alternative scenarios involving several commonly considered changes to retiree health plans offered by colleges and universities. For each alternative scenario, I re-solve the dynamic programming problem and generate corresponding simulations using optimal decision rules for each scenario. These decision rules represent the faculty member's 'best response' to each of the assumed changes in the University's health insurance coverage. It is typically easier to understand the behavior predicted by the ARM by analysing stochastic simulations rather than by studying its implied decision rules since, as I showed in the previous section, the solution to the ARM consists of four optimal decision rules for consumption, labor supply, the retirement decision and the Social Security application decision, and each of these functions depends on six variables: age, wealth, income, a retirement indicator, a health indicator, and the person's Social Security status. It is difficult to visualize these functions and see what they imply about the timing of retirement and how changes in health insurance coverage affects them. This section begins with an analysis of stochastic simulations under the base case in order to obtain further insights into the behavior implied by ARM. Then I compute simulations under the four alternative scenarios and summarize how each change affects behavior, welfare, and the university's expected discounted cost of compensation relative to the base case.

A *stochastic simulation* of the ARM starts from an *initial condition* specifying the state of the simulated individual at age 50. I use the laws of motion for the state variables and the decision rules calculated from the dynamic programming problem to generate a realized sequence of decisions and states over the individual's lifetime until death. The simulations depend on a set of *random shocks* which can be generated in advance and stored. If I re-use previously stored values of these random shocks (which are formally a $50 \times k$ matrix of uniformly distributed random numbers, where 50 is the maximum remaining lifespan of a 50-year-old simulated individual and k is the number of randomly evolving state variables in the ARM), I can re-generate the stochastic simulation and obtain exactly the same set of states and decisions that were previously generated. This provides a key method of 'experimental control' that is a major advantage of the ARM from the standpoint of evaluating the behavioral impacts of changes in retiree health insurance. By using the same random shocks for each of the four alternative scenarios that were used to generate the base case simulation, I am able to isolate the behavioral impacts of changes in health insurance coverage in each of the alternative scenarios from the effects of health, earnings, and mortality shocks. That is, if I use the same random shocks to generate the alternative scenarios, the individual will experience exactly the same realized values of the 'exogenous variables' in the ARM. In particular, the sequence of health states and the age of death will be exactly the same in the base case simulation and in each of simulations of the alternative scenarios. Realized values of the endogenous state variables and decision variables such as earnings and the labor supply and retirement decisions will change, but the changes are a result purely of behavioral changes (e.g. changes in the decision rules) and not due to 'luck' as reflected in different realized values of the underlying random health and income shocks.

Clearly, it is not possible to attain this level of experimental control in an experiment with human subjects: the same person can only be given one 'treatment' and it is not possible to observe how the same person would have behaved had they been given a different health insurance plan or if some other aspect of their fringe benefit package had changed. Thus, human experiments depend on randomly selected treatment and control groups, with sufficiently large numbers that the effect of idiosyncratic shocks can be averaged out. I also use this type of experimental control in the stochastic simulations below. I generate large numbers of independent simulations for a synthetic population of individuals, starting either from the same or a randomly generated set of initial conditions. Appealing to the Law of Large Numbers, I can average out the effects of the stochastic shocks to provide a clear view of the typical behavior implied under the base case and each of the alternative scenarios. In this analysis I use 500 independent simulations starting from the same set of initial conditions, yielding artificial 'panel data sets' that follow 500 ex ante identical individuals from age 50 until their deaths.

Figure 7.1 illustrates the results of the base case simulations, 500 simulated individuals all of whom start from the same initial condition at age

Panel A: Fraction of cohort who survive, and fraction of
survivors who are in good health

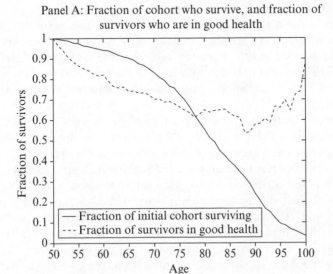

Panel B: Fraction of survivors who are working full and part-time

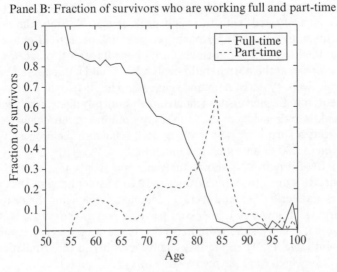

Figure 7.1   Results of simulations of the model in the 'base case' (1)

50: good health, not retired or receiving Social Security with an income of $64 857 and net worth of $581 508. Panel A of Figure 7.1 shows the fraction of survivors and the fraction of survivors who are in good health status. Although the one-year survival probabilities are high (at least 60 per cent even at age 100), the cumulative risk of death between age 50 and 100 is substantial, and only 3 per cent of the initial cohort survives to age 100. The fraction of survivors who are in good health generally declines until about age 87, and then it starts to rise. This partially reflects 'survivorship bias', i.e. healthier individuals are more likely to survive than those in poor health. However, note that the averages beyond age 90 are noisier and should be interpreted with caution since they are based on relatively few observations given the small number of survivors at these ages.

Panel B of Figure 7.1 shows the fraction of survivors who are working full- and part-time. Prior to age 55, 100 per cent of the simulation sample is working full-time, since none of these individuals have yet retired from the university. However beginning at age 55, individuals start to retire, and thus, the fraction of individuals working full-time starts to drop. We see that many of the individuals who retire start working at a part-time post-retirement job. The fraction of retired individuals working part-time increases rapidly up until age 85, and then drops off rapidly thereafter. By age 95, almost all of the survivors have stopped working entirely.

Panel A of Figure 7.2 shows the distribution of retirement ages (i.e. the age the faculty member left his/her tenured job) and the distribution of ages of first entitlement to Social Security benefits. The latter distribution is highly concentrated, with the main peak at age 70. Since the delayed retirement credit falls from 7 per cent per year to 0 per cent after age 70, it is not optimal to apply for Social Security benefits after this age. We see a secondary peak at the normal retirement age, 66, and a third small peak at the Social Security early retirement age, 62. The distribution of ages of retirement from the university is much more uniformly distributed, with the main peak in retirements at the University's minimum retirement age, 55. This reflects a surprising degree of ex post behavioral heterogeneity in a simulation of 500 ex ante identical individuals.

Panel B of Figure 7.2 shows the mean payments to faculty by the University. It is upward sloping from age 50 to 55 since none of the faculty members have retired yet, and average earnings are following their expected trajectory which involves 1.5 per cent per year real growth rates. However after age 55, faculty start to retire and average wage payments start to decline until age 85, when the last faculty member in the simulation has retired, after which wage payments are zero.

Panel A of Figure 7.3 shows average consumption and earnings, and

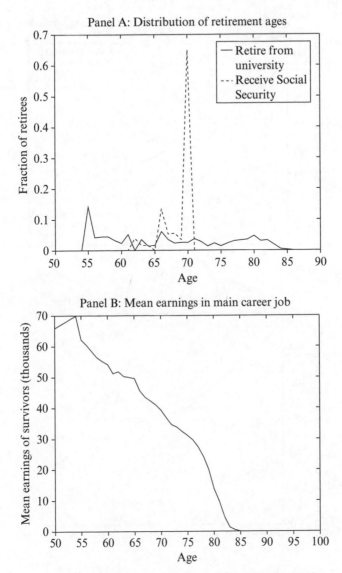

Figure 7.2   Results of simulations of the model in the 'base case' (2)

Panel B shows the evolution of net worth. Consumption declines steadily from $80 000 at age 50 to just over $20 000 at age 90. Consumption is higher than earnings initially, but between ages 60 and 80, the combination of full-time earnings from those who have not yet retired and earnings from post-retirement results in earnings that exceed consumption.

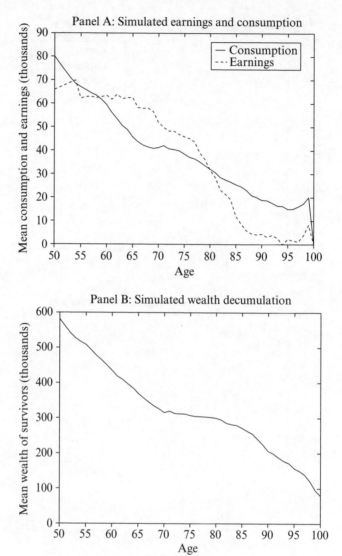

Figure 7.3   Results of simulations of the model in the 'base case' (3)

Notice that there is a slight upturn in consumption between ages 65 and 70, reflecting the additional income from the receipt of Social Security benefits. The pattern of initial dissaving, followed by net saving between ages 60 and 80 is reflected in the rate of decumulation of wealth in the lower panel of Figure 7.3. Wealth decumulates at a fairly rapid rate

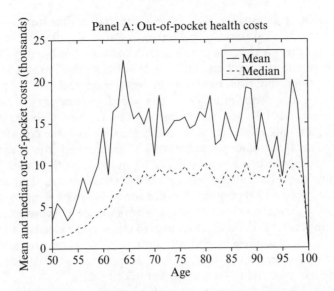

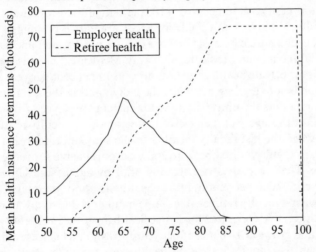

Figure 7.4   Results of simulations of the model in the 'base case' (4)

between ages 50 and 70, then it decumulates at a significantly slower rate between ages 70 and 80, and then resumes a more rapid rate of decumulation thereafter.

Why does net worth continue to decline even though there is net savings between ages 60 and 80? Figure 7.4 shows that a large part of the reason is due to health care costs. Panel A shows mean and median out-of-pocket health care costs. Consistent with the skewed Pareto distribution of uninsured health care costs, mean out-of-pocket costs are significantly greater than median out-of-pocket expenditures. We also see that, consistent with my assumptions about the escalation of health care costs, out-of-pocket expenditures are growing rapidly over this period, leveling out at a median cost of nearly $10 000 per year at age 65. Besides out-of-pocket health care costs, the only other cost that faculty must incur is the cost of their Medicare Part B insurance premiums, which I assume will grow at a rate of 14 per cent per year between ages 50 and 65 and level off thereafter. Thus, by the time these individuals become eligible for Medicare, their annual premiums will be $7500 per year. It is not surprising that the main reason why many of these individuals continue to work and do not consume more after retiring is due to concern about unpredictable uncovered health costs. This is why many of these individuals continue to save even after retiring. A secondary concern is the desire to have enough assets to last over their remaining lifespan, and to leave a bequest to their heirs.

Panel B of Figure 7.4 shows the average university payments for employee and retiree health insurance coverage, respectively. Recall that in the base case, the university is assumed to pay 100 per cent of these premiums, leaving their faculty employees only liable for Medicare Part B premiums and any out-of-pocket health care costs due to expenses not covered under the university health plan and Medicare. Similar to Medicare, I have assumed that premiums for private health care costs grow at 14 per cent per year for a 15-year period before leveling out when the individuals in the simulation turn 65. The premiums the university pays for current employees grows rapidly and peaks at this age, but then falls equally rapidly as faculty retire, reaching zero when the last faculty member in the simulation retires at age 85. However, as faculty retire, the University becomes liable for retiree health insurance. These expenses rise steadily until by age 85 the University is paying over $70 000 per year in retiree health insurance premiums for each of its surviving faculty retirees. This large number is due to my assumption that the University's premium for retiree health insurance starts out at $9000 per year, and grows at 14 per cent per year for 15 years before leveling out.

Although the rapidly increasing health care premiums may somewhat exaggerate the expectations that many employers have about future health care costs, it does serve as a graphic illustration of the problems they confront. I now present an analysis of four scenarios, representing several common strategies that academic institutions and other employers have considered as a way to deal with rapidly increasing health care costs. I use the ARM to predict how faculty will rationally respond, in terms of adjusting their retirement behavior in response to each scenario, and then simulate each scenario using the same random shocks and initial conditions that I used to generate the base case scenario. The four scenarios that I consider are:

- Case 0:   The University pays only 50 per cent of retiree health insurance premiums.
- Case 1:   The University cancels retiree health insurance completely.
- Case 2:   The University continues retiree health insurance (and pays all premiums) up until age 65, when the faculty member is eligible for Medicare.
- Case 3:   Same as case 2, except that I also assume that fairly priced high quality Medigap insurance is available for purchase in the private health insurance market.

Figure 7.5 shows a comparison of employer and employee health insurance premiums between the base case and case 0, respectively. Not surprisingly, the university's costs of retiree health benefits falls dramatically. However it may be a surprise to learn that due to delay in retirement ages the present value of the university's share of retiree health insurance falls by 80 per cent rather than a 50 per cent reduction that one might have guessed would occur in case 0. Panel A of Figure 7.5 shows the huge increase in health insurance premiums that must now be borne by retired faculty members.

Of course, faculty foresee the large increased financial burden that they will face during their retirement years and respond accordingly. Figure 7.6 illustrates the important consequences of the elimination of retiree health insurance benefits from the university's point of view. The ARM predicts that the primary offsetting behavioral response is to significantly delay their dates of retirement from the university in order to accumulate enough additional retirement savings to help cover the additional health insurance costs during retirement. This causes the university to incur higher health insurance premiums for its currently employees due to the delay in retirements (Panel A of Figure 7.6) in addition to having to pay out more in wages (Panel B of Figure 7.6).

Panel A of Figure 7.7 shows the impact of the elimination of retiree health insurance on the distribution of retirement ages: basically it delays retirement from the university by 10 years. Instead of starting to retire after age 55 as they did in the base case, faculty do not start retiring until age 66 under case 0. The last retirees remain at the university until age 94 compared to 85 under the base case. Panel B of Figure 7.7 shows that, in addition to delaying their age of retirement, faculty also reduce their consumption relative to the base case. There is also a significantly higher incidence of post-retirement work, both full- and part-time, in case 0 relative to the base case.

Panel A: Impact on employer-paid retiree health insurance premiums

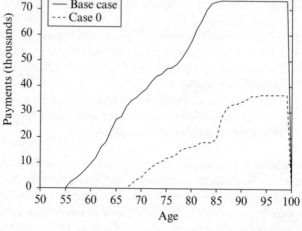

Panel B: Impact on employee-paid health insurance premiums

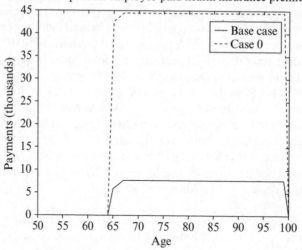

Figure 7.5　*Comparisons of base case and case 0: effects of shifting 50 per cent of retiree health insurance premiums to retirees (1)*

The decrease in consumption and increase in labor supply enables faculty to more than offset for their effective cut in compensation and acquire uniformly higher levels of wealth under case 0 than under the base case, as we see in Panel A of Figure 7.8. However this additional precautionary wealth

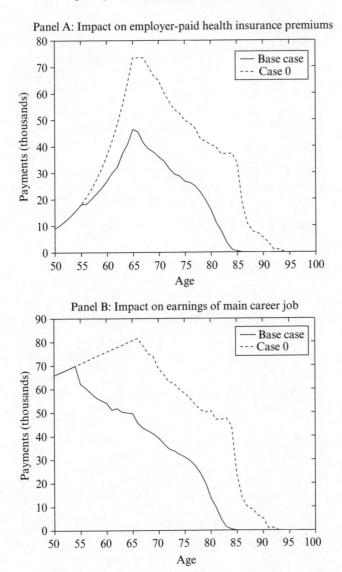

Panel A: Impact on employer-paid health insurance premiums

Panel B: Impact on earnings of main career job

*Figure 7.6   Comparisons of base case and case 0: effects of shifting 50
per cent of retiree health insurance premiums to retirees (2)*

accumulation comes at a high cost in terms of overall well-being of faculty
as we can see from the uniform downward shift in discounted lifetime in
Panel B of Figure 7.8.

Figures 7.9 and 7.10 present results from a comparison of the base case

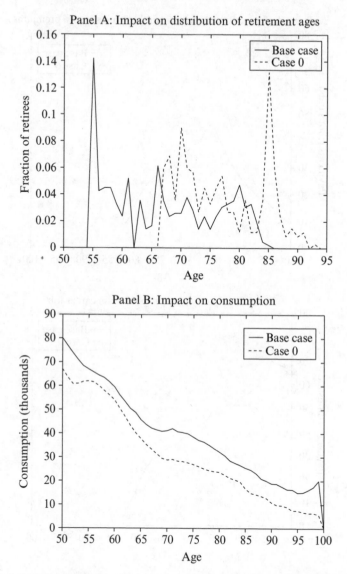

Figure 7.7   Comparisons of base case and case 0: effects of shifting 50
per cent of retiree health insurance premiums to retirees (3)

and an even more extreme alternative that the university might consider:
canceling its retiree health insurance altogether. The major direct benefit to
the university from this policy is obvious: it completely eliminates the cost
of retiree health insurance. However Figure 7.9 illustrates the two key

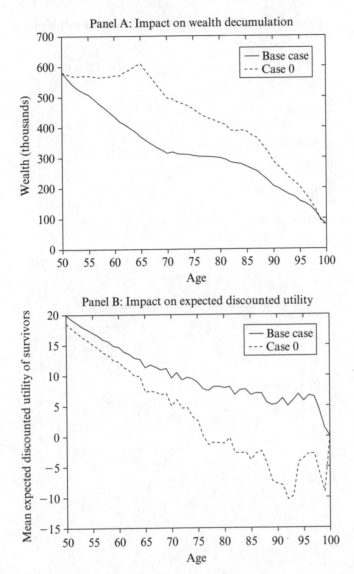

Panel A: Impact on wealth decumulation

Panel B: Impact on expected discounted utility

Figure 7.8   Comparisons of base case and case 0: effects of shifting 50 per cent of retiree health insurance premiums to retirees (4)

offsetting costs resulting from the induced delay in retirements: higher wage payments to employees (top panel) and higher health insurance premiums for its current employees (bottom panel). The overall delay in retirements is not as great under case 1 as it is under case 0, although similar to case 0

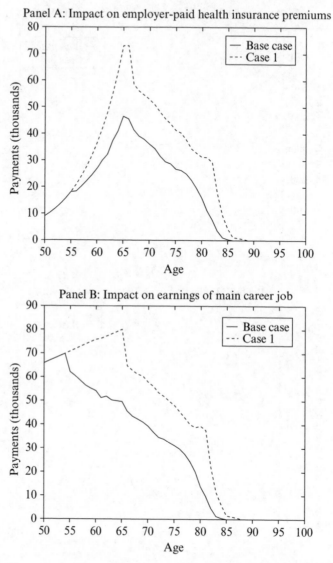

Panel A: Impact on employer-paid health insurance premiums

Panel B: Impact on earnings of main career job

Figure 7.9   Comparisons of base case and case 1: effects of canceling retiree health insurance (1)

the first retirements are postponed by 10 years, starting at age 65, which not surprisingly, is the age of first eligibility for Medicare benefits. However after age 65 retirements increase rapidly under case 1 relative to case 0, and the main peak in retirement ages is at 65, with a smaller secondary peak at

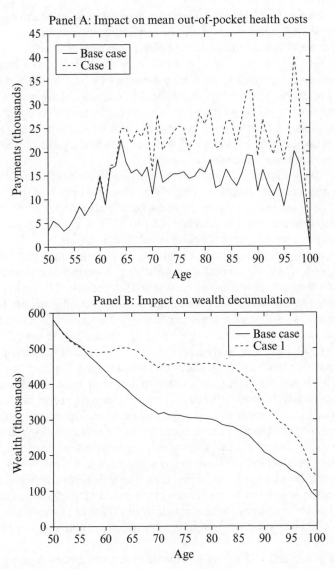

Panel A: Impact on mean out-of-pocket health costs

Panel B: Impact on wealth decumulation

*Figure 7.10   Comparisons of base case and case 1: effects of canceling
retiree health insurance (2)*

age 82, whereas the main peak in retirements under case 0 was at age 85, as
we saw in Figure 7.7.

   Panel A of Figure 7.10 shows the impact of the cancellation of retiree
health insurance on the faculty members' out-of-pocket health care costs.

As we would expect, there is no increase in out-of-pocket health care costs prior to age 65, since none of the faculty retire prior to this age, so they remain covered under the university plan for current employees, and thus do not face any higher out-of-pocket costs compared to the base case. However after age 65 they only have Medicare but do not have the additional protection provided by retiree health insurance. This leads to a significantly higher liability for out-of-pocket health care costs compared to the base case. Of course, these additional costs represent health care costs that are not covered by Medicare and were covered by the retiree health insurance coverage under the base case.

Panel B of Figure 7.10 shows the effect of the cancellation of retiree health insurance on wealth accumulation. The ARM predicts that, in addition to delaying retirements by 10 years, faculty also modestly reduce their consumption spending between ages 55 and 65. This enables them to build up a higher precautionary stock of wealth as a means of 'self-insuring' against the higher out-of-pocket health care costs that they will be facing after age 65. Thus, we see that starting at age 57, overall wealth accumulation is uniformly higher in case 1 relative to the base case. The higher wealth accumulation combined with the higher earnings actually enables individuals to have slightly *higher* consumption spending after age 65 relative to the base case. However due to the disuiltity caused by the postponement in retirement ages, the overall level of faculty welfare (as measured by expected discounted utility) is uniformly lower in case 1 relative to the base case. This is not surprising since the elimination of retiree health benefits amounts to a massive effective cut in compensation. However interestingly, the decline in welfare is not as large as in case 0. This suggests that the behavioral effects predicted under case 0 may be artificially high due to the failure to give the retiree the option to discontinue retiree health insurance coverage – in effect forcing them to pay a premium that is much higher than they would be willing to pay voluntarily. The unrealistically high levels of labor supply offered at very old ages in the case 1 scenario seems to be an artifact of having to pay for the incredibly high cost of retiree health insurance. This is why the reduction in faculty welfare is much greater in case 0 than in case 1.

Figures 7.11 and 7.12 show the simulated effects of the case 2 'compromise scenario' in which the university continues retiree health insurance and pays 100 per cent of the premiums, but only until the person reaches age 65 and becomes eligible for Medicare benefits. This option may be increasingly attractive in light of a recent decision by the Equal Employment Opportunity Commission (EEOC).

The EEOC ruled that an employer's decision to discontinue retiree health insurance after age 65 does not violate civil rights laws banning age

Panel A: Impact on employer-paid retiree health insurance premiums

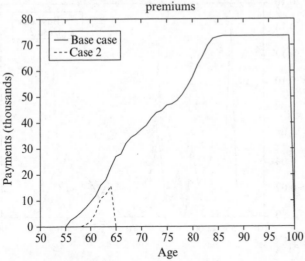

Panel B: Impact on employer-paid health insurance premiums

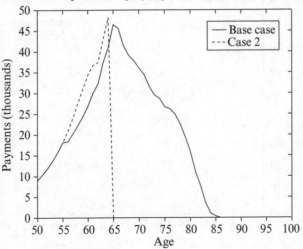

Figure 7.11 Comparisons of base case and case 2: effects of canceling retiree health insurance after age 65 (1)

discrimination. This ruling appears to be a pragmatic compromise to confronting employers with an all-or-nothing choice of 'Give all of your retirees the exact same benefits, which is incredibly difficult, or eliminate your retiree health benefits altogether' (Leo Silverman, member of the

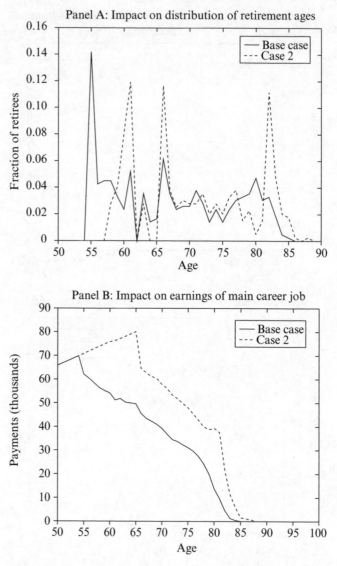

Figure 7.12 *Comparisons of base case and case 2: effects of canceling retiree health insurance after age 65 (2)*

EEOC, quoted in *New York Times* front page article, 23 April 2004). For this reason, the *New York Times* article reported that many labor organizations, including the American Federation of Teachers and the National Education Association, supported the EEOC ruling.

Panel A of Figure 7.11 shows that compared to the base case, the compromise policy of the university covering 100 per cent of retiree health insurance premiums up to age 65 results in a major reduction in retiree health insurance costs to the university. Health insurance premiums remain the same as in the base case, i.e. the retiree only has to pay for their Medicare Part B premiums, since I assume that the university covers the retiree health insurance premiums prior to age 65, and after age 65 the retiree has no affordable 'Medigap option' to supplement their Medicare coverage (so that after age 65, the retiree's only health insurance coverage is Medicare).

Panel B of Figure 7.11 shows that the impact on health insurance premiums for current employees. We also see a big decrease in these costs to the university, even though the policy of terminating retiree health insurance after age 65 does result in some delay in retirements and thus larger total wage payments to faculty. The reason that the effect is not nearly as large as in case 0 or case 1 is due to the fact that the university also terminates its coverage to *current employees* after they reach age 65. This policy has an added benefit of not appearing to discriminate against retirees in favor of current employees, and has the desirable effect of mitigating incentives to delay retirement in order to maintain the more deluxe combined Medicare/ private health care coverage that the university provides to its employees under the base case.

Panel A of Figure 7.12 shows the effect of the case 2 health coverage changes on the distribution of retirement ages. Compared to the other cases considered, this case has the least impact on delayed retirement. Compared to the base case, where the main peak in the distribution of retirements is at age 55, there are now three main peaks in retirement ages: at 62 (the Social Security early retirement age), 66 (the Social Security normal retirement age), and 83. The peak in retirements at age 65 that we observed in case 1 has disappeared, and this is because those faculty who do want to retire prior to age 65 know they can do so and still be covered under the university's retiree health plan.

Panel B of Figure 7.12 shows the impact of the case 2 coverage changes on the wages the university pays to faculty. We see that due to the delay in retirements, wage payments are higher relative to the base case, but the increase in wages is far less compared to cases 0 and 1, where the delay in retirement is much greater. The 'bridge coverage' provided by the university's retiree health plan until the Medicare eligibility age provides a sufficiently attractive option to induce a significant fraction of faculty to retire prior to age 65. This bridge seems to be a major reason why the case 2 option results a lower increase in wage costs compared to cases 0 and 1.

ARM predicts that the impact on consumption and wealth accumulation for case 2 is very similar to case 1. Up to age 55 there is virtually no change in the amount of wealth accumulation or consumption. However after 55, consumption is lower under case 2 than in the base case. Together with the additional earnings due to the delay in retirements, individuals are able to significantly reduce the rate of decumulation of wealth, resulting in significantly higher precautionary wealth accumulation at all subsequent ages, very similar to the higher level of wealth accumulation we observed for case 1. Faculty welfare is also uniformly lower under case 2, but the decrease in welfare between ages 50 and 65 is very small. Thus, faculty members at these ages would not vigorously oppose the change in the health insurance coverage. This seems consistent with the National Education Association's endorsement of the EEOC's decision to allow employers to terminate retiree health care coverage at age 65; relative to the alternative of cutting benefits completely or shifting a large share of the premiums onto retirees, the case 2 policy clearly seems to be the 'lesser of evils' from a faculty member's standpoint.

The final case considered, case 3, is the same as case 2 except that I assume that there is fairly priced Medigap insurance available for individuals over 65. I assume this Medigap coverage is twice as expensive as the Medicare part B premium, or $15 200 per year and is paid completely by the retiree. The simulation results for case 3 are similar to case 2 and are not presented here. If we compare the outcomes in Cases 2 and 3 we find that the existence of fairly priced Medigap insurance complements the compromise policy of eliminating retiree health insurance coverage after age 65. The availability of fairly priced Medigap insurance has a 'reassuring effect' on the individuals in the simulation: they are willing to retire slightly earlier than they would without Medigap. Although the average decrease in out-of-pocket expenditures is generally lower than the annual Medigap premium, $15 200, risk averse faculty members prefer to purchase Medigap due to the value of insurance it provides that reduces the risk of catastrophic health care costs in old age. Thus, although the differences between cases 2 and 3 are relatively subtle, the ARM provides intuitively plausible forecasts of how relatively subtle changes in the environment can affect individual behavior and welfare. In general, when there are more complete and more fairly priced options for purchasing health insurance in the private market (or from an expansion of government insurance programs), the better it is from the standpoint of both the employee *and* the employer. As we will see shortly, the employer can take advantage of the insurance opportunities available in the market (or from the government) to avoid the costs involved in providing these opportunities to its employees and retirees on its own.

I conclude this section with Table 7.1, which compares the expected discounted costs of compensation (both in terms of direct wages and fringe bene-

Table 7.1   Expected discounted compensation under alternative scenarios

Compensation item	Base case	Case 0	Case 1	Case 2	Case 3
Panel A: Expected discounted values (at 2%) (amounts in thousands)					
Wages	1047.2	1497.4	1370.9	1222.5	1183.1
Pension contributions	52.4	74.9	68.6	61.1	59.2
Employee health insurance	537.6	863.4	764.3	303.4	294.8
Retiree health insurance	553.1	113.6	0.0	33.8	42.4
Total compensation	2190.2	2549.3	2203.8	1620.8	1579.4
Panel B: Breakdown as a per cent of total expected discounted compensation					
Wages	47.8	58.7	62.2	75.4	74.9
Pension contributions	2.4	2.9	3.1	3.8	3.8
Employee health insurance	24.5	33.9	34.7	18.7	18.7
Retiree health insurance	25.3	4.5	0.0	2.1	2.7
Total compensation	100.0	100.0	100.0	100.0	100.0

fits) under the base case and the four alternative scenarios. Panel A presents the expected discounted values of the various components of compensation, discounted at a real interest rate of 2 per cent. These calculations take account of mortality, and in particular, all benefit payments terminate at death.

According to Table 7.1, of the various scenarios considered, the case 3 scenario is the cheapest from the standpoint of the university, whereas the most expensive is case 0, which requires retirees to pay 50 per cent of the cost of their retiree health insurance. Why is the 'compromise' policy of cutting retiree health benefits after age 65 the cheapest (to the university) of the five scenarios considered? The reason is that by cutting health benefits to employees and retirees who are older than 65 (and thus eligible for Medicare coverage), the university saves considerably on health insurance premiums and the induced delay in retirements (which increases discounted wage payments) is relatively minor and not sufficient to offset the large savings in health care costs. In fact, discounted wage payments in cases 2 and 3 are the lowest of any of the scenarios except for the base case, where the 'deluxe' health care coverage provided by the university provides a sufficient 'safety net' that faculty are willing to retire voluntarily at fairly young ages. Indeed the main peak in retirement ages in the base case is at the university's early retirement age, 55.

Case 0, where the university requires retirees to pay 50 per cent of their health insurance premiums, was the most costly of the scenarios considered. The reason is that the cost of paying for the rapidly rising premiums was so large that faculty were essentially forced to delay retiring and continue working to very late ages. This is why the present discounted value of wages under case 0 is the highest of the scenarios considered. The large delay in retirements also dramatically increased the university's cost of providing health care benefits to its current employees. As I noted above, the results for case 0 are not entirely plausible due to my implicit assumption that retirees do not have the option to cancel this expensive retiree health insurance. If retirees were allowed to cancel their retiree health care coverage (which seems to be a much more realistic assumption), then most older retirees would in fact cancel their retiree health insurance at some point rather than pay the high premiums. Under this modification of case 0, the outcomes are very similar to the outcomes in case 1, where the university cancels retiree health insurance completely.

However the interesting point to note is that the ARM predicts that it is cheaper for the university to maintain its deluxe employee and retiree health insurance package than to adopt a naive policy of trying to cut costs by cutting these benefits completely. This is due to the offsetting increase in wage and employee health insurance benefits under either case 0 or case 1 resulting from the faculty member's optimal behavioral response to the university's compensation package. The failure to account for these behavioral responses can lead to ill-advised policies that are not only greatly unpopular with existing and retired faculty, but they can actually end up costing the university more. These results support a general point that I made in the introduction: if workers are risk averse, it is cheaper to offer them a compensation package that includes insurance for their most pressing risks, rather than to force them to 'self insure' against these risks.

The other major conclusion from this analysis is that when the cost of providing insurance grows too fast and gets too high, there is a point at which some 'compromise' cutbacks in health insurance benefits become inevitable. I have illustrated a case where the university can reduce the total costs of its compensation by judiciously cutting its retiree health benefits, taking advantage of the existence of a government program – Medicare – that already provides a good deal of coverage for individuals who are over 65. The policy of cutting retiree health benefits after age 65 was the cheapest among the options considered. Furthermore, the results indicated that when faculty expect to have access to fairly priced Medigap insurance to supplement their Medicare coverage, the savings of the policy of eliminating retiree health at age 65 are even higher. This is due to the fact that the increased security level provided by the option to purchase fairly priced Medigap insurance induces faculty members to retire earlier than they would in the absence of it, and this saves the university money.

These results suggest that the recent passage of Medicare prescription drug benefit will have a similar effect: it will induce employers (including universities) to drop prescription drug coverage from their retiree health insurance benefits (at least for those over age 65), and effectively shift their employees onto the Medicare drug plan. While these actions are good from the standpoint of employers, if the financing of Medicare is not sustainable in the long run (and the most recent report of the Trustees of the Social Security System forecasts that the prescription drug benefit will add $8 trillion dollars in unfunded obligations to the $27 trillion in unfunded obligations of the pre-existing Medicare program over a 75-year horizon), the 'fix' provided by such policies may only be temporary and illusory. What is required is an intelligent, sustainable, long-term solution to the problem of runaway health care costs in the United States, and neither employees nor employers can really rest easy until it is found.

7.4   CONCLUSIONS

This chapter has developed a model of faculty retirement decisions by extending and specializing the classical 'life-cycle model' in economics to account for the presence of uncertain out-of-pocket health care expenditures and the specifics of the academic job contract and typical fringe benefit packages. I refer to this model by its acronym – ARM, for 'Academic Retirement Model'. Via solutions and simulations of an informally calibrated version of ARM I have tried to show how such a model can generate detailed predictions of how faculty respond to changes in compensation packages, and in particular, to changes in their employee and retiree health coverage.

I would like to emphasize that the results in the previous section are based on 'made up' scenarios that are not intended to be particularly realistic. I used somewhat extreme assumptions about how long current rates of inflation in health insurance costs will continue (i.e. 14 per cent rates of growth for the next 15 years) to provide a rather stark illustration of the problems that universities and colleges (and faculty retirees) face in the 'worst case', where unsustainable rates of inflation persist for much longer than many experts believe is plausible. I hope that these simulations give some indication that more realistically specified versions of the ARM could be an important tool to help academic institutions make intelligent decisions about the compensation packages they offer to their employees.

The ARM has a great deal of flexibility and can be used to predict the impact of a wide range of policy changes that were not considered here, such as the use of 'phased retirement programs' and lump sum 'buyouts' that are the subject of empirical analyses by Steven Allen and John Pencavel in this volume. More ambitiously, it is possible to use the ARM to systematically optimize over entire classes of compensation packages, in order to identify an 'efficient' (i.e. cost-minimizing) compensation package.

However before attempting to extend the model in these more ambitious directions, I would place the highest priority on collecting data on retirement decisions at specific universities that could enable me (or others) to estimate the unknown preference parameters of the ARM and statistically test its predictions. The credibility of the model rests on its ability to accurately predict retirement decisions by faculty in the past, and its ability to accurately predict how faculty will change their behavior in response to the changes in health insurance coverage and other aspects of compensation packages. An ideal data set would come from a large university (such as one of the large state systems such as University of North Carolina or California) for which we have large numbers of 'observations' on faculty retirements and where there have been interesting changes to compensation plans that provide a testing ground that can enable us to compare actual responses to changes in the compensation plan to those predicted by ARM.

ACKNOWLEDGEMENT

I thank Robert Clark, Jennifer Ma and Joseph Newhouse for helpful comments. This research was supported in part by a grant from the University of Michigan's Economic Research Initiative on the Uninsured.

REFERENCES

Allen, S.G., R.L. Clark and L.S. Ghent (2003), 'Phasing into retirement' National Bureau of Economic Research working paper no. 9779.

Ashenfelter, O. and D. Card (2001), 'Did the elimination of mandatory retirement affect faculty retirement flows?', National Bureau of Economic Research working paper no. 8378.

Freudenheim, M. (2004), 'Increases in health care premiums are slowing' article in Business Day section of the *New York Times*, 27 May, p. C1.

June, A.W. (2004), 'Medicare law may provide a lift to college health-care budgets', *Chronicle of Higher Education*, 27 February.

Kaiser Family Foundation/Hewitt Associates (2004), 'Retirement health benefits now and in the future', research report for the Henry J. Kaiser Family Foundation, Menlo Park, CA.

Royalty, Ann Beeson and J. Hagens (2003), 'The effect of premiums on the decision to participate in health insurance and other fringe benefits offered by the employer: Evidence from a real-world experiment', ERIU working paper no. 23.

Rust, J. (1996), 'Numerical dynamic programming in economics' in H. Amman, D. Kendrick and J. Rust (eds), *Handbook of Computational Economics* vol.1, Amsterdam: Elsevier, North Holland.

Rust, J. (2004), 'Impact of retiree health plans on faculty retirement decisions', manuscript, Department of Economics, University of Maryland accessed at www.gemini.econ.umd.edu/jrust/research/papers/arm.pdf.

Rust, J. and C. Phelan (1997), 'How social security and Medicare affect retirement behavior in a world of incomplete markets,' *Econometrica*, **65** (4), pp. 781–831.

8. Faculty recruitment, retention and retirement: a case study of human resources policymaking at Syracuse University

John L. Palmer, Michael A. Flusche and Myra Z. Johnson

In Chapter 1 of this volume, Robert L. Clark identifies several important human resources policy issues related to faculty recruitment, retention and retirement that he believes will be particularly challenging for universities in the near future. In addition, he argues the need for careful consideration of the diversity of educational institutions and their environments, as well as of the context of national economic conditions and key public policies, in any analysis of how universities in general might respond to these faculty labor market concerns. As they are at many other universities, human resources practices are evolving rapidly at Syracuse University (SU) in response to the concerns outlined by Clark. In this case study we discuss several relevant recent and ongoing activities at SU in which we were extensively involved,[1] with attention both to substantive outcomes and processes and to important dimensions of institutional and national context. Our major focus is on health care, but we also discuss SU's new family leave and phased retirement policies for faculty. In what follows we devote a section to each of these three areas in turn and then offer several concluding observations.

8.1 HEALTH CARE

Syracuse University has a history of providing the same health care benefits to eligible faculty and staff while actively employed, and to eligible retirees until age 70 (the old mandatory retirement age).[2] Prior to the mid-1990s, the available options for active employees (and their dependents) included the university's self-insured indemnity plan (administered by

Aetna), in which a majority of employees enrolled, and several local health maintenance organizations (HMOs). The benefits under the indemnity plan, which allowed complete choice of providers by patients, were quite generous and required minimal out-of-pocket expenditure; and both types of plans were highly subsidized by the university. Employees who formally retired from the university at age 55 or older, and had as little as one year of prior service were eligible to continue participation through age 64 under the same terms as active employees. From age 65–69 retirees were eligible – at no cost to them – for a university-sponsored, Medicare wrap-around plan that, in combination with Medicare, more or less duplicated the coverage under the indemnity plan. Starting at age 70, they were (and still are) on their own.

Several internal and external factors began to spur major changes in SU's health care benefits in the mid-1990s. A period of fiscal austerity and modest downsizing for the institution in the early 1990s, along with more rapidly rising institutional costs for medical insurance and a growing understanding of national trends in employer-based health care, resulted in strong impetus to adopt the type of utilization controls and cost-sharing in the self-insured plan that were becoming more commonplace nationwide. Also, given the modest annual salary increases in prospect for the foreseeable future for faculty and staff, there was strong interest in maximizing, to the degree possible at little or no institutional cost, the value to employees of their fringe benefits.

The first of these concerns led to a total revamping of the university's self-insured plan, with the substitution for the indemnity plan of two new options: an HMO-type exclusive provider option with no deductibles and nominal co-pays for covered medical services, and a somewhat more expensive point-of-service (POS) option with the same benefit structure for services within the primary network, but some cost-sharing for services rendered through an extended network and even greater cost-sharing for those out-of-network. The university subsidy was set at 84 per cent of total costs for both self-insured components, and the university contribution to HMO premiums was set as the same dollar amount as its subsidy for the more expensive self-insured component. The net effect was a self-insured plan with similar coverage and costs to the university and participants of the old indemnity approach on average, but also with a combination of utilization incentives and controls that it was hoped would restrain the future growth of health care costs (relative to continuation of the indemnity plan) without unduly restricting the choice of providers available to participants.

It is worth noting some important elements of the process that surrounded these policy changes. At the risk of oversimplification, it is probably fair to characterize SU's institutional approach to decision-making about benefits prior to the mid-1990s as *ad hoc*, paternalistic and insular: *ad hoc* because no processes were in place for ongoing review and planning; *paternalistic* because decisions were made almost exclusively on the basis of what the relevant administrators thought was in the best interests of employees (consistent with institutional fiscal realities) without systematic input from employees; and *insular*, both in this regard and because little effort was made to benefit from the experience and practice of other universities. This approach to decision-making also began to change in the mid-1990s under the direction of new leadership at the top of the university and in human resources. The initial manifestation of this change was the creation of an ad hoc committee to review and consider new directions for SU employee benefits that, in addition to key individuals from the human resources and business and finance offices, included two faculty with benefits expertise. Consistent with prior practice, the revamping of the health care plan was effected through a process internal to the university's human resources and business and finance offices. But the basic thrust of the new policy direction was informed by the deliberations of this committee and a study it commissioned from outside consultants with considerable knowledge of best practices among universities nationwide.

Concern for maximizing the value to employees of their benefits, at little or no net new cost, was subsequently pursued through another process that represented a marked departure from SU's paternalistic past: the creation by Chancellor Kenneth A. Shaw of a task force, broadly representative of the University's faculty and staff, to review and make recommendations on a broad range of benefit and work–life issues. In considering employee benefit plans, this task force focused primarily on issues of choice, flexibility and employee tax savings, and did not pursue a review of the basic structure or financing of the university's health plan since it had been so recently revamped. In addition to seeking input on best practices elsewhere, the task force also surveyed the university's entire workforce to ascertain employee preferences with respect to a number of options. The major outcomes from this process in the health care area were the development of a tax-sheltered flexible spending account for employee out-of-pocket expenses, the creation of a new dental insurance benefit, and some refinement in structure of employee health care premium charges in relation to the number of dependents being covered.

Things were then relatively quiescent on the health care front within the university for a few years in the late 1990s. The experience under the new self-insured plan was quite positive: employees were generally pleased with the new options available and the per capita costs to both them and the university were rising relatively slowly (in line with national trends in health care costs). But ominous clouds were gathering. The HMOs were becoming less attractive alternatives due to consolidations in the regional health care market, increasingly stringent utilization controls and more rapidly rising premium costs. Also, many firms in the region began to respond to economic pressures by cutting back on their health care benefits, leading many spouses and dependents of SU employees to move to university coverage with its more generous subsidy. The net result was a substantial increase in overall enrollment in university health care plans and an even larger increase in the self-insured components where the university's liability was not capped (as it was for HMO participants).[3] This then combined with the same resurgence in per capita health care cost inflation sweeping the country and led to a 'perfect storm' for SU health care costs: a 20 per cent increase in fiscal year 2001 with continued double-digit increases projected for the subsequent two years, which became a major contributor to rising deficits in the University's five-year budget.

In response to the growing problem, in spring 2001 Chancellor Shaw acted upon the recommendation of the Administrative Benefits Committee (ABC) – comprised of the six top human resources, business and finance officers charged with management of the university's benefit plans – to take several immediate steps (effective health care plan year 2002) to increase employee premium charges and selected co-pays to maintain the university's projected share of total health care costs at the historic target level of 83–84 per cent. He also then appointed a new body, the Chancellor's Health Care Advisory Committee (HCAC), and charged it to analyse and make further recommendations on the concrete steps the university should take to deal with the challenge of continuing to provide attractive, affordable health care options to its employees in the face of escalating costs.

So far in its three years of existence, the HCAC has proven a highly effective vehicle for facilitating university deliberation and decision-making on these matters. It has analysed, deliberated, and developed a consensus (or near-consensus) on numerous concerns informed by appropriate benchmark data and best practices elsewhere. Among the more important steps concerning health care benefits for faculty (and staff) taken pursuant to HCAC recommendations during its first two years of operation were the following:

- Employee premium charges are being adjusted upward over three years to hit a new target of a 20 per cent, rather than the prior 16–17 per cent, average contribution by employees.
- Eligibility for retiree health care benefits for newly hired employees now requires a minimum of five consecutive years, rather than

one year, of service, and the full 80 per cent university subsidy will be provided only to retirees with 10 or more years of active service.

- Increased efforts are underway to improve plan participants' awareness of the cost advantages of using generic and mail order drug purchase options and of the tax savings available to them through flexible spending accounts.
- The university is exploring the possibility of offering an affordable SU-sponsored health care plan to the part-time employee population at full cost to participants.

The HCAC, with consultant support, also undertook a study of the new so-called consumer driven health care plans to determine if there was a version the university should consider offering as an additional option for employees. A negative conclusion was reached, at least for the immediate future, on the basis that such plans were largely untested in the university environment and not likely to help SU contain health care benefit costs in any meaningful way unless a substitute for, rather than an addition to, current university plans. But it was also determined that such plans have several attractive features that should be incorporated into our current medical program over time to the extent feasible.[4] With the blessing of the Chancellor and other key university committees (discussed later in this section), the HCAC agenda in 2003–04 has focused entirely on retiree health care concerns.[5] There were several reasons for this. First, the university was informed by its actuaries in the summer of 2003 that, to satisfy appropriate financial accounting standards (under FAS 106), the liability it would have to 'book' for future retiree health benefit obligations would grow at an even greater rate than had previously been projected, despite the change in prior-years-of-service requirement for new employees noted above.[6] This, combined with the realization that SU was an outlier among employers in paying for 100 per cent of post-65 retiree health care benefits, led to a recommendation by the HCAC – and decision by the university – to institute a premium charge for the Medicare wrap-around coverage for retirees age 65–69 comparable to that charged active employees and pre-65 retirees for their coverage. Although employees already aged 55+ are exempted from this new premium charge, if and when 65–69 and retired, its imposition had the consequence of lowering the university's future FAS 106 liabilities below their previously projected levels (before all the other changes mentioned earlier in this paragraph). Second, the HCAC had previously planned to begin consideration in 2003–04 of ways the university might improve retiree health care benefits under the new eligibility criteria at no net new institutional expense. The subsequent decision to impose a premium charge on retirees aged 65–69 rendered this concern more salient. Finally, the passage of the new Medicare drug benefit legislation provided additional impetus for timely institutional consideration (to allow for final decision by early 2005) of any major restructuring of retiree health care benefits.

Thus the HCAC has been on a forced march through 2003–04 to develop a new approach to health care benefits for retirees for institutional consideration in the second half of 2004. The objective agreed upon by the committee in fall 2003 is the extension past age 69 to the end-of-life of eligibility for a SU-sponsored and partially subsidized Medicare wrap-around plan that is both affordable to participants and cost-neutral to the university. Actuarial estimates indicate this can be accomplished with a total package of benefits for those age 65+ provided through Medicare, plus a new SU wrap-around plan, that are roughly comparable to those benefits now provided to both active employees and pre-70 retirees, except for prescription drug coverage.

There are three keys to the feasibility of this accomplishment. The first is for SU to no longer subsidize a prescription drug benefit in a new wrap-around plan. Rather, participants would rely upon the new Medicare prescription drug benefit and could purchase a non-subsidized, university-sponsored supplementary prescription drug plan if they so wished. The other two keys are that SU currently (even after the recent change in policy) has much more generous age and prior-years-of-service criteria for eligibility for retiree plan participation (and the full 80 per cent university subsidy) than is typical of peers and bases its premium charges to retirees on a blended, retiree–active cost rate. Our actuarial analysis indicates that the objectives of institutional cost-neutrality and affordability for plan participants can be achieved by basing premium charges on actual (different) cost rates for retirees and active employees and by imposing somewhat more restrictive age-service criteria for eligibility and subsidy of retirement benefits that are still within the norms of peer institutions.

Whether such a new structure for retiree health benefits will prove to have sufficient appeal to faculty, staff, and institutional decision-makers to be adopted remains to be seen. (At the time of this writing, in May 2004, the HCAC report and recommendation on retiree health benefits was just completed, with broader institutional consideration yet to come.) In any event, the HCAC plans to turn its attention back to issues of cost and coverage for active employees in 2004–05, with (re)consideration of consumer-directed approaches high on the agenda in light of the provisions in the new Medicare legislation authorizing tax-sheltered health savings accounts in conjunction with high deductible plans.

The HCAC's success in facilitating university deliberation and decision-making on a wide range of issues concerning the cost and competitiveness of SU's health care benefits appears to be due to several factors beyond the fact that it has the strong support of, and reports directly to, the Chancellor. Chief among them are:

- The chief human resources officers of the university are strongly committed to it being the primary forum for in-depth analysis and university-wide consideration of all important health care policy matters, and have devoted ample staff time and other resources to this end, working in close cooperation with faculty chairs of the committee.
- Initial and subsequent appointees to the committee embody considerable depth and breadth of professional expertise on the matters at hand (e.g., in benefits, risk management, and health care finance, economics and policy), as well as reflect a broad range of important perspectives within the university community (e.g., those of deans, department chairs, other faculty, staff and administrators).
- The 15-person membership of the HCAC also includes the university's director for budget and planning (who reports directly to the Chancellor) and substantial representation from each of the other three university committees most important to deliberation and decision-making regarding health care benefits: the previously-noted Administrative Benefits Committee, and University Senate committees dealing, respectively, with the budget and with services to faculty and staff. This insures that these other bodies are well informed about HCAC deliberations and recommendations and that the latter, in turn, incorporate the concerns of the other bodies to the extent feasible.[7]
- The process of analysis, deliberation and decision-making within the HCAC and larger university community on these matters has been very open and collegial. There have been no hidden agendas. Everyone has appreciated the difficult trade-offs faced by the university and approached their resolution in a highly constructive manner.[8]

No specific time limit was set for the existence of the HCAC when it was first constituted in fall 2001, though the implicit operating assumption was to give it two-to-three years and then assess its role. Everyone involved now agrees that it should continue for at least another year or two. Given its success to-date, and the likelihood that its *raisons d'être* will only grow in importance to the university with time, it is likely to be an institutional fixture for the foreseeable future.

8.2 FAMILY LEAVE POLICY

One of the overarching recommendations of the earlier-mentioned Chancellor's task force on benefits and work-life issues was for the adoption of more 'family-friendly' policies in several spheres. This had been a long-standing concern of staff, but received additional impetus from faculty in task force deliberations, due primarily to the growing number of women in tenure-track positions with current or expected dependent care responsibilities. Several specific 'family-friendly' policies were implemented immediately pursuant to task force activities – including tax-sheltered flexible spending accounts for dependent care and medical expenses, an adoption benefit, and flex-time for staff – and the Vice-Chancellor for Academic Affairs was charged with consideration of a range of issues related to the university's medical/maternity and family leave policies. The vehicle the Vice-Chancellor chose for this purpose was a committee chaired by the Associate Vice-Chancellor for Academic Affairs and including as members, two deans, two representatives from Human Resources (the chief human resources officer and director of benefits), and two female faculty members (one senior and one junior). All but one of these six had been on the benefits and work-life task force, and the senior faculty member also sat on the Senate Committee on Women's Concerns.

From the beginning of its deliberations in spring 1998, the Committee on Parental and Maternity Benefits for Members of the Faculty (as it came to be known) focused on two concerns related to the unevenness and inadequacy of current practices, as reflected in the following quote in the introduction to its final report:

> In the absence of a formal maternity leave policy beyond those of the Salary Continuation [medical disability] Plan, various practices have arisen. The principal characteristic of these practices is unevenness, in that some members of the faculty receive greater accommodation than others, depending upon the individual's initiative in asking for consideration and the unit's ability to respond. The positive side is that deans and chairpersons try to be as responsive and as flexible as they can to meet individuals' needs and circumstances. The negative side is possible inequity or the perception of inequity and widespread uncertainty regarding what a person is entitled to. More significant, the University needs to respond to the challenge facing faculty members who are increasingly members of dual-career partnerships because of the tension between the professional expectations the University places upon them and their expectation of having children and raising a family.

As part of the process of developing a proposal for a new family leave policy for tenure-track faculty that would address these two concerns, the committee (in addition to assessing current SU policies and practices) sought information on relevant policies at other private universities around the country. It also subjected its preliminary ideas for change to both legal and financial analysis for feasibility and affordability. The committee's final proposal of December 1999 was strongly endorsed by the Academic Deans' Council, the Administrative Benefits Committee, and the University Senate and was approved by the Chancellor for implementation in 2000–01.

The university's new 'Faculty Family Leave Benefits' policy has four major elements, briefly described below.[9] The first two are new elements, whereas the third simply restates a pre-existing policy, and the forth provides for a way to combine the second and third elements.

1. Extension of tenure probationary period. Any full-time tenure-track faculty member who becomes a parent (through childbirth or adoption of a child under age 7) during the first five years credited toward tenure may receive an extension of the pre-tenure probationary period (which is normally six years) by one year. This privilege may be exercised no more than twice.
2. Parental leave. Any full-time tenure-track faculty member who becomes a parent (per above) and who, during the period of the requested leave, will be the primary caretaker for the child, may receive a parental leave at full salary beginning within the next 12 months of either a 50 per cent reduction in workload over a semester or up to one-half a semester without formal duties. (If both parents are tenure-track faculty, they may each receive parental leave during different semesters.)
3. Maternity leave. A female faculty member who, due to childbirth, receives a declaration of medical disability from her doctor or midwife is eligible for the university's salary continuation plan, which provides for full pay for up to 16 weeks of disability. (The normal period of medical disability for childbirth is presumed to be six to eight weeks.)
4. Combination of maternity and parental leaves. Any female faculty member receiving a declaration of medical disability due to childbirth which extends at least four weeks into the semester may combine her maternity and parental leave benefits to receive a full semester release from teaching duties at full pay.

Two arguments made in the committee report were particularly important to its acceptance. First, based on the prior several years' experience of births and adoptions and the projected demographics of the SU faculty, the committee concluded that any explicit financial costs resulting from the new parental leave (mainly those for teaching replacements for essential courses) most likely would be quite modest (less than $100 000 per annum in the aggregate) and could be easily absorbed within most school and college budgets. For those small schools and colleges for which it might sometime not prove possible, it was assumed the Vice-Chancellor could assist in individual cases. Second, the report contended that the new policy would not only be greatly appreciated by current faculty, but would improve faculty recruitment, retention and professional development. So far the first of these presumptions has clearly been validated. Despite substantial use of the new parental leave by younger faculty across the campus, only one small school has had any financial difficulty in accommodating it. From the feedback they have provided, there is also no doubt that faculty parents with new children, and especially two-faculty parents, have greatly appreciated the opportunity to have the reduction in professional responsibilities. Anecdotal evidence also suggests that the new policy for faculty family leave benefits has proven a useful tool in recruitment of new faculty members.

8.3 PHASED RETIREMENT POLICY

Syracuse's faculty retirement policies have followed a course similar to that of many other universities over the past 10–15 years. The university had a mandatory retirement age of 70 that was eliminated in 1994, and no new permanent personnel polices were implemented during the 1990s to address the enduring issues posed by its termination. However, two different university-wide rounds of a temporary so-called 'Supported Resignation Program' were offered between 1991 and 1998 to tenured faculty over age 55 with ten or more years of full-time service. The terms were essentially two years' severance pay at final salary – capped at the medium salary for the individual's rank and department, in order to reduce take-up among more productive faculty – along with eligibility for all standard retirement benefits.[10] Although initiated to facilitate an overall reduction in faculty size, in conjunction with a modest downsizing of the university in response to fiscal stringencies, these two rounds of supported resignations essentially served as a de facto faculty retirement policy through 1998 and strongly influenced faculty expectations immediately thereafter. Finally, a permanent personnel policy in the form of a phased retirement program was put in place effective January 2003.

The stated principal objectives of Syracuse's 'Tenured Faculty Voluntary Phased Retirement Program' are (at modest institutional cost) to support the retirement of faculty at an age, and in a way, that they individually desire and to facilitate orderly planning and transition within academic units. Its major elements are as follows:[11]

- Full-time tenured faculty with ten years of service and at least age 55 are eligible for a phase-down period to retirement of one to three years, with a work load during the transition period of anywhere from one-quarter to one-half time.

● The above phase-down terms are at the election of the individual, but the specifics of timing, workload, etc., must be mutually agreed upon by the individual and the appropriate dean (in consultation with the department chair where relevant).

● Compensation is proportional to workload, with continuation in regular university benefit plans. Most important in this regard is the usual subsidy for health care and a university contribution to the individual's TIAA-CREF retirement account of 11 per cent of (the reduced) salary.[12]

● Replacement faculty may be hired during the phase-down period, with the additional fringe benefits costs being absorbed centrally.[13]

The process by which the phased retirement program was developed was similar to that of the parental leave policy, although it had more impetus from deans than faculty. The possibility of a phased retirement option for faculty was raised in the Chancellor's task force on benefits and work–life and referred to the Vice-Chancellor. In addition, since there was no prospect of a third round of the Supported Resignation Program once the window for participating in the second round closed, several deans began to push for a more permanent retirement policy with a phased retirement option that would defuse faculty expectations for continued generous inducements to retirement and avoid a 'let's make a deal' approach that would result in both higher overall expense and very different treatment of faculty with similar characteristics. In response, the Vice-Chancellor constituted an ad hoc committee in fall 1998 under the leadership of the Associate Vice-Chancellor and charged with developing a low-cost phased retirement proposal for university consideration. Other committee members included two deans, a department chair, the Human Resources benefits director, and a faculty representative from the Senate Committee on Services to Faculty and Staff.

This committee moved expeditiously to collect information on the phased retirement policies of peer institutions and quickly developed the outlines of a preliminary proposal close to that ultimately adopted. This preliminary proposal was then referred to the Administrative Benefits Committee (ABC) early in 1999, where it languished for more than two years due to lack of support. The overt reason for the lack of support from the ABC – under whose auspices the legal analysis was done – was legal difficulties in meeting various Internal Revenue code non-discrimination tests for benefits for part-time employees. But it was also apparent that some members of the committee, all of whom were non-academic administrators, simply believed there was no institutional need for such a new faculty prerogative. Finally, in 2002 several deans pressed the case with the Chancellor at the administrative retreat held each year just before the beginning of fall semester, citing precedents of phased retirement programs at other universities similar to the preliminary proposal referred to the ABC. The Chancellor, in effect, then instructed the ABC to either forward a legally feasible, low-cost proposal for his consideration or tell him why it was not possible to do so. To no one's surprise, a constructive solution to the legal issues was quickly found and the final proposal was approved by the Chancellor (and Board of Trustees) several months thereafter.

Early indications are that the new phased retirement option is being well received by the faculty and will be used by many who retire from the university with long years of service as a transition vehicle. But it is far too early in the life of the program to reach any quantitative conclusions about its likely take-up rate and impact on age of faculty retirement and related concerns.[14] It is also clear that there is a continuing (though less pressing) need for a supplementary inducement to retirement for some portion of the small subset of older faculty, who are not making the kind of contribution their department or program requires or who are working in a field no longer required by the university. Guidelines for this purpose have recently been developed and provided to the deans. In essence, they allow up to the equivalent of one year of reassigned responsibilities or severance pay (in coordination with phased retirement, if relevant) under exceptional circumstances and with the approval of the Vice-Chancellor.[15]

8.4   CONCLUSION

We conclude with three observations. First, as we trust is evident from what preceded, the 'current state of play' at SU varies considerably across the three areas of human resources policy activities focused upon in this case study. We expect maternal and parental leave policies to remain quite stable for the foreseeable future. There may be a few wrinkles that need ironing in the execution of the new policies as concrete cases with unforeseen dimensions arise, but there appears to be no need or interest in any major policy adjustments on the horizon. At the other extreme, we expect that health care policies will remain in considerable flux for the foreseeable future, in response to continuing changes in the external environment at both the regional and national levels and the continuing challenge of providing attractive, affordable health care to employees in the face of rapidly rising costs. Finally, we expect retirement policies to continue to occupy the middle ground. The phased retirement program for tenured faculty has been in effect for little more than a year, and clear and equitable guidelines for supplementary inducements to retirement have just been promulgated. A few years' experience with both is likely to raise new issues that will require institutional attention and possibly lead to further changes in the university's retirement policy for tenured faculty.

Our second observation is that the recent success of the university in developing and implementing highly valued and/or broadly accepted changes in these policy arenas has been due in large part to the utilization of processes relying heavily upon information about practices at peer institutions and the in-depth internal involvement of representatives from key constituencies. As noted earlier, the latter, in particular, represented a marked and especially salutary departure from the university's past practice of relying primarily, if not solely, upon the judgment of benefits administrators in making changes in human resources policies. Of course, one would not expect that gaining acceptance among faculty for the new parental leave and phased retirement policies would be difficult, since they represented new benefits at no cost to participants. But the design of both in committees that included key faculty, deans and department chairs was a major ingredient. The content of the new family leave policy was heavily, and most constructively, influenced by the effective presence and leadership of women faculty committee members, who were not only committed to the project, but were also very knowledgeable about the relevant issues from personal experience, peer networks and topical publications. Similarly, the essential elements of the phased retirement policy were shaped primarily by dean and department chair committee members best positioned to understand the issues facing both individual faculty and the institution regarding retirement issues. These factors led to policies with the strongest possible support within Academic Affairs. In addition, the fact that consideration of both policies was initiated by a task force widely representative of all (non-unionized) SU employees – including staff outside of Academic Affairs – was also important to their eventual acceptance, since these new policies represented a departure from the history of equal benefits for faculty and staff at SU.

The health care area, in contrast to the other two, involved some curtailment in generosity of plan eligibility and benefits (as well as other low- or no-cost benefit improvements). Here, the role and composition of the HCAC outlined in the first section of this chapter has proven critical. Issues surrounding health care benefits are growing increasingly more complex and important for universities to deal with. Having a standing committee such as the HCAC for this purpose that is broadly representative of university faculty and staff, encompasses the relevant institutional expertise, and has overlapping membership with other key committees has much to recommend it. Appropriately adapted to local conditions, we expect it could prove a useful model for other universities as they grapple with the vexing, ongoing problems in this arena.

Our final observation is that the efforts at SU on which we have reported – and we expect analogous ones at other universities – would have benefited from much greater availability of relevant information about peer practices. For example, the only way we were able to benefit from the experience of other institutions' phased retirement programs for faculty during our planning process for such a program, was by calling our counterparts around the country and following up on useful tips. The people we contacted were generous with their time and advice, but it was a very inefficient process that still left major gaps at the time in sorely needed input that we later discovered did exist. We learned far more in a few hours of reading and discussion of the relevant papers prepared for this volume than from that very time-consuming process of ad hoc outreach several years ago. There is less of a void in important information about peer practices in areas like health care where third party consultants often have experience with, and/or databases pertinent to, a wide range of peer institutions; but such knowledge is expensive to tap and still of limited usefulness. There is a strong need for the higher education community to direct more of its expertise inward with respect to these important human resources issues and promote more relevant research along with better developed and more easily accessible repositories of information on best practices and lessons learned among its members.

NOTES

1. Johnson and Palmer were extensively involved with all the activities discussed herein, as was Flusche with those discussed in the sections on family leave and retirement.
2. A modest portion of the staff is unionized and receives somewhat different, though roughly comparable, health care benefits as the remainder of the staff and faculty, as agreed upon through the collective bargaining process. All discussion in this chapter pertains to the health care benefits shared by the faculty and non-unionized staff. In general, to be eligible for health care benefits, faculty must be employed at least 62.5 per cent of time during the academic year and staff 50 per cent of time over the calendar year.
3. The portion of SU employees opting for external HMO coverage is now quite small and largely irrelevant to future health care planning by the University.
4. These included such things as stronger incentives for employees to participate in all preventive health care screening, disease management programs and intensive health care education programs.
5. Sylvester Schieber's chapter in this volume (Chapter 6) provides an excellent discussion of the general challenges facing universities with regard to faculty retiree health benefits, many of which are directly relevant to the activities at SU discussed in this chapter. Also, one of the concerns motivating the HCAC's study of retiree health benefits was their growing importance in the retirement decisions of tenured faculty, as more generally documented and discussed by John Rust in Chapter 7.

6. Many factors have contributed to this, including the recent sizeable expansion in enrollees in the SU self-insured plan, the many years of requiring only one year of prior service for eligibility for the benefit, changes in the applicable discount rate, and a higher projected growth path for per capita retiree health care costs.
7. As a formal matter HCAC recommendations are provided directly to the Chancellor, who then refers them to the Senate and ABC for their assessment and advice at her pleasure.
8. There was initial resistance to the institution of the HCAC on the part of some members of the University Senate who preferred that the Senate Committee on Services to Faculty and Staff be charged with the responsibilities given to the HCAC. But the overlap of membership between the two committees and the openness of HCAC processes seems to have dissipated that concern.
9. A full explication of this policy can be found at the SU website http://humanre sources.syr.edu/benefits/loa2.html.
10. The most important retirement benefits were subsidized health care (as described in the section on health care), access to TIAA–CREF retirement funds, and tuition benefits for dependents. Prior to the advent of the Supported Resignation Program, all full-time faculty who retired at age 62 or older with one year of prior service were eligible for these benefits. A permanent change in this policy was made in conjunction with the Supported Resignation Program to lower the potential age of eligibility for these benefits to age 55, with only one year of prior service still required for retiree health benefits, but seven years required for tuition benefits.
11. A full explication of this policy can be found at the SU website http://provost.syr.edu/ faculty/PRdesc.asp.
12. In conjunction with implementation of the Phased Retirement Program for faculty, various amendments were made to broaden the eligibility criteria in the University's employee benefits plans as much as possible to cover Program participants without creating an IRS code non-discrimination issue. Nevertheless, isolated situations can remain where a highly compensated program participant still will be ineligible for a benefit under the so-amended plans. In such cases, the University will provide a cash payment at least equal to what it would have contributed for the benefit.
13. Fringe benefits are paid out of a central pool, not school and college budgets, at Syracuse as a routine matter, and limited only by each unit's authorized number of Personal Identification Numbers (PINs). A replacement faculty may be assigned the same PIN as a retiring faculty member during the phase-down period of the latter. The University subsidy for dual health care coverage, when it occurs, is the only significant additional institutional cost of the phase-down program, unless the combined salaries of the PIN-sharers exceed what would have been the full-time salary of the phased-down faculty.
14. As we trust is evident from our preceding discussion, the concerns leading to the introduction of the phased retirement program at Syracuse were similar to those discussed by Rust in Chapter 7 and Leslie and Janson in Chapter 11, respectively, that led other universities to earlier adoption. But since the program was introduced so recently at SU, there has not yet been any systematic effort to survey its impact.
15. In addition to providing an added inducement to retirement in an equitable manner, with these guidelines the University is trying to reduce reliance upon paid leaves as a standard method of supplementary remuneration at the time of retirement, because of the legal and tax problems that they might entail.

9. The value of phased retirement

Steven G. Allen

Higher education faces a unique challenge in the coming years as faculty who are members of the baby boom generation near retirement. There will be one set of problems if the most senior faculty stay on too long and there will be a different set if they all leave at once. With the elimination of mandatory retirement in 1994, universities and colleges are concerned about the possibility that many faculty will remain on the job past age 70. There are fears that this will have adverse consequences for teaching and research productivity and will lead to higher tuition charges to cover salaries and benefits. At the same time there is concern on many campuses that the age distribution of faculty is so heavily skewed toward the 50-and-over range that universities will face shortages in many fields by the end of this decade.

From a faculty perspective, there are serious challenges as well. Some faculty work longer than they would prefer simply because they are not yet eligible for full pension and Social Security benefits. The tenure system generally does not permit part-time work, making it difficult for older faculty to cut back on their work hours as they near retirement. In the private sector, many older workers take bridge jobs as they transition from full-time work into retirement. Although some faculty members have good options off campus, those in many disciplines will have difficulty finding opportunities to apply the teaching and research skills valued in academe to other types of work.

Phased retirement has been introduced on many campuses to help deal with these challenges. Under most phased retirement plans, faculty members resign their full-time position (and often give up tenure) in return for the right to work half-time at half-salary for a given number of years. This chapter examines how phased retirement creates value for both the university and the individual faculty member. The analysis begins in section 9.1 with a summary of the theoretical arguments about how phased retirement should be able to help both sides of the academic labor market. The chapter then turns to empirical evidence that sheds light on why universities and colleges offer phased retirement and why certain faculty accept it (and why others do not). To obtain some insights into the motivation for phased retirement, section 9.2 analyses the odds that a college or university will have a phased retirement policy. Are research universities more likely to offer phased retirement than four-year or two-year institutions? Are the odds of offering phased retirement linked to the age distribution of faculty? Section 9.3 is a detailed case study of the experience of the University of North Carolina (UNC) system with phased retirement. The discussion shows how many faculty opted for phased retirement, analyses whether it accelerates or postpones full retirement, and summarizes evidence on its overall effectiveness from the perspectives of both faculty and management. Section 9.4 concludes by summarizing which of the theoretical sources of value have been most important in practice.

9.1   SOURCES OF VALUE

In the absence of a phased retirement plan, tenured university professors have relatively few options for reducing their contracted work hours in the years before they retire. The tenure system at most universities does not allow for part-time work on campus. Faculty can resign and contract to work for the university part-time, but such contracts are usually for no more than one year and, in a world where non-tenure-track instructors provide teaching services at low cost, the financial terms of such contracts are often unattractive. Faculty with the capacity to consult or do research for the private sector or government could have attractive part-time opportunities off campus, but such opportunities may be extremely limited in some academic disciplines. Finally, even in today's wired labor market, jobs off-campus do not usually pop up after a few mouse clicks – search and negotiation costs have to be factored into any decision about whether seeking a part-time position is worth the effort.

Given these constraints, consider a phased retirement contract that allows a faculty member who has met certain age and years of service criteria to work half-time at half-salary. The value of such a contract is readily apparent for faculty who have greater earnings potential on campus than off. In purely financial terms, the promise to pay half a salary for part-time work is equivalent to an option to sell one's labor back to the university at that price. In the absence of phased retirement, faculty would have to either negotiate on their own with department heads and deans when they retire to secure a commitment for part-time work or look for work off-campus. To see the value of the phased retirement option, compare the hourly rate under each of these two choices to the hourly rate that faculty receive while working (which they also would receive under phased retirement). The financial option created by phased retirement will have no economic value for faculty who expect that they can negotiate a better deal on their own with either the university or an off-campus organization. However, if the hourly rate on campus dominates the other two alternatives, then phased retirement provides greater earnings potential for individual faculty members.

In some situations, phased retirement will enable professors to earn more income while working fewer hours. This happens whenever the sum of one-half of the academic salary and all pension income exceeds the regular academic salary (or equivalently, if pension income exceeds one-half the academic salary). The ability to make more money and work less will be highly tempting to many, but such a combination does not automatically predict movement into phased retirement. When faculty near the age of eligibility for partial or full benefits under Social Security or a defined benefit pension, there is a tremendous incentive to work an extra year because annuity income increases considerably at those ages. In such a situation, there is an economic logic behind working full-time one more year, even if it means less income and more work than phased retirement.

Faculty covered by defined contribution pensions face considerable uncertainty about their pension income because the value of their pension hinges on outcomes in financial markets. Someone who fears that the value of the assets in his or her retirement account are likely to decline could choose to retire in order to lock in an annuity on favorable terms. Eligibility to receive pension income is generally tied to severance from the university. Phased retirement allows faculty to start receiving pension income while continuing to work, thereby allowing them to make their labor supply and annuity receipt decisions with a greater degree of independence.

This discussion has emphasized financial benefits from phased retirement, but given the unique nature of academic labor markets, such a narrow focus would lead one to underestimate the true value of phased retirement for faculty. Most tenured faculty in their 50s and 60s have spent virtually their entire life in school. Phased retirement gives them extra time to collect information about retirement opportunities and potential bridge jobs outside academe before they exit the university. The psychological benefits of phased retirement will likely be substantial in many cases – faculty receive access to colleagues and academic resources, the opportunity to continue to contribute in the classroom and in research, and the ability to still call themselves members of the faculty.

Even if phased retirement is a great deal for faculty, why should a university consider offering such a benefit? Half pay for half work may seem cost neutral at first, but phased retirees will expect to continue to receive employee benefits, especially health insurance, along with their half-salary. So unless phased retirement can reduce labor costs along some other dimension, or improve professor performance, one must question whether it has any value to universities.

The first question university chancellors and presidents should ask is what happens to faculty retirement rates. Phased retirement makes bridge jobs outside the university less attractive, leading faculty members seeking to reduce work hours to stay with the university longer than they might have otherwise. However, it also creates an option for part-time work on campus where none previously existed, which will lead some faculty to enter phased retirement well before the time they would have fully retired. The one unambiguous effect of phased retirement is that it accelerates the date at which faculty start to cut back on their commitments to the university. It is also conceivable that under phased retirement they will stay on campus more years than they would have otherwise. For instance, a professor who might have fully retired at age 65 might choose to enter phased retirement at age 62 and work until age 67. Economic theory cannot predict whether the introduction of a phased retirement program will accelerate or decelerate the rate at which faculty totally sever their ties to the university. One would expect that faculty who have the option of phased retirement would start the retirement process earlier than those who do not have that option.

The second big question university leaders should ask is how will a phased retirement program affect the productivity mix of the faculty? The nightmare scenario is where top researchers use phased retirement as an opportunity to start a new business or an affiliation with another campus. The preferred scenario is where phased retirement gives unproductive faculty who have become jaded with academe but who are not yet eligible for full pension benefits a chance to exit gracefully. Phased retirement is most attractive to faculty with the worst earnings opportunities off campus, and to faculty who are least likely to be able to negotiate for themselves a satisfactory part-time salary on campus after regular retirement. Assuming a positive correlation between productivity on campus and either a negotiated part-time wage on campus or the best wage opportunity off campus, this would imply that unproductive faculty would be more likely to enter phased retirement than highly productive faculty.

Given the manpower planning challenges facing university leaders that were noted in the introduction, phased retirement also will create value if it leads to improved personnel planning and economizes on adjustment costs associated with new hires and retirements. Under a formal phased retirement program, professors announce their intention to leave typically between two to five years in advance, a much longer time horizon than would be involved under regular retirement. This should improve succession planning and thereby reduce the odds of having unfilled positions or the likelihood of resorting to early retirement buyouts or layoffs. If provosts and deans decide to use the half-salary saved by phased retirement on non-tenure-track instructors, there is the possibility of simple cost reduction as well.[1]

9.2   WHO OFFERS PHASED RETIREMENT AND WHY?

The most comprehensive source of information about phased retirement plans in higher education is the Survey of Changes in Faculty Retirement Policies (SCFRP), conducted in 2000 by the American Association of University Professors with financial support from the TIAA-CREF Institute. The survey examined US institutions of higher learning in all five Carnegie categories with 75 or more full-time faculty members. At the time of the survey, 27 per cent of the responding institutions had a phased retirement program in place.[2] These programs had the following characteristics:

- Faculty in most programs (64 per cent) must obtain administrative approval to participate.
- Most programs require faculty to reach minimum levels of age (75 per cent) and years of service (73 per cent) to be eligible for phased retirement. The modal age requirement is 55, but some programs are open to 50-year-olds whereas many others require participants to be at least 60. Programs typically require 10 or more years of service to be eligible.
- A minority of programs (21 per cent) put a ceiling on age of eligibility, in most cases 62 or higher.
- Roughly two-thirds of the programs provide special financial benefits. In most cases the special benefit is full contribution to health insurance, although some institutions provide extra salary payments or extra retirement payments or credits.
- Most plans (60 per cent) do not require professors to relinquish tenure before they enter phased retirement. Faculty members generally must lose their tenured status after three or five years in phased retirement.

One way potentially to better understand the motivation behind phased retirement plans is to compare the characteristics of universities which offer such plans to those which do not. It is reasonable to expect that the value of phased retirement to the institution should be a function of its mission. Doctoral institutions must be especially sensitive to the orderly replacement of aging faculty to be competitive for graduate students and research contracts. Presuming that phased retirement polices provide improved capacity to make long-run plans for staffing, one would expect doctoral universities to be more likely to adopt such policies. In contrast, universities and colleges that focus on teaching, especially baccalaureate and two-year institutions, have more flexibility in how they replace aging faculty members and thus may not value phased retirement as much. These patterns are borne out in the SCFRP data, as shown in Table 9.1. Phased retirement programs are most commonly observed among doctoral universities (35 per cent). The percentage of masters and baccalaureate institutions with phased retirement plans is slightly lower (29 per cent), whereas the percentage of two-year institutions is considerably lower (16 per cent).

The age and tenure structure of the faculty also should have some bearing on the value of phased retirement to the institution. Colleges and universities with a high percentage of faculty who are near retirement have much more to gain from successfully managing the transition to retirement than those with relatively fewer faculty in their 50s and 60s. There is no systematic relationship between the age structure of the faculty and the adoption of phased retirement policies across the campuses in the SCFRP sample (Table 9.1). Phased retirement policies are most prevalent among schools with 30 to 39 per cent of faculty in the 55-and-over age bracket, and least prevalent among schools with fewer than 30 per cent of faculty in this age bracket, as expected. However, phased retirement policies are least common among schools with 40 per cent or more of faculty in this age bracket, which runs contrary to expectations.

Holding age structure constant, tenure has an obviously large impact on the degrees of freedom the institution has available to manage an aging workforce. Institutions with a high percentage of tenured faculty have much less flexibility than those with relatively low percentages of tenured faculty. To the extent that tenured faculties are also highly compensated faculties, phased retirement plans also generate greater opportunities for cost savings. Empirically, there appears to be a strong relationship between the percentage of full-time faculty with tenure and the adoption of phased retirement policies. Table 9.1 shows that the percentage of schools with phased retirement steadily increases with the percentage of full-time faculty with tenure. Phased retirement policies are in place at only 16.5 per cent of the schools where less than 40 per cent of the faculty have tenure. In contrast, phased retirement is available at 25.4 per cent of the schools where the tenure ratio is 40 to 49 per cent , at 30.2 per cent of the schools where the tenure ratio is 50 to 69 per cent , and 33.7 per cent of the schools where the tenure ratio is 70 per cent or higher.

The fit between a phased retirement plan and the pension plan must be assessed carefully. Defined benefit plans are a poor fit with phased retirement for two reasons. First, the pension payment under defined benefit plans is a function of final average salary, which means that a move to a

Table 9.1   *Percentage of colleges and universities with phased retirement plans, by institutional characteristics*

Sample mean	27.0
Carnegie class	
Doctoral	35.0
Masters	28.8
Baccalaureate	28.9
Two-year with faculty ranks	14.1
Two-year without faculty ranks	18.2
Percentage of full-time faculty age 55 and over	
Less than 30	27.6
30 to 39.9	32.2
40 or more	22.9
Percentage of full-time faculty with tenure	
Less than 40	16.5
40 to 49.9	25.4
50 to 69.9	30.2
70 or above	33.7
Retirement plan	
Defined contribution only	38.2
Defined benefit only	19.4
Both combined	17.4
Both alternatives	19.3
Public–private status	
Public institution	26.7
Private institution	27.3
Other retirement policies	
Seminars on retirement planning available	29.2
Seminars on retirement planning not available	11.6
Financial incentives to retire before age 70 offered since 1995	31.9
Financial incentives to retire before age 70 not offered since 1995	22.7
Buyouts on college-by-college or individual basis offered since 1995	31.6
Buyouts on college-by-college or individual basis not offered since 1995	24.2

Source: Ehrenberg (2003).

half-time job on campus is also a move to as much as a 50 per cent cut in one's pension (unless the retiree can start receiving the annuity upon entering phased retirement or a special exemption for phased retirees can be created in the benefit formula). Second, the formulas for most defined benefit plans are set up in such a way that the present value of the pension annuity is maximized at the time the individual becomes eligible for full retirement benefits. The pension-based incentives facing these individuals for retirement are extremely powerful and are likely to reduce the value of retirement-management policies to the university. Phased retirement plans are likely to be a better fit on campuses with defined contribution plans because they offer managers a mechanism to productively influence retirement decisions. The data in Table 9.1 show a strong relationship between type of pension plan and the adoption of phased retirement plans. Phased retirement is available at 38 per cent of schools which exclusively have a defined contribution plan, versus 19 per cent of schools which exclusively have a defined benefit plan.

Private colleges and universities are likely to have more degrees of freedom to adopt phased retirement plans than their public counterparts. Public colleges and universities tend to be less autonomous, facing some degree of oversight from state government. In some states, public institutions are part of a statewide system, which would have mixed effects on the odds of adopting a phased retirement plan. On the one hand, there would be greater transactions costs associated with adopting a new policy in a statewide system than a single campus. On the other hand, a successful launch of a statewide plan would lead to earlier adoption on campuses that, left on their own, would not have adopted a plan. Further, private schools may have such an advantage in dealing one-on-one with individual faculty about their compensation and workloads that they may have little need for a phased retirement policy. In the SCFRP data in Table 9.1, there is very little difference in the odds of having a phased retirement plan between public and private institutions.[3]

The adoption of phased retirement policies is also likely to reflect the management style of the organization. Institutions that have decided to take active steps to manage the age structure of their faculty are likely to consider a variety of steps, rather than focus on a single policy. If true, one would expect campuses that have phased retirement policies to also have taken other steps, including seminars on retirement planning, financial incentives for early retirement, and targeted buyouts. These patterns are born out in the SCFRP data, as shown in Table 9.1. Phased retirement plans are available in 29.2 per cent of the schools that offer retirement planning seminars or programs, in contrast to 11.6 per cent of schools that do not offer such programs. Phased retirement policies are in place in 31.9 per cent of the schools that offered financial incentives for retirement since 1995, versus 22.7 per cent of the schools that did not offer such incentives. Phased retirement is available at 32 per cent of the schools that offered buyouts to faculty since 1995 (either on a college-by-college or case-by-case basis), in contrast to 24 per cent of the schools that did not offer buyouts.

The simple comparisons made in Table 9.1 could be misleading. For instance, it is well known that the tenure ratio is much lower at baccalaureate and two-year schools than at doctoral and master's level institutions. Probit analysis is a tool that can be used to control for additional variables. It is very much like multiple regression analysis, except that it is designed for situations where the dependent variable (odds of having a phased retirement program) is measured in binary categories (either you have a phased retirement plan or you do not). Table 9.2 reports the results of a probit analysis of the odds that a campus will have a phased retirement plan, using the variables from Table 9.1 along with number of full-time faculty. The number of full-time faculty is included in the analysis to determine whether there are economies of scale involved with developing and implementing phased retirement plans. If the costs of developing a phased retirement plan increase less rapidly with size than the benefits, one would expect that small schools would be less willing than large schools to adopt the plans.

In the probit analysis, three variables stand out as significant predictors of the odds that a campus will have a phased retirement plan. Institutions that exclusively offer a defined contribution plan have a 25 to 27 percentage point greater probability of offering phased retirement than schools that offer defined benefit plans. This reflects both the poor fit between defined benefit plans and phased retirement policies, as well as the possible use of phased retirement for strategic human resource management on campuses that only offer defined contribution plans.[4]

Schools with a large percentage of tenured faculty are much more likely to have phased retirement plans than schools with a relatively small percentage of tenured faculty. At the extreme, a school where all faculty have tenure would have a 38 to 40 per cent greater chance of having a phased retirement plan than a school where none have tenure. Percentage of faculty with tenure is strongly correlated with Carnegie categorization, so the analysis was repeated by estimating separate probit models for each Carnegie class (these results are not reported in Table 9.2; they are available from the author upon request). The decrease in sample size makes these results more fragile, but percentage tenured was still statistically significant at or near the $p = 0.10$ threshold in all levels of institutions except two-year institutions without faculty ranks. Note that whereas there is a significant relationship between the odds of offering phased retirement and percentage of faculty with tenure, there is no relationship between the odds of offering

*Table 9.2   Probit analysis of odds that a campus will have a
          phased retirement program*

	Model without retirement policy variables	Model with retirement policy variables
Number of full-time faculty	−0.001	0.000
(in 1000s)	(0.001)	(0.001)
Percentage aged 55 or older	0.098	0.065
	(0.184)	(0.184)
Percentage tenured	0.397**	0.375**
	(0.126)	(0.128)
Defined benefit plan	0.027	0.018
	(0.078)	(0.080)
Defined contribution plan	0.273**	0.253**
	(0.061)	(0.063)
Combined plan	−0.025	−0.021
	(0.083)	(0.083)
Carnegie class 1	0.028	0.035
	(0.103)	(0.106)
Carnegie class 2A	−0.035	−0.040
	(0.087)	(0.088)
Carnegie class 2B	−0.044	−0.057
	(0.088)	(0.088)
Carnegie class 3	−0.039	−0.059
	(0.100)	(0.096)
Public institution	0.104	0.095
	(0.057)	(0.058)
Retirement planning		0.119*
seminars available		(0.051)
Financial incentives to retire		0.104*
before age 70 offered		(0.045)
Buyouts of colleges or		−0.012
individuals offered		(0.049)

Notes:
Table reports change in probability that campus will have a phased retirement plan
associated with a change in the independent variable from 0 to 1 (except for line 1 which
indicates the change in the odds of having a phased retirement plan resulting from an
increase in faculty size of 1000). Standard errors are reported in parentheses.
* indicates statistically significant at $p = 0.05$ level or greater
** indicates statistically significant at $p = 0.01$ level or greater

Source: Survey of Changes in Faculty Retirement Policies.

phased retirement and Carnegie class once one controls for percentage of faculty with tenure.[5]

Phased retirement plans are much more likely to be in place on campuses which followed a management strategy of actively managing faculty retirement. Schools that have offered retirement planning seminars are 12 per cent more likely to have phased retirement plans than schools that have not offered such seminars. Schools that have offered financial incentives for retirement before age 70 are 10 per cent more likely to have phased retirement plans than schools that have not offered such incentives. There is no significant relationship between buyouts by college or individual and the odds of having a phased retirement plan. Public institutions have a 10 percentage point greater probability of having a phased retirement plan than private institutions. This effect is statistically significant at the 6 to 10 per cent level, a bit below the standard threshold used in social science.

There was no evidence in the probit analysis of economies of scale in the offering of phased retirement plans. There was also no relationship between the age structure of the faculty and the odds of having a phased retirement plan. This conclusion was robust across a number of other measures of age structure (e.g., percentage above 60, percentage below 50).

To sum up, this discussion shows that phased retirement plans have not been cropping up on a random basis. There is clear evidence that campus leaders have carefully considered preexisting conditions such as type of retirement plan and the percentage of the faculty with tenure. The fact that campuses with a high percentage of faculty members with tenure are most likely to have phased retirement plans (as well as retirement planning seminars and offers of financial incentives for retirement)[6] implies that phased retirement is being viewed as a tool to give management more flexibility to manage a difficult-to-manage workforce.

9.3 PHASED RETIREMENT IN THE UNC SYSTEM

The percentage of faculty in the UNC system who are aged 50 or higher has increased considerably in the 1980s and 1990s, following national trends.[7] In 1996 UNC President C.D. Spangler appointed a committee to study the possible need for early retirement programs. Because the university system was predicted to add 40 000 students in the first decade of the 2000s, the committee concluded that there was no need for an early-retirement program designed to reduce the number of faculty members above a given age threshold. Instead, they recommended that the UNC system consider a phased retirement program that would moderate the aging of the faculty without increasing costs.

The Board of Governors of the UNC system approved a five-year trial program in 1998 that permitted half-time work for half the final academic salary. No special payments or subsidies were provided for selection into the program. The purpose of the program was 'to promote renewal of the professoriate in order to ensure institutional vitality and to provide additional flexibility and support for individual faculty members who are nearing retirement' (*UNC Policy Manual*, 300.7.2.1 [G]). The program had three major goals:

1. Better personnel planning – institutions will be able to better anticipate position openings and make replacement plans;
2. Enhanced recruitment and retention – an additional benefit to faculty should help in this regard;
3. Increased quality of faculty – institutions will be able to fill faculty positions while retaining the skills and knowledge of experienced faculty.

Each of the 15 campuses in the UNC system that grant tenure was required to implement a phased retirement program.[8] To be eligible for the program, faculty must be tenured. When the program was launched, faculty also had to be age 50 with 20 years of service or age 60 with 5 years of service at the same institution. The criteria are now 50 years of age with 5 years of service at the current institution. Each campus was allowed to select the length of the contract for its faculty; however, the program required a minimum length of one year and a maximum length of five years. Twelve of the 15 institutions chose a three-year phased retirement contract, two institutions chose a two-year contract, and one campus chose a five-year phased retirement contract. Although launched as a five-year pilot, the program is now permanently in place.

Individuals considering entering the program negotiate their half-time duties with their department chairs prior to accepting phased retirement. Duties could be performed evenly across both semesters, or the individual could work full-time one semester and have no specific assigned duties the next semester. They may elect to start receiving pension benefits after entering phased retirement. If they begin their retirement benefits, they are eligible for the same health insurance as active employees. Since 1971, newly hired faculty in the UNC system had the ability to choose between the defined benefit plan designed for teachers and state employees or a variety of defined contribution plans. Faculty hired in earlier years are covered by the defined benefit plan.

Robert Clark, Linda Ghent and I have studied the phased retirement plan of the UNC system using the annual faculty censuses that each campus submits to the Office of the President. These are the employment records for all faculty employed as of September of the specified year. Information on each person includes age, hire date, rank, gender, race, tenure status, annual salary, and type of pension plan. The annual records are linked across years so we are able to determine whether an individual remains in his or her faculty position from one year to the next. The census data for the years 1994 until 2003 are employed in this study. The analysis is limited to faculty members who were eligible to enter the phased retirement program. This chapter briefly summarizes the key findings of our earlier papers and then reports new evidence on the experience faculty and department heads have had with phased retirement.

In the three years prior to the introduction of phased retirement, the retirement rate from UNC institutions among eligible faculty aged 50 averaged 8.7 per cent (see Table 9.3). After the introduction of the new retirement program, the total retirement rate (full retirement plus phased retirement) increased to 10.4 per cent in 1997–98, 11.3 per cent in 1998–99, and 10.4 per cent in 1999–2000.[9] The percentage of faculty selecting phased retirement was 3.2 in 1997–98, 2.3 in 1998–99, and 3.0 in 1999–2000. The full retirement rates were 7.2 per cent in 1997–98, 9.0 per cent in 1998–99, and 7.4 per cent in 1999–2000. During these years, phased retirees represented between 20 and 31 per cent of all retirements from the UNC system. In absolute numbers, about 70 faculty entered the phased retirement program each year while around 225 fully retired.

Table 9.3   Retirement rates for University of North Carolina system faculty, by year

	Phased retirement rate	Full retirement rate	Total retirement rate
1994–95	n.a.	8.7	8.7
1995–96	n.a.	8.7	8.7
1996–97	n.a.	8.8	8.8
1997–98	3.2	7.2	10.4
1998–99	2.3	9.0	11.3
1999–2000	3.0	7.4	10.4
2000–01	2.8	4.5	7.3
2001–02	1.7	4.1	5.8
2002–03	2.0	3.3	5.3

Note: These retirement rates represent the percentage of faculty eligible for phased retirement who elected to either (1) enter phased retirement or (2) resign from the university.

Source: UNC system annual faculty censuses, 1994–2003

The percentage of faculty entering full and phased retirement began to decline in 2000–01, which is the same time that the stock market began to drop. From 1999–2000 to 2002–03 the full retirement rate had fallen by more than half to 3.3 per cent . Over the same period, the phased retirement rate had fallen by a third to 2.0 per cent . In the 2000s, phased retirement accounted for 35 per cent of total retirement. In absolute numbers, 71 faculty entered the phased retirement each year in the 2000s while 130 fully retired.

Table 9.4 shows how phased and full retirement rates vary by age in the 1990s. In most years, the full retirement rate increases steadily with age, a pattern consistent with previous research. A similar pattern holds for phased retirement in 1997–98, with more faculty age 70 and over selecting phased retirement than full retirement. In 1998–99 and 1999–2000, the phased retirement rate rises with age through the early to mid-60s, but then declines. In all likelihood the very large response of the 70 and over group in 1997–98 reflects a constrained demand for phased retirement at the time it was implemented.

Ghent et al. (2001) and Allen et al. (2004) conducted an analysis of how those entering phased retirement differed from those who continued working full-time and those who entered full retirement. The following are the key findings of those two studies regarding the characteristics of those most likely to enter phased retirement:

- Those entering phased retirement were much more likely to be employed at masters and baccalaureate universities than at doctoral universities. This may reflect differences in teaching loads and a tendency to focus on teaching loads in negotiating duties under phased retirement. Faculty who teach eight courses a year can buy a lot more free time by going half-time than faculty who teach four courses a year. It is also possible that faculty on the doctoral campuses (NC State and UNC-Chapel Hill) have more opportunities for bridge jobs off campus.
- Faculty who are covered by the defined benefit plan are much more likely to enter phased retirement than those who selected defined contribution plans. This probably reflects the strong incentives to retire at the age of eligibility for full pension benefits, and may be influenced by Social Security as well. Reduced earnings during phased retirement do not adversely affect retirement benefits for faculty who chose the defined benefit plan.
- The odds of entering phased retirement by age map closely to the odds of entering full retirement by age; in both cases, there are significant upswings in retirement odds at ages 62 and 65.

Table 9.4 Percentage of eligible faculty entering retirement, University of North Carolina system, by year and age group

Age group	1994–95	1995–96	1996–97	1997–98 (total)	1997–98 (full)	1997–98 (phased)	1998–99 (total)	1998–99 (full)	1998–99 (phased)	1999–2000 (total)	1999–2000 (full)	1999–2000 (phased)
50–57	2.7	2.7	2.7	3.2	2.3	1.0	4.3	3.6	0.7	4.7	3.8	0.9
58–62	9.2	6.8	9.9	13.5	8.5	4.9	12.7	9.5	3.2	10.9	7.2	3.7
63–64	18.3	24.7	18.6	19.7	14.7	5.0	20.5	17.2	3.3	25.3	17.5	7.8
65	19.5	22.1	21.7	27.3	22.1	5.2	28.8	18.6	10.2	16.3	11.6	4.7
66–69	29.2	30.0	22.9	21.2	17.2	4.0	27.7	23.7	4.0	20.0	14.8	5.2
70+	41.7	12.0	30.8	29.5	13.6	15.9	35.0	30.0	5.0	17.0	10.6	6.4
Total	8.7	8.7	8.8	10.4	7.2	3.2	11.3	9.0	2.3	10.4	7.4	3.0

Source: UNC system annual faculty censuses, 1994–2000

9.3.1   Faculty Perspectives

Why do faculty enter phased retirement? The Office of the President of the UNC system conducted surveys of faculty in phased retirement in 1998 and 2003 to address this question. The reason given by most faculty (60 per cent in the 1998 survey and 69 per cent in the 2003 survey) is that they wanted to 'gradually transition into retirement'. Very few planned to 'pursue other employment' (6 per cent in 1998 and 1 per cent in 2003), whereas a modest share planned to 'pursue other interests' (18 per cent in 1998 and 9 per cent in 2003). The remainder cited other factors, including health, changing university policies (including post-tenure review), and inability to afford full retirement.

More insight can be obtained when one looks at how faculty entering phased retirement changed their allocation of time to university and other activities. Table 9.5 summarizes how faculty changed their on-campus workloads after entering phased retirement. The average number of courses taught per year dropped by 44 per cent from 4.3 to 2.4. In most individual cases, faculty loads dropped by exactly 50 per cent , but a few faculty had equal or even greater teaching loads, either because they were leaving administrative posts or because they cut back on time for research and service. Most faculty (60 per cent) worked at the university both academic semesters.

Table 9.5   Faculty workload on campus, before and after entering phased retirement

	Before phased retirement	After phased retirement
Mean number of courses taught	4.3 (2.8)	2.4 (1.7)
Mean percentage of time allocated to other activities		
Research	27.6 (26.8)	29.6 (36.2)
Public service/extension	7.4 (12.7)	7.3 (18.4)
Administration/ institutional service	24.2 (30.0)	9.9 (18.8)
Other assignments	16.4 (21.9)	13.8 (24.9)

Note: Standard deviations are reported in parentheses

Source: Survey of UNC Phased Retirement Program Participants

Going beyond teaching, the biggest change in time allocation on campus involved a significant cutback on administrative activities. Among the 2003 phased retirees who responded to the survey, 32 per cent had an administrative appointment. Across the entire sample, time allocated to administration fell from 24 per cent on a full-time basis before phased retirement to 10 per cent on a part-time basis after phased retirement. Faculty spent about the same percentage of their time on public service and extension activities before and after entering phased retirement. There was a slight increase in the percentage of time allocated to research, but total time allocated to research dropped significantly (28 per cent of time on a full-time basis to 30 per cent of time on a part-time basis).

With their on-campus workload reduced by 50 per cent , how do faculty reallocate their time? Roughly two-thirds of the sample (67.7 per cent) report spending more time in activities with friends, family, and community. A substantial share (42.7 per cent) report spending more time 'engaged in research or other creative or scholarly activities', spending 16.9 hours per week on such activities. Exactly one-third of the sample report spending more time on volunteer activities and family assistance, totalling 7 hours a week. Only 22 per cent report spending more time working for pay away off-campus (including self-employment) and these individuals spend 11.5 hours per week working. Phased retirees also spent more time on civic activities, taking classes, travel, and health care.

Faculty almost always begin receiving pension benefits upon entering phased retirement. In the 1998 survey, all faculty entering phased retirement started receiving benefits, whereas in 2003, 90.5 per cent started receiving benefits. The decision to start receiving Social Security as well largely depends on age. In the 2003 survey, 42 per cent started receiving Social Security, and those individuals were considerably older (68.7 years) than those who postponed Social Security or were ineligible (62.4 years).

In the 2003 survey, faculty were asked to estimate what percentage of their earnings in their last year of university employment was replaced by pension benefits (excluding Social Security). There was no small amount of noise in the responses, including a value of zero for a person who claimed to be in the defined benefit pension plan with 30 or more years of service. The raw mean response was a replacement rate of 39.2 per cent. If one trims all cases from the sample where the estimated percentage was below five (almost all of which claim 25 years or more of service), the mean replacement rate becomes 46.0 per cent.

Faculty in phased retirement came fairly close to maintaining their total level of income. For the average respondent in the 2003 survey, combined income from pensions, Social Security, and phased retirement equaled 90 per cent of university earnings before entering phased retirement. Almost half (42 of 86 respondents) reported that they had replaced 100 per cent or more of their income. The overwhelming majority (95 per cent) said that their combined income was about what they expected before entering phased retirement.

With nearly the same income and a 50 per cent reduction in work hours, one would expect most faculty entering phased retirement to be very satisfied with the arrangement. In 1998, 80 per cent said they were pleased with phased retirement, 17 per cent said they were somewhat pleased, and 3 per cent said they were not pleased. In 2003, 60 per cent strongly agreed that they were 'pleased with my participation in the Phased Retirement Program and would make the same decision again', 33 per cent agreed, 6 per cent disagreed, and 1 per cent strongly disagreed. In 1998, 89.7 per cent said they would recommend the phased retirement program to their colleagues. In 2003, 59 per cent strongly agreed that they 'would recommend the Phased Retirement Program to my colleagues', 30 per cent agreed, 6 per cent disagreed, and 5 per cent strongly disagreed.

Despite high overall levels of satisfaction, some areas of contention were revealed in the 2003 survey. One set of comments focused on the loss of on-campus amenities, including a private office, access to parking, and ability to teach summer school. Others reflected a desire to continue in phased retirement over a longer time period (usually five years instead of three). Issues concerning health care coverage (including a plan that enabled employees to use pretax income to pay for healthcare) were raised by about 10 per cent of the sample. Lastly, a few individuals seemed to have problems adjusting to a world in which they were no longer full-time faculty, as reflected by comments such as 'It's the same thing as committing suicide' and 'You will be taken advantage of constantly and consistently.'

Faculty currently working in the UNC system who are aged 50 or above have a strong interest in pursuing phased retirement in the future. In a separate survey conducted in fall 2003, 36 per cent of those responding said that they planned to enter phased retirement. This matches almost exactly with the ratio of retiring faculty who entered phased retirement (as opposed to full retirement) so far in the 2000s.

9.3.2   Managerial Perspective

The most basic question for top management in academe is whether phased retirement makes faculty leave earlier or stay longer. Table 9.3 showed an increase in the rate at which faculty left full-time employment after the introduction of phased retirement. With 2.8 per cent of faculty entering phased retirement and a decline in the full retirement rate of 0.8 per cent in the 1990s, one might reasonably infer that most of the people entering phased retirement would have continued working if the option had not been available. Ghent et al. (2001) examined this issue more rigorously using a probit analysis of data for the two years before and after the introduction of phased retirement. They rejected the hypothesis that there was a stable model that could explain both forms of retirement over this four-year period. In other words, the characteristics that predict entry into full retirement in 1995–97 do not predict entry into full and phased retirement in 1997–99. Ghent et al. could not reject the hypothesis that there was a stable model of full retirement over the same period. Equivalently, the characteristics that predict entry into full retirement in 1995–97 predict entry into full retirement equally well in 1997–99. These results imply that phased retirees more closely resemble full-time workers than fully retired individuals.

With the 2003 survey of phased retirees, a more straightforward approach can be employed – simply ask the phased retirees what they would have done if the plan had not been available. When asked if they had not chosen to enter phased retirement, the overwhelming majority (84 per cent) said they would have continued to work full-time. Phased retirees say they would have worked an average of 3.6 more years if the program had not been available. On campuses where the phased retirement contract lasts three years, phased retirees say they would have worked full-time for 3.5 more years, versus 4.2 more years of full-time work on campuses where phased retirement contracts are five years.

One further consideration from a management standpoint is that not all phased retirees work part-time for the maximum time allowed. In the 2003 survey, 11 per cent say they intend to fully retire before the end of their contract. Data on the actual duration of phased retirements are not available at this time.

Looking across all the evidence assembled, it is quite clear that phased retirement leads faculty to cut back on their workload well before the time they would have fully retired. To determine whether this is beneficial to the university, one must consider how this decreased contribution by senior faculty affects productivity and cost.

Allen et al. (2004) explored the productivity issue by examining how two different measures of productivity were related to the relative odds of full retirement, phased retirement and continued full-time work. The first measure is the average pay increase received in the three previous years. This is the most logical proxy measure for performance in the late 1990s because faculty pay raises were based entirely on merit during that period. The other measure is academic rank. Among tenured faculty in a relatively senior age and tenure bracket, full professors have been judged by their peers, department heads, and deans as more productive than associate or assistant professors.

The introduction of phased retirement increased the rate at which low performing faculty separated from the university. Consider two otherwise identical professors, one who received an average pay rise of 8 per cent and one who received an average pay rise of zero (the mean pay rise was 4 per cent with a standard deviation of 4 per cent, so this is not an unreasonable spread in the last half of the 1990s). Before phased retirement was introduced, there was a 6.0 per cent chance that a professor receiving 8 per cent rises would retire. After the launch of phased retirement, the odds changed to a 5.9 per cent chance of full retirement and a 1.7 per cent chance of phased retirement, for a combined increase in retirement odds of 1.6 per cent. Compare this to the case of a professor receiving no rises. Before phased retirement was available, this professor had a 12.0 per cent chance of full retirement. After phased retirement the full retirement odds decreased to 10.3 per cent and the phased retirement odds were 4.3 per cent, an overall retirement rate of 14.6 per cent, an increase of 2.6 per cent. Retirement probabilities went up for both, but they went up more for the least productive professors. There was a similar pattern in the change of retirement odds for full, associate and assistant professors.

The response of faculty to the introduction of phased retirement varied with the mission of the institution. Phased retirement generated a much greater response on campuses where the main mission is teaching than where the mission also included research. Allen et al. (2004) found, controlling for other factors, a phased retirement rate of 1.6 per cent on the two Research I campuses. This is much lower than the rates elsewhere: 4.0 per cent on doctoral campuses, 3.9 per cent on masters campuses and 3.2 per cent on baccalaureate campuses. This likely reflects the fact that phased retirement provides a greater increase in free time on campuses with heavy teaching loads. Full retirement rates also are lower in research-oriented than teaching-oriented campuses, possibly reflecting the greater concentration of PhDs who need to work additional years to fully leverage their investment in human capital.

What impact does phased retirement have on an academic department? So far the analysis points to earlier exits of faculty who are past their prime. But at the micro level of an academic school, college, or department, the full answer depends upon how many faculty elect to enter phased retirement, how much of their salary line gets returned to the unit, and how difficult these faculty are to replace. With only two to three per cent of eligible faculty electing to enter phased retirement in any year, most units are likely to have no more than one or two persons on phased retirement at any point in time. When only one person in the unit enters phased retirement, the savings of half a salary is generally not enough to fund a new position – and of course there is no guarantee that the salary savings will be returned to the unit. Looking across a school or college, deans have the opportunity to fund new hires in some departments, creating the opportunity for growth and renewal.

Even when funds are returned to the department, close substitutes for the services provided by tenured faculty are not always readily available. Some campuses are located far away from metropolitan areas and have relatively few options for adjunct or part-time faculty. Substitutes are more likely to be available for faculty teaching courses taken by freshmen and sopho-mores than for courses taken by upperclassmen and graduate students. Adjunct faculty can help on the teaching dimension, but are unlikely to contribute to research and departmental service. The faculty survey indi-cated that time allocated to research declined by half. Time allocated to departmental service was not directly addressed in the faculty survey, but it is difficult to imagine that faculty in phased retirement would play as active a role as when they were working full-time. Presuming the service workload stays the same for the department, this means more work for everyone else.

To address these issues, the Office of the President of the University of North Carolina system conducted a survey of deans and department heads in the 1999–2000 academic year to learn about the impact of the phased retirement plan on each campus. The number of responses relative to the number of colleges and departments varied significantly across each campus, ranging from two at UNC-Charlotte to 42 at East Carolina University. At the two largest campuses (which have the most academic programs and departments), there were only ten responses at UNC-Chapel Hill and 38 at NC State. Because of this variation in responses across campuses, the survey results do a better job of highlighting issues than of measuring impact.

A total of 231 departments and colleges responded to the survey, of which 107 departments or colleges reported that faculty from their unit had entered phased retirement. Across all campuses, 57 per cent of the deans and department heads who had phased retirees reported that some of the salary savings were made available to their unit. This percentage varied widely across campuses, ranging between 21 and 100 per cent. In units which lost a faculty member and failed to gain any resources, the depart-ment head or dean tended to have an unfavorable view of phased retire-ment. The issue that came up most frequently (mentioned on 26 responses) was the loss of resources for the collective work of the department, espe-cially service on committees and advising graduate students. Changes in teaching assignments, larger classes, class cancellations, and greater use of non-tenure track faculty were also cited in the responses. The allocation of office space was another contentious issue (cited in 35 responses), as anyone in academic administration would expect.

Improved personnel planning is a major goal of the UNC system's phased retirement plan. When the survey asked the department heads and deans if 'you believe PRP provides an additional management tool for planning', 59 per cent responded affirmatively. Although this is quite close to the 57 per cent who received released salary funds, there was no direct relationship across campuses between the answers to this question and to the odds of receiving salary release funding. Some department heads gave open-ended explanations for their response. Most of the comments were favorable and tended to note two key benefits from phased retirement: it provides the department with more time to develop a hiring strategy (cited 41 times); and released salary funds give the department head more degrees of freedom to meet staffing needs (cited 19 times). In nine cases, the respondents said that phased retirement encourages earlier retirement of less productive faculty. The unfavorable comment that came up most frequently was that phased retirement made planning more difficult by imposing constraints upon resources and creating uncertainty about when the position will be fully replaced. Such comments were most frequently made when the unit did not receive any released salary funding.

9.4   CONCLUSION

This chapter has examined the value created by phased retirement plans for both faculty members and the university that employs them. From the point of view of faculty, there are two payoffs from having access to a phased retirement program: greater opportunities for part-time work on campus, including in many cases the capacity to earn more income while working fewer hours; and the ability to make the transition to a new stage of life more gradually than permitted by the tenure system. Over the period of this study, phased retirees accounted for between 25 and 35 per cent of all retirements, indicating that many faculty appreciate having more degrees of freedom in transitioning toward retirement. In the UNC system, the take-up rates for phased retirement were significantly higher on campuses with the heaviest teaching loads, reflecting the fact that phased retirement buys more free time in those situations.

From the perspective of the university, the biggest payoff from adopting a phased retirement plan is the increased odds that low performing faculty will start the retirement process earlier. The precise payoff depends on how these individuals are replaced, but there is the opportunity for both cost savings and intellectual renewal. Cost savings arise from either pocketing the salary release or from replacing senior faculty with junior faculty or adjuncts. Given the conditions of excess supply prevailing in most academic labor markets, particularly among junior faculty, universities should expect to eventually fill these positions with highly capable new faculty.

According to a survey of deans and department heads, phased retirement is a useful tool for planning and management. Universities that have introduced phased retirement have carefully assessed the fit between this new policy and their current situation. Schools are much more likely to launch a phased retirement plan if they have a high percentage of tenured faculty, implying that the value of an additional management tool is greater in such a situation. Campuses with defined contribution plans are more likely to have phased retirement plans than those with defined benefit plans, which is what one would expect given the difficulties that come up with phased retirement under a defined benefit plan. However, in the case study of the UNC system, employees who had chosen to be covered by the defined benefit pension plan had much greater odds of entering phased retirement than those who had selected a defined benefit plan. Campuses with defined benefit plans would thus do well to develop some way to overcome the built-in conflicts between benefit formulas and the incentives for entering phased retirement, perhaps following the example of the UNC system. The main challenges associated with the introduction of phased retirement have been at the college or departmental level where administrators must scramble to find substitutes until the phased retiree becomes fully retired.

This study has shown that a phased retirement program encourages faculty to start the transition to full retirement earlier than they would have in the absence of such a program. More years of data from the UNC system will be needed to assess whether phased retirees end up entering full retirement sooner or later than they would have otherwise. The survey data of faculty in phased retirement suggest that they enter full retirement earlier, but the answer to this question can be more rigorously ascertained with data on employment patterns before and after the introduction of phased retirement, including whether those entering phased retirement stay for the maximum time permitted.

It would be helpful to learn how phased retirement rates vary by academic discipline. Accelerated exit rates from academe can be better tolerated in disciplines with an excess supply of faculty than in those where new faculty are relatively scarce. The organizational structure of the various universities in the UNC system varied so much that it was impossible to explore this issue over all 15 campuses, but it would be feasible to conduct within-campus studies at some of the largest universities.

NOTES

1. Leslie and Janson (Chapter 11, this volume) offer a different perspective for the motivation of universities that offer phased retirement. Based on a series of interviews at different campuses, they conclude that universities start phased retirement because it 'humanizes employee relations'. They conclude that most of the benefits from phased retirement accrue to the individual faculty member, whereas the benefits to the institution appear less certain.
2. Ehrenberg (2003) summarizes the key features of the programs that were in place at that time.
3. Palmer Flusche, and Johnson (Chapter 8, this volume) discuss the process through which a private university (Syracuse) adopted its phased retirement plan.
4. Pencavel (Chapter 10, this volume) finds the same thing. His model differs in that phased retirement and other retirement policies are jointly determined, which leads him to use a different set of control variables.
5. This can be easily explained by the strong correlation between Carnegie class and the tenure ratio. In Carnegie I institutions, if one takes simple unweighted averages across schools, 64 per cent of faculty have tenure in the average school. This falls to 54 per cent in IIA, 46 per cent in IIB, 45 per cent in III, and 32 per cent in IV.
6. The percentage of faculty with tenure is 51.5 per cent at schools with retirement planning workshops, versus 43.5 per cent at schools without such workshops. The tenure ratio is 52.6 per cent on campuses that have offered financial incentives, versus 48.2 per cent on schools that have not offered such incentives.
7. This discussion borrows heavily from Ghent et al. (2001).
8. The NC School of the Arts is also a member of the UNC system, but it does not award tenure.
9. The retirement rates represent the percentage of eligible faculty in census year t who were retired in census year $t+1$.

REFERENCES

Allen, Steven G., Robert L. Clark and Linda S. Ghent (2004), 'Phasing into retirement', *Industrial and Labor Relations Review*, **58** (1) (October), 112–27.

Ehrenberg, Ronald G. (2003), 'The survey of changes in faculty retirement policies', American Association of University Professors, accessed at www.aaup.org/Issues/retirement/retrpt.htm.

Ghent, Linda S., Steven G. Allen and Robert L. Clark (2001), 'The impact of a new phased retirement option on faculty retirement decisions', *Research on Aging*, **23** (6), November, 671–93.

10. Faculty retirement incentives by colleges and universities

John Pencavel

10.1 INTRODUCTION

The ending of mandatory retirement has given tenured faculty a new job privilege.[1] Except for faculty dismissed for cause, a tenured faculty member's decision to leave a university or college is now entirely at the discretion of the faculty member. At one time, the implicit contract between a university and a professor involved tenure for a certain number of years followed by its termination at a specified age. The professor was protected from job dismissal for his views, but in return the institution was permitted unilaterally to sever its association with him at a particular age. With the end of mandatory retirement, this university-initiated severance has been ended.

Yet academic tenure was not intended to provide a guarantee of lifetime employment. In 1940, the American Association of University Professors provided a classic statement about academic freedom and tenure:[2]

> Institutions of higher education are conducted for the common good and not to further the interest of either the individual teacher or the institution as a whole. The common good depends upon the free search for truth and its free exposition. Academic freedom is essential to these purposes and applies to both teaching and research . . . Tenure is a means to certain ends; specifically: (1) freedom of teaching and research and of extramural activities, and (2) a sufficient degree of economic security to make the profession attractive to men and women of ability. Freedom and economic security, hence, tenure, are indispensable to the success of an institution in fulfilling its obligations to its students and to society.

The argument here is that society's well-being is enhanced by protecting the employment of the scholar who expresses unpopular views. In addition, this statement perceives that guaranteed employment requires a pay policy and so it expresses the importance of adequate 'economic security.' The statement is silent about mandatory retirement.[3]

The end of mandatory retirement of college and university faculty in January 1994 has increased the employment of older faculty. In a comprehensive analysis of institutions whose faculty participate in TIAA-CREF, Ashenfelter and Card (2002) reported that, whereas the retirement rate of 70-year-old faculty was about 75 per cent prior to the lifting of mandatory retirement, this fell to below 30 per cent in the two years from 1994 to 1996. These changes were similar across different types of colleges and universities and across disciplines. Similarly, Clark et al. (2001) report that, at the three North Carolina research universities, retirement rates of tenured faculty aged 69 years dropped from 61 per cent in the years 1988–92 to 38 per cent after the elimination of mandatory retirement, while those aged 70 years fell from 77 per cent to 13 per cent.

With the end of mandatory retirement in academia and the rise in employment of older faculty, colleges and universities have resorted to other means to induce employment separations. The purpose of this chapter is to review these other means and to consider how else universities may be expected to respond to the changes resulting from the end of mandatory retirement. Though the literature sometimes portrays universities' policies to induce employment separations as if they are distinctive to academia, in fact there are many examples from other types of labor markets of employers devising procedures that respond to constraints placed on their ability to terminate the employment of workers.

In labor markets in general, though employment-at-will was once the prevailing doctrine in this country governing employer behavior with respect to employment separations, it has now been eroded to such an extent that a large part of the personnel or human relations departments of many businesses are devoted to specifying and implementing policies to facilitate the dismissal and layoff of employees. Various pieces of statute (such as the 1935 National Labor Relations Act, Title VII of the 1964 Civil Rights Act, and the 1990 Americans with Disabilities Act) have placed constraints on the behavior of employers with respect to the separation of their employees. Furthermore, decisions in state courts have recognized exceptions to the employment-at-will rule.[4] Most collective bargaining contracts in this country require managements to go through explicit procedures to end the employment of any worker covered by these contracts, and sometimes there are mandatory severance payments that the employer must pay the terminated worker. What operates for unionized workers in this country obtains for a large number of workers – unionized or not – in many countries of the world. Seen in this light, the constraints implied by the end of mandatory retirement on universities provide just another example of a set of policies that restrict what employers may do to terminate the employment of employees.

What policies do colleges and universities now use to affect the employment decisions of their tenured faculty? And what do we know about the relative effectiveness of these policies? This chapter takes up these questions by exploiting two bodies of data. The first consists of the data collected from the 'Survey of Changes in Faculty Retirement Policies' conducted by Ronald Ehrenberg and his colleagues at Cornell University.[5] The survey was conducted in August and September 2000 and it collected information from 608 institutions. I augment this useful survey with information on these institutions kindly provided by the American Association of University Professors.

In addition, I draw upon the administrative data taken from the faculty payroll and benefits offices at the University of California (UC). In the early 1990s, the UC system engaged in the largest 'buyouts' (voluntary severance payments) of any academic institution in history. Why were these buyout programs instituted, how did they operate, and what was their effect? What may be learned from these buyouts about the appeal of buyout programs as mechanisms to effect the employment of tenured faculty?

I shall argue in this chapter that the employment problems presented to colleges and universities resemble those faced by employers in other labor markets, and the phased retirement programs and buyouts that have become common in higher education have been used by other types of employers too. Buyouts seem to have special appeal to colleges and universities because they hold the prospect of effecting a cut in payrolls and of changing the demographic structure of the faculty quickly. However, forecasting the consequences of buyouts is difficult to determine with any confidence, especially when faculty speculate that an 'unsuccessful' buyout now may be followed by a more generous buyout in the future. In an environment of volatile expectations, buyouts may not yield the outcomes that university administrations seek.

More generally, contrary to the predictions of observers writing about twenty years ago when the Age Discrimination Act was being discussed, the end of mandatory retirement has not brought about the attenuation of tenure in higher education. The system of tenure remains very much the same as it was and, for the most part, it has not been replaced with long-term employment contracts or other features that compromise guaranteed employment for the tenured faculty member. The reason for this may well be that colleges and universities have found that the measures at hand are adequate to deal with the conjunction of tenure and the aging of faculty. Among these measures has been the growth of part-time faculty and instructors without tenure-track status (see Ehrenberg and Zhang, Chapter 3 this volume). So while the system of tenure has remained broadly untouched by the end of mandatory retirement, it is now extended to a smaller share of the instructional employees of universities and colleges. The growth of contingent employment that has characterized many labor markets in recent decades has also been a feature of the labor markets of higher education.

10.2   PENSION PLANS AND RETIREMENT PATTERNS

College and university procedures relating to the employment of older tenured faculty are usually called *retirement* policies. However, of course, only an individual can determine whether he or she retires from market work; more precisely, the university designs incentives for such faculty to relinquish tenure. The individual may 'retire' from the university, but not necessarily from labor market work. Indeed, it is not uncommon for faculty who have accepted a 'retirement' incentive to return to work at the very same institution from which he/she has just 'retired'. What has happened is that the individual faculty member has relinquished tenure, and his/her status has changed markedly upon return to university employment. In what follows, although we shall refer to an individual retiring or leaving employment, in many instances what is involved is the surrender of tenure.

The monetary incentives to induce the renunciation of tenure and the separation of a tenured faculty member from the university, are often linked to the pension program or are financed out of the pension fund, and this is why the universities think of them as 'retirement' incentives. However, there is nothing preventing the individual from engaging in market work after 'retirement' from his/her tenured employment at a university. Indeed, in a survey of all older wage and salary workers, Brown (2000) found that nearly half of those who accepted temporary retirement incentives were employed for pay two years later.[6] The corresponding percentage for university faculty may well be lower than this, but nevertheless, the point remains that 'retirement' incentives are more precisely separation incentives.

Many university policies designed to induce older faculty to relinquish tenure are linked to the characteristics of the pension plan, so it is not surprising that the terms of the individual's pension plan has a marked effect on whether the individual elects to retire.[7] There are two broad classes of pension plan: a defined benefit (DB) plan and a defined contribution (DC) plan. A typical DB pension plan specifies the annual flow of pension benefit usually as depending on an individual's pre-retirement salary and on other variables (often, years of service). It is the employee's benefit that is *defined*. A typical DC pension plan specifies the payments made by the individual and employer into a fund which is invested in securities. The value of the accumulated assets is determined at the time the worker retires when it is usually converted into an annual flow of income (an annuity). With a DC plan, it is the employer's payments that are *defined.*

One theme running through this chapter is the important consequences of choice of pension plan. Many features of an institution's retirement policies are associated with the institution's pension plan type. Although generalizations are sometimes difficult, in many cases for older faculty, a typical DC plan embodies greater incentives to remain at work than a DB plan. This is best understood by considering the comparative returns to one more year of work for a faculty member under a DC plan and then under a DB plan.

Under a DC plan, with each year of work an employee adds another year of contributions to his pension wealth, he earns returns on his prior pension wealth, and his monthly annuity will be larger at an older age reflecting the shorter life expectancy remaining. Under a DB plan, one more year of work adds one more year of service to the formula defining pension income (unless the individual has already reached the maximum benefit). However, the addition to pension income from one more year of work under a DB plan is typically not as large as the consequences for the pension annuity under a DC plan of one more year of work. Indeed, the expected present value of pension benefits under a DB plan often falls with one more year of work for someone aged over 60 years.

For this reason, other things equal, a university that has elected to operate with a DC pension plan is likely to find it has a lower retirement rate of older faculty and, perhaps, a greater need to devise explicit retirement incentives than a university that uses a DB pension plan.[8] Indeed, we shall note below that colleges and universities with DC pension plans are more likely to operate a permanent phased retirement program, and to have offered faculty buyouts, than colleges and universities with DB pension plans.

The most common pension plan offered by educational institutions is an exclusive DC plan although it is not unusual for different varieties of DC plans to be available. In Ehrenberg's (2003) survey, some two-fifths of responding institutions reported offering their faculty one or several DC plans only. Fifteen per cent offered a DB plan only.[9]

The incidence of DC pension plans is markedly different between private and public institutions. According to Table 10.1, virtually all private institutions offer a DC plan only. Most public institutions offer faculty a choice between a DC plan and a DB plan. This is generally effected by allowing faculty to enroll in pension programs available to all state employees and these are often DB type plans. In addition, these public colleges and universities offer their faculty a DC plan.[10]

Table 10.1   Type of pension and private–public status: percentage of all institutions

	Public	Private	Total
Defined Contribution (DC)	8.1	33.1	41.2
Defined Benefit (DB)	13.8	1.5	15.3
Combined DC-DB	7.1	0.5	7.6
Both DC and DB offered	35.7	0.2	35.9
Total	64.7	35.3	100.0

Source: Ehrenberg (2003)

Because of the sharp differences in the incidence of pension plan type between private and public institutions, in examining various features of institutions' retirement programs, it is important to differentiate between the effect of any pension plan type and the effect of the private–public distinction. In other words, when two variables are highly correlated (as is the case here involving pension plan type and the private–public character of the institution), it is important to identify whether, in analysing various features of retirement programs, the principal variable is the pension plan type or the private–public nature of the school. We shall accomplish this through multivariate analysis that separates the correlations associated with pension plan type from the correlations associated with the private–public status of the institutions.

To be specific, suppose (as we shall do below) we analyse the incidence of phased retirement programs across institutions and we want to determine those features of these institutions that are associated with the incidence of phased retirement programs. Thus, let y be a variable that takes the value of unity for those institutions with a phased retirement program and of zero for those institutions without a phased retirement program. In the research reported below, we focus on three classes of variables to determine their association with the occurrence of phased retirement programs: the type of pension program, the type of institution (as measured by the Carnegie classification),[11] and whether the institution is private or public. We may write this as

$$\text{prob}(y = 1) = F(DC, DOCTORAL, PUBLIC). \qquad (10.1)$$

In other words, the presence or absence of a phased retirement program can be interpreted as the probability that an institution has a phased retirement program. DC takes the value of unity for those institutions that operate only a defined contribution type of pension plan and of zero for others. DOCTORAL takes the value of unity for those institutions classified as doctoral granting institutions and of zero otherwise. PUBLIC takes the value of unity for public colleges and universities and of zero for private colleges and universities. F is the logistic distribution, a distribution that ensures the implied probabilities are neither greater than unity nor less than zero. This equation (and others that are modifications of this specification) may be fitted to the 600 or so institutions that provided information to Ehrenberg (2003), and maximum likelihood estimates of the implied effects of these three classes of variables on the incidence of phased retirement programs may be derived.

In this example, y stands for the incidence of phased retirement programs and, indeed, this will be one of the variables whose patterns will be investigated below. In addition, we shall examine the incidence of buyout programs and assess the separate effects of DC, DOCTORAL, and PUBLIC on buyout programs. For both the incidence of phased retirement programs and the incidence of buyouts, we shall find that there is a separate and distinct role for each class of variable. That is, the pension plan type is associated with, say, the incidence of phased retirement, even holding constant the separate effect of being a public or private university.

We turn first to a consideration of existing retirement incentives available to colleges and universities with special attention later to phased retirement and buyout programs.

10.3 WHAT RETIREMENT INCENTIVES DO UNIVERSITIES USE?

10.3.1 Temporary and Permanent Policies

It is useful to distinguish two types of retirement incentives. Some incentives are in place for a specific period of time in response to a particular and *temporary* set of circumstances. These aspire to effect a discrete change in the size and/or age composition of the faculty within a few months or years. On the other hand, some incentives are viewed as part of an institution's *permanent* personnel policies designed to address the enduring issues posed by the end of mandatory retirement. Because these policies are, in fact, never permanent and can be changed, the distinction between the two types of policies may blur. For example, the terms of the permanent policies may be changed at a time when the university is experiencing budgetary problems and, although the new 'permanent' policies may be introduced without specifying that they will operate only for a certain time, in practice they may well be altered again when budgetary conditions change.

The temporary policies are sometimes described as 'window' policies because they apply for a specified period of time. This is a suitable distinction provided it is understood that there are two different meanings to 'time': calendar time and age. Usually, the window policies are responses to transitory budgetary problems and they offer severance opportunities for faculty who leave (or, sometimes, promise to leave) between one calendar date and another calendar date. However, they usually apply to faculty at specified ages and, in this sense, some have used the word 'window' to describe policies that operate for faculty only within a designated age interval. Used in this sense, permanent retirement policies are also 'window' policies because they are often specified for faculty in particular age groups. That is, there may be permanent severance incentives for faculty who retire within the window of ages 60 to 65.

In general, a university provides inducements for an employee to quit by changing his returns to university employment compared with his returns to leaving this employment. The returns to university employment are affected by the age profile of earnings. Among workers in general, median real earnings tend to fall after a certain age.[12] The age at which this happens is later for well-educated workers than for poorly-educated workers, but it tends to be the case for all such workers.

Among university teachers and researchers, nominal earnings increases tend to be smaller for faculty aged in their 60s, and a series of meager pay raises can serve as a clear signal for faculty to expect further modest increases. Although every organization must avoid the appearance of its pay policies being tied to age rather than to productivity, in practice the university's salary policies are an adjunct to its retirement policies because for many disciplines an age–productivity association is strongly suggested with productivity falling with age after a certain point.[13] Expressed differently, just as upward-sloping earnings–age profiles may discourage employee turnover at younger ages, so downward-sloping age–earnings profiles later in life embody incentives to leave employment.[14]

10.3.2   Explicit Retirement Incentives

In addition to the implicit incentives provided by their pay policies, universities may put in place explicit incentives for faculty to retire. These incentives take different forms, but some are characterized by various severance pay opportunities for quitting by a certain age. A typical severance incentive pays a retiring faculty member an amount that is proportional to his or her most recent salary and the factor of proportionality declines with age. Usually faculty are eligible only if they have recorded a certain number of years of service at the university.[15] Another type of monetary incentive takes the form of some sort of pension credits.[16]

These are examples of monetary incentives accompanying a transition. There are also non-monetary inducements to enhance the returns to relinquishing tenure. For many academics, the 'social' aspects of work – the daily contact with colleagues and students, the sense of being part of a shared enterprise – are closely intertwined with the 'job' aspects. Hence the opportunity for an individual upon retirement to retain an office or lab space and remain a respected figure in the collective venture can be an important inducement to retire. Moreover, for many scholars, their work is an integral part of their identity and the opportunity to continue their work in a social setting can be a very important component of their well-being. They are often ready to waive tenure and the administrative chores of being a faculty member, but they do not want to forgo the social aspects of employment and the explicit connection to their scholarly work. For these people, the opportunity to retain an office or lab space or be eligible to apply for research grants makes the transition to retirement more attractive.

Ehrenberg's (2003) survey asked whether the institution offered various benefits to retired faculty and the summary of responses are given in Table 10.2. This table presents the responses for doctoral/research universities separately from the other categories of colleges and universities, because our multiple regression analysis indicated that the only consistent difference among institutions was that between doctoral/research universities and all others, and there was no persistent correlation between the incidence of these benefits and the public–private nature of the institution, or the incidence of these benefits and the type of pension plan that operated. In every instance in Table 10.2, the incidence of benefits provided to retirees is very much greater at doctoral/research universities than at others. For example, three-quarters of doctoral universities report they grant retirees office space whereas only two-fifths of other colleges and universities claim to do so.[17]

Of special concern to retirees is health insurance and four-fifths of the institutions responding to Ehrenberg's (2003) survey reported that retirees were eligible for group medical insurance. Yet only three-fifths of these institutions actually contributed to the cost of this health insurance. Ehrenberg (2003) noted that 'the failure of institutions to contribute to retiree health insurance may provide an incentive for their faculty members to delay their retirements and institutions would profit by seriously considering this issue' (p. 7).

Most institutions allow some retired faculty to carry on teaching on a part-time arrangement. However, once a faculty member retires and loses

Table 10.2   The percentage of institutions offering various benefits to
retired faculty

Benefit provided to retired faculty	Doctoral/research universities	All other colleges & universities	All colleges & universities
Office space	75.6	40.4	47.6
Secretarial assistance	54.5	29.3	34.4
Access to institution's computer system	88.6	61.2	66.8
Telephone	65.9	36.2	42.3
Travel funds	22.8	8.0	11.0
Parking	86.2	62.8	67.6
Lab space	42.1	13.0	21.9
Apply for research grants	81.1	42.9	54.5

Notes:
The question on lab space is, 'Are retired professors who are scientists assigned lab space using the same criteria that are used for tenured faculty members?' The question on research grants is 'Are retired faculty eligible to continue to apply for research grants through the university?' In these two cases, the numerical entries in the table represent the answers 'yes' as a percentage of answers 'yes' plus 'no' (eliminating 'not applicable').

Source: Ehrenberg (2003)

tenure, colleges and universities are in a position to be quite selective in determining who is permitted to teach. Some faculty negotiate part-time teaching arrangements before (and sometimes as a condition of) retiring.

10.4   PHASED RETIREMENT PROGRAMS

One type of permanent retirement policy concerns the modification of the terms of employment to permit phased retirement. With these programs, faculty do not move discontinuously from full-time employment to full-time retirement, but rather for a period of time they occupy an intermediate state in which their teaching and advising responsibilities are reduced over those responsibilities associated with full-time employment. According to Ehrenberg's 2003 study, 27 per cent of institutions responding to their survey reported the existence of such phased retirement programs. In those phased retirement programs, about one-third of institutions had procedures that did not require individuals to seek and obtain administrative approval to take advantage of them whereas, for the remaining two-thirds of institutions, individual faculty members needed some sort of administrative sanction to avail themselves of this benefit.

The typical phased retirement program specifies an age window (both minimum and maximum ages) for eligibility and a length of service requirement. Usually the faculty member participating in such phased program gives up tenure and commits to move into full-time retirement after a given number of years (usually three or five). Faculty in phased retirement are paid less than their full-time salary although non-salary fringe benefits are often comparable to full-time employment. For instance, institutions usually pay into the individual's health insurance program at the same rate as if the individual were a full-time faculty member. One survey of universities (Leslie and Janson, Chapter 11 this volume) suggests that, by providing older faculty with more employment options, a phased retirement program boosts morale among long-serving employees.

Allen et al. (2004) provide an excellent case study of the phased retirement program introduced at the 15 campuses of the University of North Carolina system in 1997–98.[18] To be eligible for the UNC phased retirement program, faculty must be tenured and aged at least 50 years with 20 years of service or at least 60 years with five years of service. Most campuses selected a period of three years for the intermediate state of semi-employment (phased retirement). At UNC, those occupying the state of phased retirement are not eligible for most fringe benefits. By comparing the characteristics of the faculty who opted for phased retirement in 1997–98 with the characteristics of those who in 1995–96 elected to remain fully employed and those who in 1995–96 chose to retire full-time (i.e., at a time when part-time employment was not an option), Allen et al. (2004) argue that the people choosing phased retirement in 1997–98 appear more similar to those who remained at work in 1995–96 than those who retired completely in 1995–96. The suggestion is that, in the absence of the phased retirement option, most of those faculty who chose phased retirement would have remained full-time faculty members. This is a key issue in assessing the value of phased retirement programs: in the absence of such programs, what fraction of the phased retirees would be working full-time and what fraction would be retired completely? Those who criticize phased retirement programs often presume to know what the alternative activity would have been.

Data from Ehrenberg's (2003) study were analysed to determine the institutional variables associated with the incidence of phased retirement programs. As described in Section 10.2 above, three categories of variables were examined for their association with the occurrence of phased retirement programs: the type of pension program, the type of institution (as measured by the Carnegie classification), and whether the institution was private or public. We may write this as:

$$\text{prob}(PHASEDRET = 1) = F(DC, DOCTORAL, PUBLIC)$$

where PHASEDRET takes the value of unity for an institution with a phased retirement program and of zero otherwise; DC takes the value of unity for those institutions that operate only a defined contribution type of pension plan and of zero for others; DOCTORAL takes the value of unity for those institutions classified as doctoral granting institutions and of zero otherwise; PUBLIC takes the value of unity for public colleges and universities and of zero for private colleges and universities. F is the logistic distribution and the equation is fitted to data on 607 institutions.

Maximum likelihood estimates of the implied effects of these three classes of variables on the incidence of phased retirement programs are contained in column 1 of Table 10.3.[19] These results are to be interpreted as follows: holding each of these groups of variables constant, phased retirement programs are more likely in institutions:

- with defined contribution (DC) pension plans. Holding constant the private–public distinction and the Carnegie classification, an

Table 10.3   Maximum likelihood estimates of institutional variables associated with the incidence of phased retirement programs and the incidence of faculty buyouts

	Phased retirement programs		Buyouts	
	(1)	(2)	(3)	(4)
Right-hand side variables				
Defined contribution = 1	0.239	0.236	0.126	0.130
	[0.000]	[0.000]	[0.030]	[0.002]
Doctoral = 1	0.099		0.173	
	[0.020]		[0.000]	
Public = 1	0.073	0.087	−0.183	−0.200
	[0.199]	[0.146]	[0.030]	[0.002]
Masters = 1		−0.056		−0.164
		[0.245]		[0.002]
Baccalaureate = 1		−0.100		−0.210
		[0.066]		[0.001]
Two-year institutions = 1		−0.149		−0.158
		[0.008]		[0.005]
−2 × (maximized log likelihood)	673.7	670.6	697.8	696.8

Note: *p* values corresponding to two-tailed tests that the estimated logistic coefficients are not different from zero are reported in square brackets

Source: Ehrenberg (2003)

institution with a pure DC plan is 24 per cent more likely to operate a phased retirement program than an institution that has some sort of defined benefit program. As argued in section 10.2 above, this reflects the programmatic features of a DC program that offers fewer incentives to retire compared with a DB program, so that institutions with DC plans are induced to resort to other schemes (such as phased retirement programs) to encourage retirement. In addition, because DB retirement benefits are often linked to an individual's salary immediately prior to retirement, faculty on DB plans do not want to conclude their employment earning less than full pay, as is implied by the typical phased retirement program.

- that are classified by the Carnegie system as doctorate-granting institutions. These research universities have an 10 per cent greater probability of offering a phased retirement program than other types of colleges and universities.
- that are public institutions. Holding other variables constant, public institutions have a 7 per cent higher probability of offering phased retirement programs than private institutions.[20]

The specification in column 1 of Table 10.3 treats all institutions other than doctoral institutions as the same with respect to the incidence of phased retirement programs. The specification in column 2 allows for different effects across the other types of Carnegie-classified institutions with separate categories for master's degree institutions, for baccalaureate institutions, and for all two-year colleges. It does appear as if phased retirement systems are least common in two-year colleges.[21]

In addition to the equations whose results are reported in columns 1 and 2 of Table 10.3, other equations were estimated to describe the incidence of phased retirement programs. For instance, we examined whether the private–public distinction described above varied with the Carnegie classification so that, for instance, public doctoral schools were different from other types of public institutions. In fact, no further meaningful statistical differences were obtained.

10.5 BUYOUT PROGRAMS

Sometimes educational institutions determine that an abrupt reduction in the level or composition of faculty employment is called for. In these circumstances, a common technique is a buyout program that offers certain faculty for a specified period of time greater returns to relinquishing tenured employment. These are sometimes called 'retirement windows' although this language may be misleading. 'Retirement' connotes leaving all paid employment whereas these buyouts are opportunities for eligible faculty to give up tenured employment and the individual faculty member does not necessarily retire from market work. In addition, the word 'window' has a double meaning: it refers to a specified period of calendar time during which this separation opportunity is in effect; and it refers also to an age window of eligible faculty.

These buyouts are often prompted by an unexpected change in the institution's financial situation such as, in the case of a public university, a large cut in the state's support for higher education. Of course, private institutions are subject to the vagaries of their financial environment too. These financial motivations for buyouts are sometimes complemented by the need that some universities feel to change the demographic composition of their faculty.

These reasons for a university or college instituting a buyout program are no different from those that impel any business to institute such a policy. In other words, many firms and businesses experience fluctuating fortunes and, at times, they face the need to made sharp reductions in their labor costs. For conventional businesses, these labor cost reductions are often effected by a combination of layoffs and nominal pay cuts, options that are usually denied to colleges and universities in dealing with their tenured faculty. Nevertheless, outside of higher education, some conventional for-profit firms have chosen to use buyout programs in preference to layoffs and wage cuts. These firms view themselves as engaged in a long-term (though usually implicit) contract with their employees and the effectiveness with which their employees work depends crucially on how management deals with its labor force. In these circumstances, offering severance incentives (buyouts) to employees is more likely to maintain worker morale and preserve incentives to workers to acquire firm-specific skills.

Evidence that buyouts are not restricted to college and university faculty is provided by the surveys of individuals from the Health and Retirement Study, a nationally representative longitudinal survey of individuals aged 51–61 years in 1992. In these data, Charles Brown (2000) found that, in the first half of the 1990s, an estimated 8.8 per cent of workers had been offered at least one buyout opportunity. Among those workers who had left their employers in a two-year period, one-tenth had quit upon accepting a buyout. This indicates that separations prompted by buyouts represent a non-trivial component of all such turnover. The individuals offered such buyouts were a select group of the workforce: they were much better educated than the typical worker and tended to be professional or managerial workers who had worked for a long time for a large (often unionized) firm.

Those who received buyout offers earned about 40 per cent more than those who did not.

With respect to educational institutions in particular, Ehrenberg (2003) reported that some 35 per cent of colleges and universities had offered buyouts since 1995. Some of these buyouts were part of a permanent program to induce separations while, in other cases, they were temporary programs presenting faculty with more attractive separation opportunities for a particular period of time. Ehrenberg (2003) reported the interesting finding that there was a tendency for some institutions to have offered more than one temporary buyout plan and he conjectured that, 'once a window plan is adopted and then expires, faculty believe that future window plans will be adopted and threaten to delay their retirements until a subsequent plan is adopted. This puts pressure on institutions to adopt a subsequent plan if they want to encourage their older faculty to retire' (p. 4). The role of expectations in influencing the operation and effectiveness of these buyout programs will be returned to in the discussion of the programs at the University of California below.

Some buyouts take the form of lump-sum cash payments and others represent an addition to the individual's retirement contributions especially when the pension plan is of the DB type.[22] However, it is not the case that, overall, buyouts were more common in institutions that operated a DB pension plan. This conclusion was arrived at from multivariate analysis of the data from the Cornell study which were investigated to identify the institutional variables associated with the incidence of buyouts. As described earlier, three classes of variables were examined for their association with the incidence of buyouts: the type of pension program, the type of institution (as indicated by the Carnegie classification), and whether the institution was private or public. In particular, the following equation was specified:

$$\text{prob}(BUYOUT = 1) = F(DC, DOCTORAL, PUBLIC)$$

where BUYOUT takes the value of unity for an institution that had reported any buyout since 1995 and of zero otherwise; DC takes the value of unity for those institutions that operate only a defined contribution pension plan; DOCTORAL takes the value of unity for doctoral granting institutions; and PUBLIC takes the value of unity for public colleges and universities. F denotes the logistic distribution and the equation is fitted to data on the 595 institutions providing information on buyouts. Maximum likelihood estimates of the implied effects of these three classes of variables on the probability of buyouts are contained in column 3 of Table 10.3.[23]

These results have the following interpretation: holding each of these groups of variables constant, buyouts are more likely in institutions:

- that are private. Public institutions were 18 per cent less likely than private institutions to have offered a buyout program over the previous five years.
- that are classified as doctoral. Such research universities are about 17 per cent more likely to have offered a buyout program than other types of colleges and universities.
- with a pension program that is exclusively of the defined contribution type. Institutions offering just a defined contribution plan are 13 per cent more likely to have offered a buyout program during the five years prior to the survey than institutions with at least some type of defined benefit plan.

As was the case with respect to the incidence of phased retirement programs, institutions operating DC plans appear to be those that find the need to introduce incentives to faculty to retire.

The estimates in column 4 of Table 10.3 go beyond the simple distinction between doctoral and non-doctoral institutions and they allow for differences among master's degree institutions, baccalaureate institutions, and all two-year colleges. In fact, as far as the incidence of buyout programs is concerned, the other three types of institutions are similar and, according to conventional statistical tests, the specification that allows for these finer differences does not provide a superior description of the data.

10.6   A CASE STUDY OF BUYOUTS: THE UNIVERSITY OF CALIFORNIA, 1990–94

10.6.1   The Appeal and Drawbacks of a Buyout Program

A buyout program has clear intrinsic appeal. The basic notion is to provide monetary and non-monetary incentives to induce faculty to renounce tenure and quit employment with the institution. Often, pension fund reserves are drawn upon to effect the severance payments. In this way, a discrete change is effected in both the level and the composition of the institution's employment. If people are sensitive to the incentives offered (that is, if only small monetary incentives are required to induce the required change in employment), then the budget savings can be considerable. Also, because the buyouts are usually offered over a short interval of calendar time, the employment effects (and, therefore, the budget savings) are realized quickly.

There are two principal concerns with buyouts. First, there is the issue of the computation of payroll savings and pension expenditures. Although buyout programs will reduce payrolls and may do so swiftly, they raise disbursements from pension funds both now and in the future. The appropriate intertemporal calculations need to be made to ensure that, on balance, this is a prudent use of reserves. These calculations involve an assessment of whether pension reserves are adequate or projected to be adequate. Colleges and universities need to be able to forecast accurately the size of the reduction in payrolls accompanying any buyout program. What is known about the ability of colleges and universities to forecast the number of quits in response to the incentives offered?

Second, even if the *number* of tenured faculty accepting the buyouts is predicted accurately, what about the composition of retirements? Is there an adverse selection problem, meaning that the most productive senior faculty accept the severance incentives and the least productive remain in employment? The concern here is that the more productive faculty are likely to have the more attractive alternative employment opportunities and, therefore, are more inclined to accept the severance incentives, quit the organization, and move to another college or university.[24] This will be less of a concern if faculty view their principal option as one of retiring from all paid work rather than becoming re-employed somewhere else.[25]

The appeal of buyouts as a means to effect employment reductions may be severely compromised by these two defects. These shortcomings probably explain why most employers in the economy do not use such severance incentives to effect employment reductions: most firms implement employment reductions by layoffs or dismissals, that is, by the employer initiating the separation. Most employers do not choose to present their employees with a menu of severance payments and then leave the decision to their employees of whether to accept these payments and to quit. Because tenure prevents colleges and universities from laying off significant numbers of senior faculty (except when the institution is in dire circumstances), employer-initiated separations are not an option for institutions of higher education. However, these two possible defects with buyouts remain for universities: the number of separations may be 'too' high or 'too' low; and the mix of separations (the adverse selection problem) may have undesirable consequences for the institution.

10.6.2 The University of California's verips

What is known about the importance of these two concerns? To address this issue, consider the following case study that involves the largest number of faculty accepting buyouts in any group of institutions of higher education; the early retirement programs used by the University of California for tenured faculty in the first half of the 1990s.[26] These buyout programs were induced by a state budget crisis that brought about sharp reductions in the state's appropriations for higher education. Though the UC system responded in different ways to this reduction in support, its most important response (measured by the cost reductions that were effected) was to provide incentives to tenured faculty to relinquish their tenure. In the first half of the 1990s, almost 2000 tenured faculty (over 20 per cent of all faculty in 1990) accepted the monetary inducements and left their positions.

The essential idea behind the scheme was as follows. While the university's operating budget was in a desperate position, its pension reserves (the UC Retirement Plan) were very well funded. By statute, income could not be reallocated from the pension fund to the current operating budget so, instead, people were induced to switch from current payrolls to receiving pension income. In this way, because *dollars* could not be transferred from one account to another, *people* were induced to switch from receiving income from one source to another source.

Because the severance payments were funded out of pension reserves, the buyouts were portrayed as early retirement programs. Indeed, the common name for them was verips: voluntary early retirement incentive programs. Anecdotal evidence suggests that, indeed, some of those who accepted the buyouts did cease paid employment. However, we also know that some faculty accepted the severance incentives and did not cease work. Indeed, many returned to teach in their original departments although they were no longer tenured and their status was quite different.

The first verip (named Plus 5) was extended in academic year 1990–91 and offered additional pension benefits to those who quit employment by 1 July 1991: call this verip 1. The second verip (named Take 5) was offered in 1992–93 and the resignation date was 1 January 1993: call this verip 2. The third verip (named verip 3) was introduced in 1993–94 and the separation date was 1 July 1994: call this verip 3. Data from the payroll and benefits offices of the UC system were used to analyse the acceptance rate: the probability of an individual accepting the severance incentives offered to him or her.[27] Because administrative data are used in this analysis, information about each faculty member's health status or income from other sources (such as the spouse's income), variables relevant to the severance decision, is not available. This would be a serious shortcoming if we sought a full account of severance decisions. In fact, our research goal is the narrower one listed above, that is, to evaluate the university's ability to forecast the consequences of its buyout program and, for this objective, the information on employees we have is precisely what any university administration would have.

UC's pension program at the time of the three verips was a DB plan that offered cost-of-living adjusted annual payments proportional to a faculty member's highest UC salary over a three-year consecutive period. The factor of proportionality rose with age at retirement and years of service. The severance incentives changed the formula for computing pension benefits by operating separately on the age and years of service factors. Suppose, for each eligible faculty member i, we define S_i to be the ratio of i's verip monetary bonus to i's pension income in the absence of the verip. S_i is an indicator of the magnitude of the severance incentive. S_i varied across individuals and, indeed, for the same individual, S_i varied across verips because the terms of the verips were not the same. In verip 1 and verip 2, the mean and median values of S_i were about 19 per cent, but in verip 3 the mean and median values of S_i were 46 per cent. Indeed, in verip 3, at some age and seniority levels, the value of S_i could reach as high as 90 per cent.[28]

10.6.3 The Consequences of the verips

In the UC verips, is there a relationship between the magnitude of the severance incentive and the probability of its acceptance? Suppose, for each individual faculty member eligible for a severance payment, we form the ratio of pension income offered by the verip to the individual's income from work at UC. This is the replacement ratio.[29] For each verip, organize faculty by their ages. For all faculty of the same age in a given verip, average their replacement ratios and compute the fraction of faculty who accept the verip bonus.[30] Figure 10.1 presents these observations in a scatter diagram: the horizontal axis measures the average replacement rate for faculty of a given age in a given verip; the vertical axis measures the fraction of age-specific faculty eligible for the verip who accepted it.

The positive slope to the relationship in Figure 10.1 is unmistakable: as pension benefits increase relative to salary, so a larger fraction of faculty of a given age accept the severance incentive.[31] The convex shape to the relationship suggests that increases in the replacement ratio have a larger effect on acceptances at higher replacement rates. Figure 10.1 strongly suggests that faculty are responsive to monetary incentives. Approximately, at a replacement ratio of 0.75, a 1 per cent increase in the replacement ratio is associated with a 3.7 per cent increase in the acceptance rate.

10.6.4 Forecasting the Response to Severance Incentives

However, this finding does not address the issue of whether the overall severance or acceptance rate can be predicted with some confidence. Because

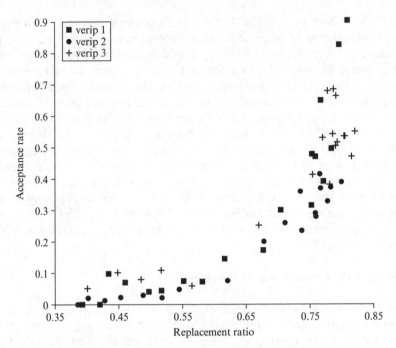

Note: Each observation in this figure shows the replacement ratio and verip acceptance rate for a given verip at each age of the faculty. There are nineteen ages for each verip: age 52 years or less, age 70 years or more, and each single years of age from 53 years to 69 years.

Figure 10.1   The relationship between each verip's replacement ratio and the acceptance rate by age

the observations in Figure 10.1 describe *average* behavior (averaged in each age group), *individual* variations in replacement rates and in acceptances are concealed. Each observation in Figure 10.1 does not represent the same number of individual faculty; more faculty were eligible at older ages where replacement ratios were higher than at younger ages where replacement ratios were lower. It is at the individual level that the cost of the program needs to be assessed. If the acceptance rate can be forecast with accuracy, the cost of the program can be calculated with some reliability. To determine a program's cost, what needs to be predicted is not so much the aggregate severance rate, but the response of individual severances to different alternative monetary incentives.

These buyout programs at UC provide a rare opportunity to address this issue because there were three such programs, and we may ask whether the behavior displayed in one verip may be used usefully to predict severance behavior in later verips. One might think that the prospect for reliable prediction in this setting is auspicious: in each instance, one is forecasting from behavior revealed by one group of faculty members to subsequent behavior by the faculty at the *same university* – in some instances, the very *same people* – no more than 18 months later.

To assess this, I used the individual observations in verip 1 to estimate relationships between, on the one hand, the buyout acceptance decision and, on the other hand, a large number of characteristics of the faculty members, including the size of each individual's severance incentive, income, base pension, age, UC campus, and academic department. These estimated relationships were then used to forecast severance probabilities for each eligible individual in verip 2. These predicted probabilities are aggregated for all faculty of a given age. The implied severance rates by age are then compared with actual severance rates by age. Similarly, using the data on eligible individuals in verip 2, equations relating their severance decision to sets of independent variables were fitted. I then asked how well verip 3's severance probabilities could be forecast using the verip 2 behavior thus embodied in these fitted equations.

In each instance, the forecasts were not at all encouraging. Severance rates by age in verip 2 were substantially below those predicted on the basis of behavior revealed in verip 1. Similarly, severance rates by age in verip 3 were noticeably lower than those forecast by the severance equation fitted to faculty eligible for verip 1 and, *a fortiori*, were considerably lower than those forecast by the severance equation fitted to faculty eligible for verip 2.[32] To provide a particular example at the aggregate level, compared with actual acceptance rates, verip 3's acceptance rates were about 21 per cent lower when using verip 1's estimated equation to predict verip 3's acceptances and were about 49 per cent lower when using verip 2's estimated equation to predict verip 3's acceptances. On the basis of this evidence, our ability to forecast severances is defective.

Why are such forecasts flawed? There are two explanations. The first concerns divergent expectations. Verip 1 was unprecedented at UC and faculty tended to believe this was a singular, not to be repeated, event. Then verip 2 demonstrated that it could be repeated and, indeed, because UC's budget woes continued, faculty conjectured that another buyout program was probable. When buyouts operate in a context of volatile expectations and when these expectations vary across individuals in a manner that is essentially not identified, it is not surprising that behavior in one buyout may not effectively describe behavior in the next buyout.

A second reason thwarting accurate forecasts is the changing composition of the eligible faculty across the buyout programs. The problem is that, when faced with the same monetary incentives to quit, individuals differ in their responses and the reasons for these differences contain an element that is intrinsically unobserved; that is, a key variable affecting the severance decision – each individual's 'taste' for remaining a tenured faculty member – varies across individuals and makes the eligible population of faculty heterogeneous. When the population of faculty eligible for the severance payments changes from one buyout program to another, the pattern of these different and unobserved propensities to accept the buyout changes in unknown ways and this obstructs prediction.

In what sense was the population eligible for the buyouts different across the verips? First, eligibility conditions were less strict from one verip to the next. In addition, verip 2's eligible faculty consisted in part of those who had been offered incentives to quit in verip 1 but had rejected them. So, holding constant the monetary inducements to quit, the distribution of verip 2's eligible faculty consisted of more people with a high 'taste' to remain a UC faculty member than those in verip 1. Those with a high propensity to quit had already accepted verip 1's severance incentives and relinquished their tenure. So, from verip 1 to verip 2, the distribution among the eligible faculty of unobserved propensities to accept the severance incentives changed.[33] A similar argument can be offered with respect to the eligible faculty in verip 3.

10.6.5   The Adverse Selection Problem

Were the more valuable members of UC's faculty particularly inclined to accept the buyouts? If so, the 'quality' of UC's faculty changed with the loss of the more productive faculty and the retention of the less productive faculty. There are two pieces of information relevant to this.

First, consider the relation between severance rates and salaries. Faculty salaries vary for many reasons including age, length of service, academic discipline, and campus. However, holding these factors constant, there ought to be a residual association between an individual's salary and his or her worth to the institution. So one may ask whether, holding other factors that are correlated with salary constant, were those people who enjoyed higher salaries (and, under these circumstances, appear more valuable to the institution) more inclined to quit UC. The unambiguous answer is 'no'. On the contrary, other things equal (including the severance incentive), those individuals with higher salaries were less inclined to accept the buyout program,[34] a finding that is commonly found in studies of the relationship between pay and quit rates (for instance, see Farber 1999).

Second, Kim (2003) collected information on the research publications and citation rates of faculty eligible for the verips. He documented that, measured over the years immediately before the verips, those faculty with lower research output were more inclined to accept the severance incentives than other faculty. In addition, using the ratio of each individual's research output in the three years prior to each verip to the individual's research output over the previous fifteen years, Kim found that those faculty whose research output had slowed down in recent years were more likely to choose the buyout opportunities than faculty whose research output had remained the same.

These two pieces of evidence do not support the notion of an adverse selection problem. It does not appear to have been the case that the more productive and valuable faculty were more inclined to accept the severance incentives.

10.6.6 Conclusion on the verips

The experience of the verips certainly confirms that large reductions in tenured faculty employment can be effected by offering individuals inducements. Although individual faculty display considerable heterogeneity in their behavior, on average, faculty are responsive to severance incentives. The reductions in employment by age achieved at UC are pictured in Figure 10.2. They show sharp reductions at older ages: declines were 25 per cent among those aged 56–60 years, 55 per cent of those aged 61–65 years, and 71 per cent of those aged 66 or more years. Also, the fear that the more valuable members of the faculty would be more apt to quit seems unfounded. Given the reductions in employment that were effected without the loss of some of the more productive faculty, UC administrators appear to believe the verips were a success. However, I know of no careful cost–benefit analysis to support this conclusion. Administrators appear to have arrived at this judgment by noting (1) the sharp reduction in payrolls, (2) the ability of the pension fund to absorb the number of faculty accepting the severance incentives, and (3) the absence of an adverse selection problem. In other words, even though severances were very difficult to forecast, and the inability to forecast accurately helps to explain why there were three buyout programs rather than simply one, the verips were a very important component of the solution to UC's budgetary problems. However, the UC system must have been a less effective teaching and research institution during and after these years and I am not aware of a study that has tried to assess these scholarly losses.

There does seem to be a problem in making accurate predictions of the severance rate and, therefore, of the program's cost. Different forecasting schemes were analysed and they were wanting in providing reliable predictions. Unfortunately UC did not form or make public estimates of

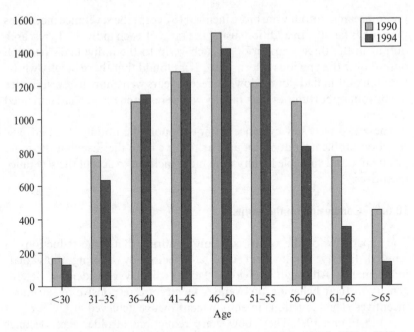

Note: Employment of faculty enjoying tenure protection fell from 8368 in 1990 to 7333 in 1994, a 12 per cent reduction.

Figure 10.2   Tenured faculty employment by age at the University of California before and after the buyouts

the severance rate they anticipated with each verip so it is impossible to compare their projections with outcomes. I did unearth one UC document calculating the cost implications of verip 2, and it describes a 'worse case scenario' as one with a faculty severance rate of 20 per cent. In fact, the actual severance rate in verip 2 was 18 per cent, substantially lower than the central tendency of their 'scenarios' of 25 per cent. The suggestion here is that UC had problems in forming accurate forecasts. Indeed, this is compatible with the fact that another verip, verip 3, was devised shortly after verip 2 was offered.

10.7   CONCLUSION

The labor markets of higher education are sometimes characterized as being unlike all others. In particular, the conjunction of tenure and the absence of mandatory retirement are often seen as posing distinctive problems to institutions of higher education. I have tried here to emphasize the similarity of the problems facing higher education and those facing many other employers, that of devising incentives to induce employees to quit. Policies such as buyouts and phased retirement programs that have been used in higher education to address their employment problems are found in other parts of the economy.

What may be surprising is the extent to which the end of mandatory retirement has seen so little reconsideration of tenured employment contracts in academia. If one goes back to the literature of 15 to 20 years ago, when the consequences of the end of mandatory retirement in higher education were being discussed, many observers predicted that, without mandatory retirement, universities would start to challenge tenure and to devise new contracts designed to circumvent the problems of inducing senior faculty to quit. For example, some proposed supplanting tenure with fixed-term contracts of 10 or 15 years, while others devised schemes to allow nominal salaries to fall with seniority to attenuate the rewards to continued university employment.[35] Though there have been challenges to tenure, for the most part they have been atypical.

I interpret this to mean that, for the most part, the costs imposed on universities by the end of mandatory retirement have been manageable, and the programs to induce the retirement of older faculty have been sufficiently effective that colleges and universities have not been motivated to undertake more fundamental changes in the nature of tenured employment contracts in higher education.

One reason why tenure has remained virtually intact is that the adjustments have been borne by those who are neither tenured nor on the tenure track. The ratio of non-tenure-track (often part-time) faculty to tenure-track faculty has increased, and the salaries of full-time non-tenure-track faculty have declined relative to those of full-time tenured and tenure-track faculty (Ehrenberg and Zhang Chapter 3, this volume). Increasingly, the teachers at American colleges and universities are separated into two groups: the 'insiders' consist of a relatively cosseted and privileged group who enjoy the entitlements of tenure and of being on the tenure track; the 'outsiders' are part-time and full-time non-tenure-track faculty who often have the appearance of contingent workers. The end of mandatory retirement imposed on colleges and universities additional costs of employing tenured and tenure-track faculty, and so the drop in their relative use and the increase in the relative employment of those off the tenure track should not be surprising. By combining phased retirement and buyout programs with greater use of instructors off the tenure track, colleges and universities appear to have avoided the drastic re-thinking of tenure arrangements that observers forecast 20 years ago.

ACKNOWLEDGEMENT

I am most grateful to Ronald Ehrenberg for access to data collected from the *Survey of Changes in Faculty Retirement Policies* and to John W. Curtis, Director of Research at AAUP, for providing information on colleges and universities. This paper benefitted from comments from Morley Gunderson on a preliminary draft and from participants at the Three R's Conference.

NOTES

1. Mandatory retirement was rendered illegal by amendments to the Age Discrimination in Employment Act of 1986. Colleges and universities sought and won an exemption from this and were permitted to impose a retirement age of 70 years. This exemption came to an end in January 1994. Since this time, tenured faculty may or may not retire at any age.
2. This can be found at http://www.aaup.org/statements/Redbook/1940stat.htm.
3. For a more recent assessment of the issues regarding tenure, see McPherson and Schapiro (1999).
4. For instance, see the discussion in Dertouzos and Karoly (1992).
5. This survey was a collaborative effort involving the American Association of University Professors, the TIAA-CREF Institute, the American Council of Education (ACE), the College and University Professional Association for Human Resources (CUPA-HR), the National Association of College and University Business Officers (NACUBO), and Cornell University. Of 1382 institutions that were surveyed, 608 provided useful replies. The response rate was higher for doctoral institutions especially those in the public sector. See Ronald G. Ehrenberg (2003).
6. The characteristics of these subsequent jobs were different however. The jobs involved less work and lower pay. More precisely, those who had accepted their separation offers and then returned to paid employment worked, on average, about eleven fewer hours per week and four fewer weeks per year compared with their pre-buyout work level. On average, their hourly pay was about 40 per cent lower than their pre-buyout wage. These data are from the first two waves of the Health and Retirement Study in 1992 and 1994.
7. Lumsdaine and Mitchell (1999) provide an excellent review of research on retirement and pension plan types.
8. This conjecture finds support in Allen et al.'s (2004) analysis of retirement behavior of tenured faculty at the University of North Carolina's campuses. Since 1971, newly hired UNC faculty may select between a DC plan or a DB plan. The authors find those faculty in a DB plan are more likely to retire and to enter a phased retirement program than those in a DC plan. Though this is consistent with the reasoning in the text, one should also note that there is some simultaneity here: other things equal, those faculty with greater tastes for leisure are more likely to select a DB type of pension plan so the inherent work–leisure preferences of the faculty are revealed in both the choice of pension plan and the retirement behavior. That is, rather than the pension plan type inducing different retirement behavior, the choice of pension plan and retirement behavior are joint outcomes of faculty work–leisure preferences.
9. In these data, institutional contribution rates to DC programs were mostly between 5 and 12 per cent with 10 per cent being the most common value. About 15 per cent of institutions with DC plans had rates of contribution that varied by age, years of service, or salary. The faculty member's contribution rate also varied across institutions with 16 per cent of institutions requiring no contribution from the individual, 21 per cent requiring 5 per cent, and the remaining specifying rates from 1 to 20 per cent (though the lone 20 per cent was a distinct outlier).

10. Table 10.1 reveals that almost 8 per cent of institutions (almost all public) offer a com-
     bined DC-DB plan. In these cases, it seems as if the basic pension is a DB plan which
     requires mandatory participation. Then individuals are given the opportunity to sup-
     plement this DB plan with a contribution to a DC plan.
11. The Carnegie Classification of Institutions of Higher Education covers all US colleges
     and universities that grant degrees and that are accredited by an agency recognized by
     the US Secretary of Education. The classification is made at the level of a campus even
     if a college or university is part of a larger institution. In this chapter the following cat-
     egories are used: Doctoral/research universities that provide a wide range of baccalau-
     reate and doctoral programs; master's colleges and universities, institutions that offer a
     wide range of baccalaureate programs and graduate education usually concludes with a
     master's degree; baccalaureate colleges, primarily undergraduate colleges with principal
     emphasis on baccalaureate programs; and associate's colleges that are mainly two-year
     institutions and usually award no baccalaureate degrees, some with faculty ranks and
     some without faculty ranks.
12. I emphasize that the description of the age-earnings relationship here is in terms of real
     earnings (that is, earnings deflated by some relevant price index). Nominal earnings often
     continue to rise with age. However, even though basic nominal salaries may not fall with
     age, various supplements to salaries (such as paid summer months and opportunities
     within the University to augment one's income) do tend to fall with age, and this is why
     even total nominal compensation declines after a certain age.
13. See, for instance, Oster and Hamermesh (1998) and Stephan and Levin (1992).
14. For arguments regarding the incentive effects of the slope of age-earnings profiles, see
     Lazear (1981).
15. My own institution furnishes an example. Stanford University's Faculty Retirement
     Incentive Program specifies faculty as eligible who have at least 15 years of service and
     aged between 60 and 69 years. Currently, if such faculty retire, each receives a severance
     payment equal to twice his annual salary if aged between 60 and 66 years at retirement
     or equal to his salary if aged between 67 and 69 years.
16. Examples of different types of early retirement incentives are provided in Chronister and
     Kepple (1987).
17. Equation (10.1) in Section 10.2 above was fitted for each benefit provided to retirees.
     That is, for each of the eight benefits listed in Table 10.2, the left-hand side variable
     related to its presence or absence in an institution and the right-hand side variables indi-
     cated the pension plan type, the category of institution (using the Carnegie classifica-
     tion), and whether the institution was public or private. The only meaningful results
     concerned the distinction between doctoral/research universities and all other colleges
     and universities. This is why we neglect the other variables and in Table 10.2 focus on the
     difference between doctoral universities and other institutions.
18. My own institution provides another example. The School of Humanities and Sciences
     at Stanford University operates a 'Retire Then Phase-In' program in which a faculty
     member officially retires and then is called back at no more than 50 per cent for up to three
     years as an emeritus professor. In another option, a faculty member reduces his appoint-
     ment to half-time for up to three years and then officially retires. The second option is less
     popular as the individual remains a faculty member and is liable for administrative duties.
     During the three-year part-time appointment, salary increases are locked in at 3 per cent
     per year. For other programs, see the contributions in this volume of Steven Allen
     (Chapter 9) and of John Palmer, Michael Flusche, and Myra Johnson (Chapter 8).
19. These estimates are those implied by changing the value of the right-hand side dichoto-
     mous variable from zero to unity and evaluating the implied change in the probability of
     phased retirement (where the point of evaluation is at the sample mean values of the
     right-hand side variables). The numbers in square brackets in Table 10.3 are the *p*-values
     of the null hypothesis that the associated logit coefficients are different from zero on a
     two-tailed normal distribution test.
20. The null hypothesis that the incidence of phased retirement programs association is
     uncorrelated with whether the institution is private or public can be rejected at only the

20 per cent level. After examining the data he collected, Ehrenberg (2003, p. 2) reported that 'programs to encourage phased retirement are more likely to be present at private institutions' and this is true on the basis of simple cross-tabulations of the data. However, upon controlling for the incidence of DC plans (which are much more prevalent at private institutions), the link between phased retirement programs and private institutions is closer to being the opposite of what he reported; that is, though strong inferences are inappropriate, it appears as if, holding constant pension plan type, public institutions are more likely to offer phased retirement programs.

21. However, on a joint test and at the 5 per cent significance level, the specification whose estimates are reported in column 2 would not be judged as providing a superior fit to that in column 1.

22. The enhancement of retirement benefits is effected by furnishing the individual with the benefits from more years of service or by granting the individual a terminal leave (during which retirement benefits accumulate) prior to retirement. Augmenting an individual's DC retirement benefits is less advantageous because additional employer contributions to a DC plan are regarded as cash payments that are subject to federal income tax in the year the payments are made.

23. As for Table 10.2, these estimates are those implied by changing the value of the right-hand side dichotomous variable from zero to unity and evaluating the implied change in the probability of phased retirement (where the point of evaluation is at the sample mean values of the right-hand side variables). The numbers in square brackets in Table 10.3 are the p-values of the null hypothesis that the associated logit coefficients are different from zero on a two-tailed normal distribution test.

24. Canadian friends report a story that illustrates the adverse selection problem. A well-known Canadian university is said to have offered its faculty a uniform buyout package. All eligible members of the Computer Science Department left and no-one left from the Classics and Philosophy Departments. I have not been able to find confirmation of this story.

25. Indeed, if faculty view the choice presented to them as that between continuing employment at the institution or retiring from paid work (not of obtaining work at another institution), then the question becomes that of whether more productive faculty value their leisure time in retirement more or less highly than less productive faculty. If the more productive faculty have a lower value of their leisure time upon retirement, then the adverse selection problem does not operate; the less productive faculty are more inclined to accept the severance incentives and quit paid work.

26. The discussion that follows draws heavily on Pencavel (1997, 2001). Valuable perspectives on the verips are provided by Kim (2003) and Switkes (2001).

27. The acceptance rate is also called the take-up rate or quit rate or severance rate. Eligibility criteria were eased with each subsequent verip and depended on the sum of a faculty member's age and years of service. In verip 1, this sum had to be 80 or more; in verip 2, the sum had to be 78 or more; and in verip 3 the sum had to be 73 or more.

28. This particular value of S_i would be presented to a faculty member who was aged 57 years and had 20 years of service and who was at any UC campus except Berkeley. In verip 3, the terms of the severance incentives differed somewhat between Berkeley and other UC campuses.

29. So if S_i is the ratio of i's verip monetary bonus to i's pension income in the absence of the verip, if p_{oi} is i's pension income in the absence of the verip, and if y_i is i's UC salary, then the replacement ratio is $p_{oi} (1 + S_i)/y_i$, the fraction of i's salary that the verip's pension income will replace.

30. There are nineteen age categories: the youngest are aged 52 years or less and the oldest are aged 70 years or more; in between, there are seventeen more ages from 53 through to 69. With nineteen age categories per verip and three verips, there are 57 observations in all on the replacement rate and the verip acceptance rate. Figure 10.1 is a scatter diagram of these 57 observations.

31. The replacement ratio so measured is one year's pension and one year's salary, but of course what matters to each individual are pension benefits and income in future years

too. We lack information on future income so an explicit calculation of future income cannot be undertaken. However, a key variable in calculating that future income will be each faculty member's age with younger faculty computing their income and their pension over more years. Tacitly, Figure 10.1 recognizes this by computing the replacement ratio separately for faculty at each age. In other words, each observation in Figure 10.1 corresponds to faculty of a given age in a given verip.

32. A crude suggestion of this is indicated in Figure 10.1 by the fact that, at a given replacement ratio, the square entries (corresponding to verip 1) tend to be higher on the vertical axis than the circles (corresponding to verip 2) and to the crosses (corresponding to verip 3), especially at high values of the replacement ratio. This is 'crude' for two reasons. First, each 'observation' in Figure 10.1 corresponds to different numbers of underlying individuals. Thus, at a replacement ratio of 0.45, the observed acceptance rates in verip 1 (the square) and in verip 3 (the cross) are close. However, only 3.7 per cent of verip 1's eligible individual faculty members and only 5.6 per cent of verip 3's eligible individuals are observed at this point. Many more individual faculty are observed at higher values of replacement ratios where the vertical difference between the observations is greater. A second reason why this inference is 'crude' is that other variables affecting the severance decision are not being held constant in Figure 10.1. This is important because these other variables (such as age and campus) are correlated with the replacement rate measured on the horizontal axis.

33. Indeed, we may compare the behavior in verip 2 of those faculty who had rejected verip 1's severance incentives (call these the 'repeaters') with the behavior in verip 2 of those faculty newly eligible for a buyout. Almost two-thirds of verip 2's eligible faculty were repeaters. Other things equal, the repeaters had a 6.5 per cent lower probability of accepting verip 2's severance incentives than the non-repeaters. This lower acceptance rate of verip 2's repeaters supports the notion that the distribution of severance probabilities in verip 2 differed from that in verip 1 and, more specifically, that verip 2's eligible faculty consisted of those with a greater propensity to retain their tenure at UC.

34. Reasoning along these lines is contained also in Allen et al.'s (2004) investigation of retirement behavior at the University of North Carolina's campuses. They find that, other things equal, the probability of faculty moving to phased or total retirement is lower among more productive faculty where an individual's productivity is measured by the magnitude of his pay increases over the previous three years. In their sample of faculty who participate in TIAA-CREF, Ashenfelter and Card (2002) report that, at any age, faculty with higher salaries are less likely to retire.

35. For a discussion of some of these ideas, see Oi (1979) and Weiler (1987). Thus, one suggestion was to divide a faculty member's salary into two components, one of which could not fall in nominal terms while the other would be adjusted to reflect the individual's contributions to various aspects of the university's activities. A frequent proposal is to replace tenure with long-term but fixed employment contracts.

REFERENCES

Allen, Steven G., Robert L. Clark and Linda S. Ghent (2004), 'Phasing into retirement', *Industrial and Labor Relations Review*, **58**(1), 112–27.

Ashenfelter, Orley and David Card (2002), 'Did the elimination of mandatory retirement affect faculty retirement?', *American Economic Review*, **92** (4), 957–80.

Brown, Charles (2000), 'Early retirement windows', in Olivia S. Mitchell, P. Brett Hammond and Anna M Rappaport (eds), *Forecasting Retirement Needs and Retirement Wealth*, Philadelphia: Wharton School of the University of Pennsylvania, University of Pennsylvania Press, pp. 253–73.

Chronister, Jay L. and Thomas R. Kepple, Jr. (1987), *Incentive Early Retirement Programs for Faculty: Innovative Responses to a Changing Environment*, ASHE-ERIC Higher Education Report no. 1, Washington, DC: Association for the Study of Higher Education.

Clark, Robert L., Linda S. Ghent and Juanita Kreps (2001), 'Faculty retirement at three North Carolina Universities', in Robert L. Clark and P. Brett Hammond (eds), *To Retire or Not? Retirement Policy and Practice in Higher Education*, Philadelphia: Pension Research Council, Wharton School of the University of Pennsylvania, University of Pennsylvania Press, pp. 21–38.

Dertouzos, J.N. and L.A Karoly (1992), 'Labor market responses to employer liability', Rand report no. R-3989-IC, Santa Monica, CA: Rand Corporation.

Ehrenberg, Ronald G. (2003), 'The survey of changes in faculty retirement policies', American Association of University Professors, acessed at http://www.aaup.org/Issues/ retirement/retrpt.htm.

Farber, Henry S. (1999), 'Mobility and stability: The dynamics of job change in labor markets', in Orley Ashenfelter and David Card (eds), *Handbook of Labor Economics*, vol. 3B, Amsterdam: Elsevier Science, pp. 2439–83.

Kim, Seongsu (2003), 'The impact of research productivity on early retirement of university professors', *Industrial Relations*, **42** (1), 106–25.

Lazear, Edward P. (1981), 'Agency, earnings profiles, productivity, and hours restrictions', *American Economic Review*, **71** (4), 606–20.

Lumsdaine, Robin L. and Olivia S. Mitchell (1999), 'New developments in the economic analysis of retirement', in Orley Ashenfelter and David Card (eds), *Handbook of Labor Economics*, vol. 3C, Amsterdam: Elsevier Science, pp. 3261–307.

McPherson, Michael S. and Morton Owen Schapiro (1999), 'Tenure issues in higher education', *Journal of Economic Perspectives*, **13** (1), 85–98.

Oi, Walter Y. (1979), 'Academic tenure and mandatory retirement under the new law', *Science*, **206** (4425), 21 December, 1373–78.

Oster, Sharon M. and Daniel S. Hamermesh (1998), 'Age and productivity among economists', *Review of Economics and Statistics*, **80** (1), 154–6.

Pencavel, John (1997), 'The response of employees to severance pay incentives: Faculty of the University of California, 1991–94', unpublished paper, Stanford University.

Pencavel, John (2001), 'The response of employees to severance incentives: The University of California's Faculty, 1991–94', *Journal of Human Resources*, **36** (1), 58–84.

Stephan, Paula E. and Sharon G. Levin (1992), *Striking the Mother Lode in Science: The Importance of Age, Place, and Time*, New York: Oxford University Press.

Switkes, Ellen (2001), 'The University of California Voluntary Early Retirement Incentive Programs', in Robert L. Clark and P. Brett Hammond (eds), *To Retire or Not? Retirement Policy and Practice in Higher Education*, Philadelphia: Pension Research Council, Wharton School of the University of Pennsylvania, University of Pennsylvania Press, pp. 106–21.

Weiler, William C. (1987), 'Economic issues in faculty retirement plans in American higher education institutions', *Economics of Education Review*, **6** (3), 207–26.

11. To phase or not to phase: the dynamics of choosing phased retirement in academe

David W. Leslie and Natasha Janson

With the abolition of mandatory retirement, academic institutions are increasingly exploring alternative retirement options for their faculty. Early retirement, phased retirement, and other arrangements extending employment beyond the traditional retirement age(s) are alternatives that have emerged during a period best described as unsettled and exploratory. While approximately half of all colleges and universities now offer phased retirement options to their faculty, phased retirement is still a relatively new development and has not been studied to the point that any clear assessments of its effectiveness are available. This chapter focuses on the experiences thus far of a small sample of institutions with phased retirement policies.

Our study, sponsored by the Alfred P. Sloan Foundation, was conducted during 2003–04 and is based on extensive interviews at twelve institutions and two state systems. We interviewed a wide array of faculty members who had elected for phased retirement and institutional leaders including department chairs, deans, provosts, and system-level executives. We supplemented the interviews at (predominantly) comprehensive and research universities with a survey of (principally) smaller liberal arts colleges. Altogether, we have responses from approximately 150 individuals. This chapter is a preliminary report about selected findings.

Our project's original purpose was to explore institutions' and individuals' experience with flexible employment arrangements – focusing on phased retirement. We expected to learn how providing more flexible working conditions for late career faculty might lead to new ideas that could benefit early career faculty who are more often faced with the many demands of family and career. In fact, that aspect of our project has served to refocus our attention on retirement patterns. On the whole, retirement appears to be a distinct stage of life and career. Essentially, what may work to help faculty retire is sufficiently different from what junior faculty may want or need in the way of flexibility, that few explicit connections are

239

warranted. Therefore, in this chapter we will address only the following questions: how and under what conditions do American academics prefer to (and choose to) retire? What options may be most appealing to which faculty? And what have institutions and individuals experienced and learned from the past decade's experiments with phased retirement?

11.1   RETIREMENT PATTERNS AMONG FACULTY: NATIONAL DATA

We analysed data from the National Survey of Postsecondary Faculty (1998) administered by the National Center for Education Statistics to generate descriptive data about faculty retirement patterns.[1] This survey of roughly 18 000 faculty and a large sample of institutions includes items asking about retirement plans and preferences. The 1998 survey was the first to be administered following expiration of mandatory retirement in 1994. These data are therefore the first look at how individuals and institutions were adapting to a watershed change in policy.

Half (50 per cent) of all surveyed institutions reported offering a phased or early retirement option in 1998 (up slightly from 48 per cent in 1993 when the previous survey was administered). Research institutions and public institutions were the more likely to offer phased retirement options to their faculties. Our analysis suggested that institutions offering phased retirement intended it as an incentive for their relatively 'tenured' faculties, and that the incentive had been at least partially successful. However, institutions that did not report offering incentive programs experienced an increase in retirements between 1993 and 1999, suggesting that other factors (such as the overall aging of the faculty population and economic conditions) may play as substantial a role as incentives in the decision to retire.

On the whole, faculty responding to the NSOPF survey reported intending to retire at about age 65 (women) or 66 (men). We have dealt with the difference between men's and women's retirement patterns in more depth elsewhere.[2] For the purposes of this chapter, we focus briefly on how faculty who choose early retirement differ from those who elect to retire after age 70, and on characteristics of those who plan to choose for phased retirement.

Roughly 14 per cent faculty intend to retire at age 60 or earlier, and roughly 14 per cent intend to retire at age 70 or later, with women far more likely to consider early retirement. Women in this group reported relatively high household incomes and relatively heavy teaching loads. Men who planned to retire *later* than 70 were among the highest paid, the most 'successful' by traditional measures (e.g., publications), the least likely to have heavy teaching loads, and the most satisfied with their jobs. Without going into more detail, these two patterns indicate varied motives and circumstances affecting retirement decisions, and suggest that whatever policies institutions may adopt should leave room to accommodate individual variability. Wealth, work-related concerns, and overall morale or satisfaction were among the factors that differentiated (to varied degrees) faculty according to their retirement plans.

The data did not sort in particularly meaningful ways in our search for patterns related to the likelihood that an individual would opt for phased retirement if it were available except where strong financial incentives exist. Overall job satisfaction was the most 'significant' discriminator, although it was far from determinative. We would expect to find, holding other things equal, job satisfaction might tip the scale toward opting for phased retirement.

But other things are clearly not equal. This was perhaps the principal conclusion of the interview/survey phases of our study. Faculty who approach retirement age vary dramatically on almost every measure and their choices about how to retire reflect two kinds of interactions: First, aspects of their personal and professional lives interact to predispose them differently to retirement options and opportunities, and, second, their personal economic circumstances interact with the incentives and penalties they confront in deciding when and how to retire.

Using the data from our interviews and surveys, we examine why institutions offer phased retirement plans and the results of that choice. We also review individual choices and satisfactions with phased retirement.

11.2 WHY DO INSTITUTIONS OFFER PHASED RETIREMENT?

Institutional rationales for offering phased retirement programs are of two kinds. On one hand, institutions have felt the need to (and in some cases have been directed to by their boards or other sources of policy oversight) provide incentives to assure that retirement – no longer mandatory – is attractive to older faculty. A balance must be struck to assure that plans are non-discriminatory, yet are sufficiently attractive to faculty approaching or past traditional retirement age. Phased retirement is seen as one tool that can help institutions plan and control their academic workforces and as a benign way to help long-standing employees make difficult decisions about when and on what terms to retire. Phased retirement policies also provide consistency and fairness in an essentially unstructured environment that tempts institutions to 'wheel and deal' with individuals over retirement packages that, as Palmer, Flusche, and Johnson in Chapter 8 of this volume point out, may 'result in both higher overall expense and very different treatment of faculty with similar characteristics'.

11.2.1 Planning and Controlling

Older faculty are, of course, among the highest paid at just the time when institutions are suffering economic reverses – and at a time when they both foresee the need to and have begun to compete for the newer generation of academics. The bulge of faculty hired in the 1960s and 1970s will inevitably retire in the near and very predictable future, just as enrollment pressures are bearing down on institutions and as states struggle just to continue level funding of colleges and universities. The pressure to offer more higher education at lower cost leads inexorably to the payroll. Leaders we interviewed often noted that they hoped phased retirement plans would attract enough 'takers' to allow banking of half-salaries that could be allocated to new positions.

Institutions also faced additional pressures to shift faculty positions from fields that had been more popular 20 or 30 years ago when current senior faculty had earned tenure. Newer fields needed more faculty positions, and those positions could only come from vacated lines. Also, without mandatory retirement, institutions felt they had lost some ability to plan and control the distribution of positions and salary dollars. Phased retirement plans typically commit individuals to a firm retirement horizon – say, 5 years – that helps institutions clarify and control the flow of both dollars and positions. This assumption, however, only holds when sufficient numbers of faculty commit to phasing, which has not been the experience of most of our case-study institutions. Phased retirement policies are usually one-sided as to when individuals may terminate their active employment, meaning that phased retirees can decide to opt out of their jobs at their own discretion. One of our respondents said, 'I can walk away if things aren't as I'd like.' When random departures mount up, institutions may be left with too many vacancies for which they had not planned.

Also, patterns of work, funding, and staffing profiles differ so substantially from discipline to discipline that any given policy will serve only certain interests well. For example, one vexing problem has emerged in the hard sciences. The start-up costs for a new faculty member's laboratory may far exceed the continuing cost of retaining a seasoned scientist with an established laboratory. The institution is reaping returns on their (usually relatively small) investment in the older laboratory that produces a continuing flow of grants, while it would have to re-invest at a much higher (and more speculative) level in a new laboratory for a junior faculty member without an established track record. In either case, the institution's ability to obtain an individual's commitment to retiring at a pre-established time, as with phased retirement, may provide the institution with increased foresight and thus allow administrators to engage in improved financial and administrative decision-making.

11.2.2 Supporting Loyal Employees

The catalyst for widespread institutional implementation of phased retirement programs may have been the 1994 federal prohibition of the mandatory retirement age. The policies we have reviewed almost all condition eligibility on a combination of age and length of service, a combination that reflects institutional loyalty. For example, eligibility might be restricted to individuals with 15 years of service who have attained the age of 55, or any other combination of age and service equaling 70 'years'. But phased retirement may also be seen (perhaps perversely) as one resourceful way to encourage the retirement of 'curmudgeons', as one administrator infelicitously – but with real feeling – termed them, who would otherwise remain indefinitely and work for years beyond their most productive capacities.

However, institutions also calculate that phased retirement programs may work as an incentive to retain those individuals who continue to add value to the institution. One administrator declared, 'We aren't as anxious to get rid of the older faculty as we might once have been', largely because of their experience and institutional memories on which the college or university depends. Ideally, phased retirement would provide an environment where the productive stay longer and the non-productive leave earlier, thereby increasing the overall effectiveness of departments, programs, and institutions. Allen (Chapter 9 this volume) reports evidence showing exactly this result of one state system's phased retirement policy.

Administrators at many of the institutions we visited conveyed sincere interest in phased retirement programs simply as a reward for an individual's continued and productive service to the institution, especially at a time when financial and other benefits are in short supply. This motivation was clearly articulated by an administrator who believed phased retirement serves to cultivate faculty morale by promoting, 'A more humane working environment [that] represents a caring attitude on the part of the university.'

These two imperatives – improved planning or control and provision of a humane retirement process – are not always mutually compatible, nor even mutually reinforcing, although our interviews suggested they do complement each other in both intended and unintended ways. Clearly, there are cases where individuals have taken advantage and 'gamed' the system – often those individuals whom the institution would prefer to have retired.

Other individuals simply choose to extend their employment as long as possible without regard for how this arrangement serves the institution.

Perhaps more difficult, though, is how faculty salary compression has eroded whatever financial gains the institution expected from early or phased retirements. Quite simply, half of a senior person's salary is no longer adequate to hire a junior replacement, especially if that junior person expects a laboratory or other research support. Also, because half of a senior person's salary is relatively high, the rest of that salary (the vacated amount) is not enough to hire a full-time replacement at the same rank. These facts have led to increased hiring of temporary or adjunct faculty on at least some campuses, the unintended consequences of which may include a delay in hiring full-time replacements, and as one institutional leader called it, 'a squeeze on mid-career faculty between [phased retirees] and lecturers'.

Terms and conditions on which faculty 'phase' are, more often than not, mutually satisfying for both the individual and the institution, as our respondents reported. But there are ways for the relationship to go awry. Pencavel, in Chapter 10 in this volume, indicates that phased retirement is more attractive to individuals in a defined benefit plan. Indeed, the Faculty Early Retirement Plan (FERP) offered by the California State University System's contract with its faculty union provides incentives that are very attractive to participants in the California public employees' (defined benefit) retirement system (CALPERS). We found that roughly 80 per cent of all retirees in the CSUS now elect to phase, an indication that the terms and conditions are so generous that the result is indiscriminate participation. And that, of course, means indiscriminate results that constrain institutions' capacity to plan and control the size and deployment of their faculty workforce. In another case, a new department chair indicated that he felt seriously hamstrung in his efforts to realign his faculty with the teaching and service demands on his department. His predecessor had agreed to terms and conditions with phasees that absolved them of certain duties, and left the new chair struggling to manage. Misunderstandings between individuals and their deans or department chairs also led to discontent in some cases. Heavier work loads than anticipated – or less productivity than expected – accounted for some of this discontent.

11.2.3 Effects on Departments

We found some divergence of views between central administrators and department chairs about the impact of phased retirement. When individuals choose phased retirement, institutions can more efficiently plan ways to recapture and reallocate the resources associated with the individual's commitment to retirement. However, for the phasee's particular department, phased retirement can create a sort of financial limbo wherein the department is left scrambling for itself to cover the full workload of the part-time phased retiree with fewer funds.

For example, at many institutions the monies freed-up by the part-time status of phased retirees are reclaimed by the central administration for distribution to other areas and departments. As one department head noted, 'Departments [with phased retirees] get a raw deal.' Departments in which several faculty had elected to phase felt especially deprived. As one institutional leader with several phased retirees in her department noted, when a 'cascade of health problems hit' it was 'harder to adapt and fill in'.

Department heads also report mixed satisfaction with the varied and unpredictable productivity of phased retirees. One administrator declared, 'They [phased retirees] can't advise graduate students or serve on committees because that is a continuous, full-year process. Nominally, they are carrying half FTE load, but functionally they are really working less than that.' Another administrator agreed, stating that because of phased retirement, 'Departments have had to scramble to find instructors.' Departments are further inconvenienced when more unproductive individuals opt for phased rather than full retirement. One administrator claimed, 'Many good full-time faculty members are not so [good] during their phased retirement' and another asserted that the reality of phased retirement is that, 'Tired and less effective people can still hang on longer than they should.' Other departmental problems have also been noted when, as one institutional leader observed, phased retirees 'have tried to maintain control over departmental affairs, which is awkward'.

Conversely, some department heads reported great satisfaction with the productivity and value added by their phased retirees. One administrator asserted, 'Many who enrolled in the [phased retirement] program were the "backbone" of [the institution] and have been "good citizens".' Another administrator noted, 'The program gives the department a chance to hold people for their . . . talents and their reputations.' At one institution we were told that 'Keeping older faculty here preserves institutional memory, expands the pool of potential mentors for junior faculty, provides a pool of experienced people to take on service assignments, and preserves departments' pools of expertise.'

Thus, for departments where phased retirees pull their weight, managing phased retirement appears to be less difficult than for departments faced with unproductive phasees, or too many phasees. But, problems notwithstanding, the institutions we visited predominantly reported that their phased retirement policies had served both sides benignly – neither a cure-all to the abolition of mandatory retirement nor a wasteful activity of which faculty took undue advantage. The one exception occurred in the California State University System where most retiring faculty elected to phase as a matter of right, removing all discretion and flexibility from institutions.

11.3   INDIVIDUALS AND OUTCOMES OF PHASED RETIREMENT

By far the most satisfied partner to phased retirement agreements, individuals expressed very positive views of their phased retirement experiences. Overall, those who had elected to phase were pleased with the financial security they were able to assure for themselves, with the balance found between more free personal time and the time spent at work, and with the ability to gradually ease into full retirement. However, the emergent reality of participation meant – to some – that there are unintended negative consequences, such as working more than anticipated or feeling marginalized within the department, which may challenge individuals' pre-conceived notions regarding phased retirement.

11.3.1   The Financial Reality

The terms and conditions offered under the many varied phased retirement policies we reviewed differentially affect the financial attractiveness of the option for individuals. Institutions differ on how they structure the reduced-pay, reduced-work package. Policies vary on whether, for example, the institution will continue to contribute to pensions and other benefits at full-time (or part-time, or not at all) rates during the phased period, as well as on whether phasees are eligible for merit and other raises.

Individuals who are eligible to draw from Social Security and who are covered by Medicare or continued health benefits, and who are eligible to receive annuities from their pension provider during the phased period while they are also receiving half or more of their full-time salaries, may actually make more money than they had while working full time. As one faculty member reported, 'The college was quite generous in its offer to pay me a lot of money to work half-time.' Another stated, 'I get 160 per cent pay [in phased retirement]. It is a godsend.' Of these types of financial windfalls at certain institutions with generous phased retirement plans, one administrator remarked, 'Enough years in the system with the possibility of [phased retirement] and you'd never want to leave.'

Also, choosing to phase, as opposed to retiring fully, sometimes appeals to individuals who participate in defined contribution plans that experienced setbacks during market downturns. For these faculty, deciding to phase allowed more time to add to retirement funds. More often, however, individuals experience a real reduction in pay during the phased retirement period. Their pay may be prorated based on their reduced work assignment and the consequences must be balanced against the decision to continue to work full time for full pay and benefits. As one individual reported, 'the deal is not as good' as it had seemed.

Some institutions, however, provide bonus pay or balloon incentives that make phased retirement more attractive. Two institutions among those we visited scaled their pay to phasees at a higher level than others. (In one case, individuals typically received 75 per cent of their full-time pay for a 65 per cent work assignment.) One institution provided a balloon payment to all fully retired faculty that amounted to about 165 per cent of an individual's annual salary. (Individuals would commit to retire two years in the future without any work assignment during these remaining two years, but they would remain on contract and receive a reduced paycheck in exchange.) These bonus and balloon policies were generally seen as win–win propositions by all involved.

11.3.2 The Element of Time

Most individuals expressed contentment with the newfound time for balance between personal and work obligations afforded by their reduced work schedules in phased retirement. As one faculty member noted, ' . . . [the terms of phased retirement are] reasonably attractive enough where buying time for yourself is more important than the pay.' Phasees largely echoed one individual's sentiment that phased retirement 'Allowed me to spend more time with my family and extended family [as well as provided me with] more time to travel.' Also, the reduced time spent at work was more selective and focused, allowing individuals to concentrate on more rewarding aspects of their jobs while avoiding the more annoying duties. One respondent remarked that the more rewarding aspects of phased retirement involved 'teaching two favorite courses, still seeing colleagues, but without the usual distractions or responsibilities of departmental matters, faculty politics, etc.'

Nevertheless, for some individuals the phased retirement period turned out to be less of a winding-down period than hoped for. An administrator at one institution noted, 'Lots took phased retirement . . . but many found the continuing obligation to teach relatively heavy loads to be too painful and didn't continue for the full [phased retirement] period.' One phasee also noted, 'I have to keep telling myself the problems of the department are not mine to worry over [and I have to] force myself to stay home because I'm not able to finish everything' in part-time mode. Another individual stated of his purported half-time phased retirement assignment, ' . . . it is only the actual classroom teaching that has been cut in half; advising of various forms continues unabated, so that on balance I am working probably about 75 per cent of full-time'. A different phasee agreed with this reaction asserting, 'I am continuing to do research [while phasing], which I love – but I should be paid for this. My work and its success accrue to the benefit of [my institution] . . . I feel some bitterness at this.' Thus, perceived time inequities affected some phasees' satisfaction with phased retirement.

11.3.3   The Psychological Effects of Phasing

Phasees overwhelmingly believed that phased retirement was providing them with the psychological transition they required to ease into full retirement. One reported, for example, 'I feel badly that I'll soon have no job, no professional status, and no identity as a faculty member . . . but tapering off by phasing is a lot better than going cold turkey into retirement.' Another said:

> The pervasive dread of facing life without contact with . . . undergrads makes me want to break down and weep. I love what I do – and can still do it well. I receive so much energy and enthusiasm from walking into a classroom of bright, motivated, and personable young people that the thought of NOT teaching causes the bile to rise and fester.

One unintended negative psychological consequence of the phased retirement period was a reported feeling of marginalization within the department. One individual declared, 'Our colleagues treat us differently – they know exactly when we are retiring and that we no longer have tenure. This has affected how they think of us – whether they realize it or not.' Other phasees felt this marginalization as they were forced out of their offices to temporary spaces. One individual stated, 'We [phased retirees] usually have to vacate [our regular] offices, and I didn't learn about my new assignment until the last minute. It is harder to work from temporary or shared offices,' (a transition that no doubt has a negative psychological impact as reiterated by other phasees).

11.4   CONCLUSION

The principal reason cited by institutional administrators for initiating and promoting phased retirement among faculty is that phased retirement humanizes employee relations. As one interviewee noted, phased retirement

'Allows the institution to get beyond the bottom line of money,' while another said, 'The benefits [of phased retirement] accrue mostly to individual faculty. Phasing into retirement has psychological benefits, health benefits, morale benefits, and represents a more humane way (organizationally) to deal with the inevitable.' Thus, institutional administrators repeatedly refer specifically to the individual benefits provided by phased retirement programs when asked about the overall benefits of such programs.

Administrators were far less certain that phased retirement advantaged the institution financially, programmatically, organizationally, or strategically. In fact, one institutional leader stated of the institution's phased retirement policy that it 'Is a huge giveaway to faculty, and was not thoughtfully rationalized from the system perspective. It is costly, hurts campuses, and disrupts departments.' But at a time when colleges and universities are pressed to keep salaries at a level commensurate with the market, and when both individuals and institutions are still exploring how best to navigate the new policy environment regarding retirement, the option to phase is more often seen, at least in theory, as an attractive benefit to prospective faculty as well as a useful option that attracts some who might otherwise find retiring to be a more difficult process.

Our general analysis suggests that phased retirement policies fill a niche, but that they are not a universal solution to whatever problems institutions may face in the absence of mandatory retirement. Experience is now sufficient – without mandatory retirement – to affirm that individuals will 'normally' retire in their mid-60s, commensurate with their eligibility for Social Security and Medicare, and commensurate with the prospective payout from their retirement plans. Relatively small percentages of faculty elect to retire earlier or later than the norm, and these individuals often do so because their financial, health, family, or career situations are atypical.

Phased retirement policies that aim for 'conventional' retirees with a generic set of terms and conditions probably will not attract large numbers, nor have the desired budgetary or human resource impacts. They do represent a humane and attractive side-benefit for faculty who find the prospect of retirement difficult for both financial and other reasons. But we were struck by the degree to which the policies had less impact than might have been intended, except in cases where the phased retirement package offered by the institution was considered inordinately generous. The unintended consequences of too many faculty opting for phased retirement have been discussed elsewhere in this chapter.

While it is premature to offer recommendations, we conclude that phased retirement policies should focus more purposefully on particular institutional or individual needs and be made, as one administrator suggested, 'to fit the culture of the institution'. We suggest the following questions as starting points in considering more tightly focused policies:

- Could phased retirement opportunities be offered selectively to departments based on their staffing and enrollment levels?
- Could phased retirement eligibility be expanded to all faculty, regardless of longevity of service to the institution, but be qualified by waivers of certain obligations on the part of the institution (e.g., by limiting phasees' pay to adjunct pay rates if they do not meet eligibility standards?) Some faculty have enough assets or other income (from consulting, for example) to make working at more than a bare minimum unnecessary. They might accept adjunct pay rates in return for minimal duties.
- Could phased retirement be made more attractive to faculty whose pay has eroded, either because of inflation or because they have not received full merit increases, by more creative use of bonus or balloon payments?
- Could phased retirement be arranged cafeteria-style, allowing individuals to trade benefits (like health insurance) for pay?
- Could phased retirement be made more attractive if more counseling support – financial, personal, and career – were available to help faculty and their spouses come to grips with the realities of retirement? (One of our surveyed institutions provided $3000 credit toward services of a financial advisor. Some faculty might be willing to consider out-placement services or marital and personal advice to help them face what they genuinely fear – life beyond their careers.)
- Could, as one administrator suggested, some sort of 'mutual benefits analysis' be conducted for the individual and the institution when a faculty member is considering phased retirement (to ensure that fully informed choices are made on both sides)?
- Could department chairs be provided with better information (e.g., training sessions on negotiation) on how to approach faculty members when they near retirement (again, to help ensure that faculty are fully aware of their choices and consequences)?

NOTES

1. For a full report of this analysis, see Leslie and Conley (2003). Technical information about the National Study of Postsecondary Faculty is posted at www.nces.ed.gov/surveys/ nsopf/.
2. See Leslie and Conley (2003).

REFERENCES

Leslie, David W. and V. Conley (2003), 'Early and phased retirement plans among tenured faculty: a first look', presented at the annual meeting of the Association for the study of Higher Education, Portland, OR, 13 November.

12. Phasing out of full-time work at the University of California

Ellen Switkes

This chapter describes a multiyear discussion between the administration and the faculty at the University of California about the transition between full-time work and full-time retirement. The story begins with a phased retirement program instituted in 1980, and ends in the spring of 2004 with ongoing discussions between faculty senate committees and campus provosts about provisions for recalling faculty following retirement mediated by staff in the system-wide Office of the President. The faculty, represented by a system-wide senate faculty committee, wanted the option of a phased retirement program which they viewed as a humane and generous benefit to transition between full-time work and full-time retirement. Academic managers, represented by campus provosts, had serious concerns about any program that might encourage faculty to retire early. Campuses regularly recalled retired faculty to teach, and the provosts saw no reason to make these individual arrangements into a 'program.'

The Berkeley campus recently sponsored a seven-session series on retirement planning. During the first session, several retired faculty gave a picture of their retirement activities. All these retirees, even those who had been retired for ten years remained professionally active. They had retired to finish a book, to study, and in some cases to avoid meetings, committees or teaching. It's clear that many faculty who retire do not plan to give up their scholarly lives. In fact, at this program it became clear that many faculty have no clue what to do after retirement other than more study. For these reasons, a program that provides a transition from full-time work may be attractive to many older faculty who aren't prepared to retire fully.

To put this discussion in context, the University of California has ten campuses around the state, the newest at Merced opening in the fall of 2005, with almost 9000 tenured or tenure-track faculty. Enrollment growth has been spectacular and is not expected to level off until 2010, so that in recent years all campuses have had high levels of faculty recruitments to meet increasing retirements and increased enrollment. UC sponsors a defined benefit retirement plan that allows retirement from age 50 up, with five years of full time service. The plan is structured so that the age factor in the pension formula reaches its maximum at age 60. Faculty who are 60 or older with 40 or more years of service have full salary replacement in retirement. The plan is well enough funded so that no employer or employee contributions have been made since 1990. Annuitant health benefits are also provided with some vesting requirements.

In 1980 a formal phased retirement program was adopted for purposes of faculty renewal in anticipation of an increase in the mandatory age of retirement to age 70. This program was available to faculty and staff age 60 or older with 20 or more years of service. It was designed so that the retirees could take all or part of their pension during the phase period and also earn additional retirement service credit for part-time work. It required administrative approval. Only 304 volunteers participated, almost all faculty. The program was discontinued in 1990 because of legal concerns about favoring the highly compensated, limited participation and in-service distribution.

In the early 1990s due to a serious budget crisis, a series of three special Voluntary Early Retirement Incentive Programs (verips) reduced the regular faculty by 2000 members (or about 25 per cent of existing faculty), and campuses are still replacing positions vacated during that period (Switkes 2000; Pencavel, Chapter 10, this volume). After the end of mandatory retirement in 1994, many universities developed retirement incentives including phased retirement programs to encourage faculty turnover. This was not a concern at the University of California due both to the large number of older faculty who had retired during the verips and also because the University was experiencing rapid enrollment growth and was having trouble hiring faculty fast enough.

In fall 2000, faculty at the Berkeley campus started talking again about developing a phased retirement program and decided a system-wide program would be better. While limited options for phased retirement could be developed at a single campus, a program for all campuses provided a much broader range of possibilities, including use of the UC Retirement Plan and changes to system-wide policies which require approval of the President or possibly even the Regents. In addition, faculty at other UC campuses were also interested in phased retirement. Successful programs at the University of Washington and the North Carolina system were models for the Berkeley faculty. These faculty expected that this type of program would be attractive both to faculty and academic managers for several reasons:

1. to encourage faculty to retire who don't otherwise think about it;
2. to provide a transition from full-time work to full-time retirement;
3. for purposes of planning, to know when faculty were going to retire.

The Berkeley recommendation was referred to the system-wide academic senate committee, the University Committee on Faculty Welfare – UCFW, which proposed a generous phased retirement program as a two-part 'partial retirement and retirement/recall'. This plan was designed to permit paid work during part of the year and continued retirement service accrual and partial retirement – to reduce normal duties and receive retirement benefits for the balance of the year. It would also provide guaranteed recall for up to five years after full retirement for combinations of teaching, research and/or professional and community service. UCFW suggested the possibility that the phased retirees might do their teaching during the summer term since encouraging regular faculty to teach during the summer school program was a university goal. UCFW modeled its proposal after a Faculty Early Retirement Program (FERP) at the California State University (CSU) system. The CSU FERP is open to any faculty choosing it, and has proven to be a very popular transition between full-time work and full-time retirement at CSU campuses.

The UC provosts had several concerns. Although many retirees remain active scholars, only a few do their research on pay status and then, only if an extramural grant supports the salary. The provosts did not want to pay retirees from university funds for research, but rather only for teaching and occasionally for a special service assignment. The provosts did not know if they could predict which faculty might be interested in phased retirement. In addition, salaries proposed by UCFW would be higher than campuses were paying to most retired faculty who were recalled to teach. Also, campus provosts saw no need for a 'program.' Individuals could phase down by working part-time and then retiring or by retiring and then being recalled. Space for office/labs was also not addressed in the UCFW proposal, and office and research space for retirees is always a problem.

The UCFW marketed their plan as one that would encourage faculty to 'remain at UC rather than retire and move to other institutions where they could pursue their research and teaching interests while drawing UC retirement benefits.' However, there was no evidence that such behavior was occurring. The UCFW plan was not well received by campus provosts. How could they establish any program that would encourage faculty retirements at a time when campuses had high recruitment goals and needed instead to increase faculty ranks? During verip, some older faculty declined to retire under very generous incentive programs. It became clear that some faculty don't want to retire under almost any circumstances. They do not work solely to maximize their income. Otherwise, the university would experience an exodus of faculty when they reach age 60, which provides the maximum age factor in the pension formula. Therefore, the campus provosts were doubtful that any incentive program was needed to keep most faculty from retiring and leaving. There was no evidence of a high attrition rate for retirements or other separations.

A major concern with developing any phased program was in-service distribution – paying out retirement income while still employed. For faculty below the normal retirement age, which was defined as age 70, making post-retirement arrangements before actual retirement is seen as continuing to work – hence in-service distribution concerns. University officials realized that the retirement plan design could redefine the normal retirement age from 70 to 60 with five years of service with no fiscal or accounting consequences. This would allow post retirement work arrangements to be made *before* retirement for faculty and staff at age 60 or greater with five or more years of service. This change was made in the summer of 2003 to allow for the development of a phased retirement plan and also to permit individual arrangements for recall following a retirement. Campus provosts liked this change, but were unprepared for its sudden announcement and were concerned about an onslaught of requests to make recall arrangements in exchange for retirement, although that did not actually happen.

As a response to the UCFW phased retirement proposal, Office of the President staff then prepared their own model phased plan. There were several reasons for doing so. Since many other universities have some phased program, UC could view a phased retirement program as another benefit it could provide to faculty (see Chapter 11). Phased retirement also provides a transition for senior faculty from full- to part-time work and then to full retirement. Based on experiences elsewhere, these plans do not appear to have a major impact on individuals' decision to retire much earlier than they would otherwise do so. This program was designed for faculty aged 60 or more with five or more years of service. Each phased arrangement would be designed individually, approved by mutual agreement and would include immediate retirement, recall arrangements of 25 per cent to 50 per cent time for up to three years with duties, pay and space all negotiated. Individuals would receive their full pension plus a recall salary. At the end of the phased period, the pension would be recalculated to add the extra 1.5 years (three years of recall at 50 per cent time) additional service credit. This would be a trial program for five to eight years, which could be extended, modified or discontinued.

Benefits office staff worked hard to figure out how to implement this program including addressing whether phased retirees would receive retiree or employee benefits and how to recalculate retirement benefits at the end. They considered whether staff would be included or only faculty should be eligible. These and many other technical problems were identified. The proposal was not well received by either the provosts or the UCFW.

The Office of the President staff made a pitch to the campus provosts arguing that (1) a phased retirement program had been in place in the 1980s which was not widely used, so that a new plan may not encourage many early retirements; (2) many other universities had phased retirement programs; (3) phased retirement could be considered a benefit for senior faculty who otherwise might not know how to transition from full-time work to full-time retirement; (4) a phased retirement plan would be responsive to faculty's interest and allow for a cadre of experienced part-time teachers. Approval would be for each individual, and campuses could establish criteria or set quotas. However, the campus provosts had many concerns about this program, including the possibility of facing grievances if they said yes to some phased arrangements and no to others. In the end, they rejected this plan entirely.

During this period, the financial picture for the University of California experienced a rapid change. In the early part of this story, starting fall of 2000, state budgets were robust and enrollment growth and faculty growth were rapid. By the fall of 2003 it was clear that the budget situation had changed completely and that the university was facing major cuts in state appropriations. Campuses started to slow faculty hiring and undergraduate admissions, closing major programs in outreach, and making other cuts.

Faculty as a whole were growing older, with an average age greater than the average age was before the first verip in 1991. Some campuses became interested in encouraging retirement of older, more expensive faculty and encouraging hiring of assistant professors to replace them. The Berkeley campus developed a modest retirement incentive plan for faculty to foster this.

The UCFW remained very interested in the phased retirement proposal but also did not like the latest proposal presented by the Office of the President staff. UCFW wanted another round of discussions to develop a program that would be open to any eligible faculty member with up to five years recall following retirement, where the recall salary was proportionate to per cent time of recall set at the Professor's salary rate at the time of retirement, and with the possibility of additional merit increases following retirement. The campus provosts were clearly not interested in adopting these provisions. UCFW then modified its proposal to make it appear less generous, so as not to encourage too many retirements by modifying the recall salary for teaching only to use a lecturer workload calculation with no office/lab space guarantee, and a five-year recall maximum.

The campus provosts still did not like it. They countered with a three-year maximum period of recall which could be further extended, truncating the recall pay for teaching only at $10 000 per course for quarter system for highly paid faculty who had retired, mutual agreement by the faculty member and the campus administration to participate rather than having the program open to anyone who applied, plus immediate retirement followed by a 90-day period of retirement before the recall appointment started.

The UCFW was disappointed with the provosts' salary offer. Some faculty threatened 'union style' activity to tell colleagues not to agree to a recall appointment at such a cheap rate. However, UCFW really liked the three-year guaranteed recall. Under current policy, recalls of retired faculty may be for only one year at a time so that a three-year program was seen as a major concession. The proposal also changed at this point from being a 'phased retirement program', although it has many of the same features, and became instead 'Guidelines for Recall for Teaching' for faculty who were retiring.

The campus provosts seemed willing to compromise and the UCFW did as well. Campus provosts did increase the highest salary for teaching in retirement to $12 000 per quarter or $18 000 per semester. The provosts, however, still wanted to preserve the right to set recall salaries at rates higher or lower than those suggested in the proposal when circumstances warranted (such as for teaching a freshman seminar with only one unit of credit).

At this same time, the University President announced that there would be no new verip for at least another three years and that there were no plans for one after that. Campuses anticipated that some faculty had delayed retirement on rumors that the University would deal with the difficult budget cuts by instituting another verip as it did in the 1990s. This new announcement may result in more retirements in 2004 and a 'pent up' interest in recall arrangements when the 'Guidelines for Recall for Teaching' are adopted.

In anticipation of final agreement with the faculty Senate, campuses were urged to prepare for requests to retire under this new policy by developing guidelines for implementation. Campus guidelines could address whether to institute a departmental quota, clarify who has authority to approve these arrangements, and set guidelines on how to handle salary, space, and teaching assignments.

Final approval has now been given by both the UCFW and the provosts, and the new guidelines should be issued in the summer of 2004. The new guidelines may pressure campuses to make more deals for recall following retirement than they do now; it may pressure some departments to pay more than they do now; and it may encourage a few more retirements than normal. Given the current budget climate in California, that may be welcome.

REFERENCE

Switkes, Ellen (2000), 'The University of California Voluntary Early Retirement Incentive Programs' in Robert L. Clark and P. Brett Hammond (eds), *To Retire or Not? Retirement Policy and Practice in Higher Education*, Philadelphia: University of Pennsylvania Press, pp. 106–21.

13. The costs and benefits of early retirement plans

John B. Shoven

13.1 INTRODUCTION

Mandatory retirement had certain advantages for higher education. It facilitated planning for faculty renewal, it avoided delicate issues of competency and, for many faculty, it provided an automatic answer to a difficult question – namely when to retire. Many colleges and universities believe that fresh ideas often result from new appointments of young faculty, and that the number of slots available for such new hires would be seriously curtailed if senior faculty remain on the job far longer than before the elimination of mandatory retirement. For these and other reasons, many colleges instituted early retirement incentives following the lifting of mandatory retirement in 1994. The purpose of this chapter is to describe the features of those plans and to assess the costs and benefits that they offer. While the plans will be described generally, I will outline the Stanford plan in some detail as it is the one that I know best.

13.2 DESIGN FEATURES

I am going to describe early retirement plans that can be used in an environment of defined contribution pension plans. Defined benefit (DB) plans, such as those at many state universities, have their own set of issues. Quite typically, DB plans offer a pension benefit at age 65 depending on final salary and years of service. Early retirement incentives are easy to incorporate into such plans, both permanent and temporary ones. The DB formula can simply be adjusted, for instance by giving qualified participants a few extra years credit in their years of service, or initiating full payments before age 65. Essentially, the retirement benefit formula can be either temporarily or permanently changed in such a way as to encourage retirement of those in particular age or seniority categories. In the defined contribution (DC) world, there is no formula to alter. Without introducing some early retirement incentive, the additional contributions that accompany additional work in DC plans implies that such plans encourage additional tenure. In fact, delaying retirement increases the expected monthly retirement benefit for two reasons. Delayed retirement means higher investment accumulations and it also means a larger monthly annuity payout due to the shorter life expectancy of late retirees. Many colleges and universities have responded to these features of DC plans by introducing supplemental early retirement incentives. In the DC world, almost all early retirement programs take the form of a one-time cash payment if retirement is chosen by a faculty member with sufficient seniority and within a particular age range.

There are a number of things to consider in designing such an early retirement system. How large should the payment be? For instance, should it be sufficient to materially supplement the retirement resources of the faculty member, or should it simply be enough to cause the individual to review his or her retirement plans? What should the initial age of eligibility be, with what minimum level of years of service? For instance, Stanford decided that the minimum age of eligibility for its plan should be 60 with 15 years of service. The Stanford administration was worried that it might lose some of its most productive scholars if the age of eligibility were any younger. This does raise a point that needs to be emphasized. These early retirement plans are not really retirement plans at all. They are simply incentives to leave the current employer. Nothing prevents someone from taking an early retirement incentive and moving to a different college or university or starting a new, separate, career. The one thing that most universities fear is that this type of plan might cause some of the best faculty to leave.

Another dimension of choice is whether the early retirement incentive should be continuing or temporary. A temporary or 'window' plan might be chosen if the college or university thinks of it as a way to deal with a particular budget crisis. For instance, senior faculty might be eligible for the bonus cash payment if they retired within a 24-month window. On the other hand, a continuing plan might be more appropriate if the university felt that there was a continuing need for senior faculty of a particular age range to consider retirement to open slots for junior hiring.

One feature of early retirement incentives in the higher education institutions with defined contribution pension plans is that the real inducement to retire does not come from eligibility for a bonus, but from the phase-out of eligibility at more advanced ages. For instance, say that a plan has a cash bonus attached to it of $100 000. There is no real retirement incentive to retire or leave if the faculty member is eligible for the $100 000 this year, but would also be eligible for it next year and the year after that.

The real retirement incentive comes from the phase out of eligibility. For instance, if delaying retirement by a year causes the cash payout to shrink to $50 000 and a two-year delay eliminates the cash entirely, then for each year of additional work the faculty member is foregoing $50 000 in potential early retirement bonuses. It is this take away that may cause someone to retire sooner than they would otherwise. In the Stanford plan, which I will describe in detail, the take away does not begin until age 67.

The tax treatment of the bonus money may affect the design of the plan. In general the bonus money is fully taxable as ordinary income. If the money is paid out as a life annuity, the present value of the annuity may be taxable when it is granted. The tax considerations are complicated and changing, so I only alert the reader that they may be a design issue.

Two issues that are important to many senior faculty are whether they can be 'called back' to part-time service after they have retired, and whether they are allowed to keep their office. The one thing that is necessary in all plans that I know of is that the faculty who participate give up their tenure in order to receive the payment. In fact, you can consider the whole trans-action as a payment by the college or university to buy out the tenure of the faculty member. Once a faculty member has given up tenure, she or he is free to negotiate a term appointment with the institution. At Stanford, it is quite common to work half-time for three years after having taken early retirement. Typically, the people in the 'call back' status are not voting members of their departments. Similarly, they are usually not given key administrative assignments in the department. The office space issue is part of a broader issue of the attractiveness of the status of emeritus professors. One has to assume that current faculty are knowledgeable about how current retirees are treated. Retirement is a much more attractive choice if retired professors are invited to seminars, consulted for advice, asked to teach on occasion and treated like valuable members of the academic com-munity. My observation is that retired faculty do not want to be housed in a separate building for retired faculty; rather, they want to remain attached to their disciplinary department.

The need for early retirement programs may have increased with the rela-tively recent removal of the Social Security earnings test after the normal retirement age. The normal retirement age will soon be 66. After that age, faculty can begin to collect Social Security without retiring. Their earnings as a faculty member do not cause a reduction in their monthly Social Security check. This is a relatively recent change in the Social Security rules. It is as if Social Security has also removed mandatory retirement after the age of normal retirement. While there is an advantage to participants in separating the liquidation of pension assets from retirement itself, it does make institutional planning considerably more difficult.

13.3   POTENTIAL BENEFITS OF EARLY RETIREMENT PLANS

There are a number of potential benefits of early retirement plans for both the eligible faculty and their institutions. One benefit stems from my observation that most faculty – like most Americans – are not very financially sophisticated. They may not know whether they can afford to retire or not; after all, they usually have had no practice at decisions of this sort. The eligibility for a significant cash bonus or, even more, the possible reduction of a potential cash bonus if they work beyond particular ages may stimulate an assessment of the household's finances. Stanford's plan encourages this effect by its willingness to pay a limited sum for a professional financial advisor. My own guess is that many faculty are in better financial shape (in terms of being able to finance retirement) than they may have realized. Certainly, encouraging the collection and assessment of personal financial information is in the interest of the faculty members. The employing college or university may benefit as well. Quite frequently faculty voluntarily convey their retirement plans to the department or university after they have completed such a financial check-up. Simply knowing the plans and expectations of the faculty members helps the institution in its own hiring programs.

In many cases, the biggest benefit to the college or university is the potential for intellectual rejuvenation that comes with the hiring of additional young faculty. While some academics do their best work at advanced ages, it is not the usual pattern. Real breakthroughs are frequently made by those in the first stages of their academic careers.

A related and often important benefit of early retirement programs is the potential to lower the ongoing salary expenses of the institution. Quite typically, entering junior faculty earn about half as much as veteran senior faculty in the same field. If the institution strictly replaces retiring senior faculty with junior faculty, they can reduce total salary significantly. In fact, in some cases, the salary reductions along with the inherent delays in completing the replacement hiring can more than offset the cost of the bonuses, leaving the total budget of the institution in better shape. Even if the salary reductions just match the cost of the bonuses, the whole program seems to be a winner. In that case, the senior faculty are offered a valuable option at zero net cost to the institution. Remember, these early retirement programs are options. No one is forced to participate. At least at the straightforward level, having this additional option unambiguously benefits the senior faculty. The appeal of these programs is that if they can be designed properly, they have the potential to invigorate the academic environment, introduce a valuable benefit for the senior faculty, all at no cost and perhaps even a budget reduction for the employing institution.

13.4 POTENTIAL DRAWBACKS OF EARLY RETIREMENT PLANS

Some of the potential drawbacks of early retirement plans for faculty members have already been alluded to. First, there is the problem of adverse selection regarding which faculty members utilize the plan. The best faculty presumably would have the easiest time finding employment at other universities. What was intended as an early retirement incentive can become an incentive for the best faculty to leave. These talented and active faculty members can pick up the bonus and continue their career at a competing institution. The incentive for the least productive faculty to participate is lower because they have much more limited reemployment possibilities. Those whose productivity has tailed off really would have to retire. Stanford partially addressed this problem by setting the youngest age of eligibility at 60 whereas some early retirement plans at other institutions (and outside academe) allow participation as early as age 55. Second, Stanford doesn't begin to lower the cash bonus until age 67. Age limits don't solve the adverse selection problem, but it has been our experience that they mitigate it.

A second drawback from the employer's point of view is simply the cost of the bonuses themselves. In order to trigger the type of lifetime financial planning that I have described, or in order to actually have the potential of affecting the affordability of retirement, the bonuses must be significant. While many programs may be less generous, Stanford sets its early cash retirement cash bonus at twice the annual salary of the senior faculty member. This certainly is enough to cause faculty to consider whether they should take it or leave it. In some cases, it may be enough to top off pension accumulations and cause retirement to be affordable at a younger age.

A third drawback is that the institutions may lose the ability to influence the retirement choices of their most elderly faculty. Since the whole plan is designed to encourage faculty turnover, this drawback is slightly ironic. The power of the cash bonus plans is in withdrawing them if you work beyond particular ages. In the Stanford plan, the cash bonus drops from two years' salary for those retiring between 60 and 66, to one times salary for those retiring at 67, 68 or 69, to no bonus for those retiring at 70 and beyond. The withdrawal of the bonus provides the incentive to retire. If the institution routinely provided cash bonuses for faculty at ages 70, 71, and 72, for instance, it would completely undermine the program. Suddenly, those who are considering retirement at age 69 would realize that they don't really lose a cash bonus of one times salary – if they don't retire they will simply pick up one of the deals being offered those in their early 70s. To make the plan effective, you have to refrain from offering extra retirement incentives for those too old to participate. If on the other hand, the institution made sure that those in their 70s kept full teaching, research and administrative duties, it might further encourage retirement. In this regard, Stanford usually refuses to allow faculty to move from full-time to half-time, without first retiring and giving up tenure. Half-time jobs are possible, but not with tenure.

13.5   THE STANFORD PLAN

The Stanford Plan has been described piece by piece in the previous sections. Here I will describe it in its entirety, but in a concise manner. It does have the beauty of being very simple. It was first introduced in 1994. Between 1994 and 2002 there were five possible bonus levels. In order to participate, you had to have 15 years of service. The schedule of one-time payments is shown in Table 13.1.

Table 13.1   Schedule of one-time payments

Age on date of retirement	Salary multiple
60–65	2.0
66	1.8
67	1.5
68	1.1
69	0.6

Since 2003, the program has been simplified so that there are only two possible bonus multiples. One reason for the change was to make the take-away more discrete to cause people to consider their optimal retirement plans. The current plan has the following schedule of salary multiples:

Age on date of retirement	Salary multiple
60–66	2.0
67–69	1.0

That's it. As I said, it is a very simple program. As part of the assessment that led to the 2003 simplification, the retirement pattern of Stanford faculty under the 1994–2002 plan was examined. It is difficult to know what the retirement experience would have been in the absence of an early retirement program. However, the number of retirements by age had a noticeable peak at age 65, just as the bonuses began to be reduced. There was no peak at 62, the age of eligibility for Social Security, as there would be for employees in the overall economy. The age distribution of retirements under the Faculty Retirement Incentive Program (FRIP) is shown in Figure 13.1.

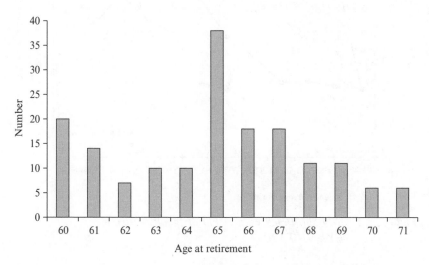

Figure 13.1   FRIP participant age distribution, FY1994–FY2002

The statistics are not sufficient to know for certain yet, but the general consensus at Stanford is that the program has influenced retirement behavior in a way that is beneficial to the institution. The retirement behavior at Stanford has changed less since the lifting of mandatory retirement than at other private research universities and FRIP is given considerable credit for that.

Another matter that came up during the 2002 review of the plan is the influence of the stock market's performance on faculty retirements. This is another issue on which there is limited statistical evidence, but what evidence there is indicates that some retirements were accelerated by the very strong stock market returns in the late 1990s, and that some are now being postponed by the decrease is asset values. In Figure 13.2, we plotted the percentage of the faculty retiring and the level of the S&P500 stock index. The retirement percentage peaks one year after the stock market peak, suggesting the link between the two. Many people lost more in the market in their pension accumulations than the bonus cash in the early retirement plan.

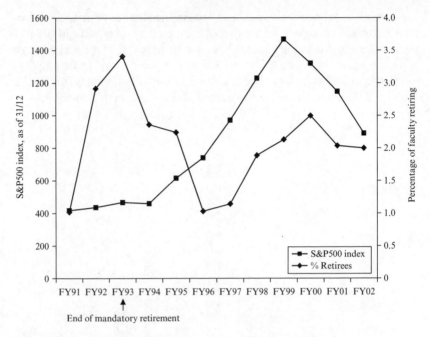

*Figure 13.2   S&P500 Index vs. per cent of faculty retiring,
FY1991–FY2002*

This simply illustrates the limitations of bonuses, even ones that are as large as in the Stanford plan.

13.6.   CONCLUSIONS

The statistical evidence is far from ideal, but it appears that early retirement programs can be designed that are in the interest of both the faculty and the employing colleges and universities. This chapter has reviewed some of the important design considerations and has described Stanford's plan in some detail. Stanford feels that its plan has served it well, that it has permitted more hiring of young faculty, has provided a valuable benefit for long-term senior faculty, and has proven cost-effective. The most compelling evidence of this is that when the plan was reviewed and modified after eight years of experience, it was left almost completely intact. Hopefully, this experience at Stanford will be useful for the rest of academe.

14. Recruitment, retention and retirement: institutional research and the need for data

Michael A. Baer, Deborah A. Freund, Charlotte V. Kuh, David E. Shulenburger and Richard R. Spies

There is a long-standing need for research to inform administrative or institutional policy decisions that too often tend to be based on assumptions or 'conventional wisdom' with little or no supporting data. As issues involving faculty recruitment, retention, and retirement become increasingly urgent, the advantages of having a repository of data on these matters based on shared institutional research are clear. To establish such a resource will require developing or inventing better ways to measure the effectiveness of faculty employment policies in light of immediate and long-term institutional goals.

While the need for this research is apparent, defining or identifying its exact nature presents a challenge. At this point in the history of higher education and the professoriate, it is difficult to know exactly what questions researchers should be posing.

That was not always the case. As recently as the late 1980s and early 1990s, the questions were more direct: what for instance should (or could) be done about the impending elimination of mandatory retirement for faculty? Indeed, with the growth in adjunct and part-time faculty, the definition of a faculty member has blurred. The issues have become more subtle and open-ended, and the possible solutions more complicated and less prescriptive.

The TIAA-CREF Institute conference on the Three Rs shed considerable light on these issues, while making apparent the extensive resources available through TIAA-CREF and its affiliates to develop programs based on gathering and sharing comparable data. Simply comparing data collected in similar ways across institutions would give participants great insights about their own faculties. The challenge here is to establish a framework that allows the sharing of data to take place.

14.1   THE STARTING POINT: FACULTY DEMOGRAPHICS

If there is a constant in the evolution of these questions, it is the need to accurately chart (or at least take snapshots of) ever-changing faculty demographics. The process might begin by asking baseline questions to determine the current age distribution of the faculty, how that distribution has changed over the past decade, and how it is likely to change over the next. Investigation at this level would help identify the policies available to institutional leaders to influence those changes, and provide a valuable context for a discussion and some decisions about which changes would be most desirable.

14.2   INSTITUTIONAL RESPONSES

The value of this kind of information is apparent. It would provide a broader, clearer understanding of how faculty demographics influence an institution's ability to meet such goals as education, scholarship, and service. Specific research agenda items might include understanding how the demographic makeup of the faculty affects an institution's ability to realize its goals in these areas. How, for instance, can the mix of faculty best be structured to provide students with a quality education while carrying out research that meaningfully contributes to the advancement of society? Or, in teaching, is it really true that having more adjunct faculty and fewer tenured and tenure-track professors in the classroom results in a diminished educational experience for students? Is there a desirable level of turnover of faculty that will bring in 'new blood' without raising concerns about employment security?

Take, for example, the relationship between age and scholarly productivity, a relationship that is complex and undoubtedly varies by field. Very little is known about how faculty age structure relates to student learning. In the popular mind, an aging faculty is associated with dated knowledge and yellowed notes; however, senior faculty may be highly skilled in teaching, a craft that is learned through practice.

This is not simply about bodies; it is also about the quality of scholarship. For example, research about the relationship between reputational measures of quality (such as the NRC rankings), quantitative measures of productivity (such as citations), and faculty age may help to determine whether age diversity within the faculty does, in fact, improve the learning process for students. To gain a true understanding of this relationship would require data on faculty demography, the changing structure of the academic workforce, and measures of learning.

Other research topics include how an institution might structure fringe benefits (e.g., health insurance, pension contributions, and housing options) or even non-pecuniary factors in response to faculty demographics, in order to increase an institution's ability to attract desirable faculty on the one hand, and influence an individual faculty member's decision as to when to retire on the other. In addition, academic institutional leaders need a clearer understanding of the mechanics for firing faculty, or 'counseling them out.'

Another item for this hypothetical research agenda would be to investigate the division of labor within the academy. At many of today's colleges and universities, full-time staff fill essentially all administrative roles, including all the non-academic – and much of the academic – advising of students. Post-doctoral students and professional research staff increasingly are the front-line researchers who fulfill an institution's obligations under sponsored research grants and contracts and on whom the expansion of knowledge depends. Much of the teaching of undergraduates now falls to graduate students and adjunct faculty. Researchers should ask whether there are different ways to divide up that work that might serve better the needs of both the 'consumers' of those services – primarily students – and the 'producers' – i.e., faculty at different stages in their academic careers?

14.3 INTERACTION OF RECRUITMENT, RETENTION AND RETIREMENT

The Three Rs do not exist independent of one another. For example, if a university intends to keep its workforce at a constant size, higher retirement rates would make it possible to recruit more faculty. On the other hand, if a university wishes to increase recruitment but has no vacancies from retirement, then untenured faculty turnover rates will have to be increased. However, if the university feels that high rates of untenured turnover hurt morale, it will have to consider enhancing retirement inducements so that newer faculty members can be retained. One way to influence the balance of these variables is through the use of adjunct and part-time faculty. But research using data that are comparable across institutions might uncover other methods, other incentives or disincentives for institutions to consider.

14.4 FUNDING AS A BASIS FOR RECRUITMENT AND RETENTION DECISIONS

Administrators are often 'faith-based' when it comes to making decisions about faculty employment: given the ability to express their own preferences, provosts at AAU-level institutions clearly would prefer to employ as high a proportion of tenure-track faculty as permitted by the budget. Provosts believe that such faculty members produce the best outcomes in student learning and are more likely to produce important research findings.

Unfortunately, provosts are constrained by the belief systems of regents, legislators, and trustees who tend to hold a different faith. These institutional overseers increasingly appear to favor the reduced costs associated with producing research and student credit hours with temporary personnel. Administrators need sophisticated research that explores the types of personnel employed, relating that information to outcomes in the classroom. Such data would help determine whether the least costly method of producing a credit hour is also the most effective. In the absence of such research, university decision makers will face pressures to produce credit hours with lower-cost personnel. Unfortunately, unlike the private sector's profit measure, higher education does not produce outcome measures that are as easily understood. Identifying outcome measures that are themselves persuasive and understood by policy-makers should also be a research focus.

The decision to hire tenure-track faculty versus temporary faculty is influenced not only by the relative costs but also by the type of funds available to hire faculty. A tenure-track appointment might well be a 40-year commitment. One does not enter into such a commitment unless there is a reasonably predictable source for funding the position in the long term.

The four principal types of funds generally available for hiring instructional personnel are state appropriations, endowment receipts and earnings, tuition, and external grants. The last few years have demonstrated that state appropriations, long felt by public universities to be the most stable source of funding and hence the most appropriate funding base against which to hire tenure-track faculty, are indeed quite volatile. Reductions of up to one-third have been common in recent years.

Endowment earnings and receipts have also been found to be highly erratic. The 'miracle market' of the 1990s gave way to the bear market of 2001–03. Sustained very low interest earnings further confounded the predictability and stability of returns.

The instability of the first two sources of earnings led both public and private universities to increase tuition charges dramatically beginning about the year 2000. Revenue from tuition is uncertain, however, as many state governments have directly limited the amount that tuition can be increased, and the Federal government has threatened to do the same. Demographic projections have raised concerns about the number of future, qualified students able to pay higher tuition charges. Thus, the predictability of tuition receipts in the long run is in question.

Finally, the last five years have seen National Institutes of Health appropriations double, and Congress has committed to doubling National Science Foundation appropriations in the next five years. This huge infusion of research funds has increased the probability that faculty in the sciences can be at least partially supported from grant funds. However, the burgeoning federal deficit and war expenditures have caused many to wonder how predictable federal support for research funding will be in the future.

Future research agendas should examine how variation in the proportion of federal funds in recent years has affected decisions to hire various types of instructional professionals (including a cross-sectional study). One would expect such research to explain how any policy decision to increase or decrease one of the four types of funding (state appropriations, endowment receipts and earnings, tuition and external grants) affect demand for tenure-track faculty and lecturers. Research that examines how fluctuation in the equity and capital markets affects the demand for faculty would be of great value and add to the existing knowledge base.

14.5   CHARACTERISTICS OF THE DATA USERS

The data collected will be used by a wide variety of end users. For example, economists, demographers, and policy analysts focus on questions of overall faculty supply and demand; thus, their analysis tends to the macroscopic, looking at faculty as a single, large entity without the detail that would permit analysis at the institutional level. These researchers are concerned with age-specific data about new hires, retirement rates, and the rates at which mid-career academics are leaving the academy.

By contrast, high-level university administrators (deans and provosts) need data specific to their institutions, including such details as the faculty age structure and the age at which faculty members typically retire. Beyond the demographics, administrators need to know the cost of retirement to their university in terms of health care coverage and other 'perks' offered as retirement incentives. These costs must then be weighed against the savings in wages and benefits that accrue from hiring less experienced junior faculty.

Department chairs must contend with a set of issues perhaps even more complex than those facing deans and provosts. Responsible for determining the 'output' for their departments – that is, the course loads, course coverage, research quality and so on – they must make these decisions in light of the university's retirement policies, knowing full well that each faculty member is weighing workload against retirement incentives. Non-pecuniary factors such as course assignments can be used quite effectively to encourage faculty to stay or to retire.

Individual faculty members ultimately make decisions about retirement. They rarely act on impulse, and the bases for their decisions are often not financial. To make informed decisions, prospective retirees need to know the financial dimensions of retirement, as well as the kinds of non-pecuniary arrangements (teaching, office and library privileges and so on) that will be available after retirement. Many faculty members are unwilling to simply abandon the work they have done for the previous 30 years or more, and such non-financial arrangements may be almost as important as the financial. Institutions need to understand those non-pecuniary incentives and to shape them according to their workforce needs.

14.6   STANDARDIZING MEASURES AND SHARING DATA

No single institution could possibly get a handle on the education marketplace using solely its own internal resources. Data availability and the role of institutional research vary greatly from school to school. For those reasons, the sharing of data among institutions is essential to developing a serviceable understanding of the greater marketplace, which ultimately will result in better recruitment, retirement and retention programs and policies.

Before this can happen, the research community must define common standards and measures, and be willing to share these findings. Bruce Johnstone, former chancellor of the State University of New York (SUNY) system, noted the need for this kind of collaboration by outlining the disconnect between scholars of higher education and policy-makers. While academic research by its very nature is detailed and nuanced, research prepared for presentation by and for policy-makers and senior institutional leadership must be simple and unambiguous, should include policy recommendations, and must list potential consequences.

Johnstone observed that, from the perspective of higher education, institutional or governmental policy-makers, the academic researchers were not asking – and certainly not answering – the questions they, the policy-makers, were asking. On the other hand, the administrators – the college and university decision makers – are less concerned with the long-term policy implications of complicated issues, and instead are looking for quick answers to support immediate decisions. The point here is that policy and decision makers at different levels throughout higher education require different kinds of information.

Recognizing this situation, the American Council on Education (ACE) recently convened a group of foundation leaders, higher education scholars and university presidents to identify key issues that were of common interest to all three groups. One of the more surprising discoveries of the conference was that the university presidents were unaware of much of the research that was available, or they found that the available information existed in formats they could not use.

In response, ACE implemented a publication series called 'informed practice' to provide a digest of research on a number of issues of common interest for different groups of senior administrators and researchers. Subjects covered to date include access and persistence, diversification of campus revenue streams, and high school-to-college transitions. The ACE approach might be a model for future Three Rs research. Ideally, this research will be presented in a way that relates various models for faculty recruitment, retention, and retirement to the cost of providing education, tuition prices, research productivity (for research institutions), and the quality of student learning.

14.7   ELICITING COOPERATION FROM RESEARCH FACULTY

At the same time, universities should consider looking internally for 'hidden' or underused research resources. Most modern universities have tremendous resources for both institutional and academic research. However, relations between institutional and academic researchers – that is, faculty members devoted to single-topic research – are not always harmonious. In order for a given institution to get the most out of its institutional and academic research resources, relationships that are both candid and reciprocal need to be fostered.

To begin to overcome this divide, faculty researchers who work on recruitment, retention and retirement projects must participate in the construction of the datasets that will be used in institutional research. At the same time, issues involving the security and confidentiality of sensitive, personnel-related data should be resolved to the satisfaction of the institutional researchers, eliminating a potentially show-stopping impediment to collaboration. Put another way, research faculty need to have access to institutional data; institutional researchers must be confident that their proprietary data and publication rights are secure.

14.8   A MODEL FOR COLLABORATIVE RESEARCH

Institutions by their very nature are tradition-bound, and often the rationale for continuing a given practice or policy is 'it's always been done that way'. Every university is unique. What works at one in terms of faculty recruitment, retention or retirement policy may not work at another. However, it is impossible to make comparative assessments without common data in these areas. Without such data, it is particularly difficult for an institution to redefine personnel or benefit policies that allow it to efficiently recruit or retain faculty, or determine how retirement incentives should be structured.

The problem with basing these decisions on internal institutional research alone is that generalizations are not possible: You can't explore a 'what if' when the new policy you're exploring is radically different from what you're doing now.

To address this need will require a national database on recruitment, retention and retirement. The database would draw on data from individual colleges and universities and link them to policies at many different institutions. Information from this database would provide the broad range and variety of data necessary to allow policy-makers and administrators to examine how changing benefit X will impact outcome Y – based on data that otherwise would be unavailable. Establishing a central repository of information about the Three Rs that contains data contributed by many universities is key to making such a resource a reality.

Sharing institutional data and collaborating on methodologies and models can only enhance the value of research into the Three Rs. Such shared endeavors will permit institutions to compare data and results, which in turn will add greater depth and validity to institutional self-evaluations. All institutions are served by looking beyond their immediate campuses for answers to questions about the effectiveness of faculty and other institutional practices. To do that, decisions makers need new and more effective tools.

A few years ago, the National Association of College and University Business Officers (NACUBO) sponsored a study on college cost (which was also supported by the TIAA-CREF Institute). The purpose of this study was to develop a common methodology for calculating the actual cost of undergraduate education at different colleges and universities. While that project has not resulted in as much inter-institutional soul searching as originally expected, it has demonstrated the feasibility of institutional collaboration to produce standardized, comparable data. The NACUBO example at least demonstrates that individual institutions are likely to gain a better understanding of their own issues if their internal analysis is augmented with comparative data from a large sample of institutions.

ACKNOWLEDGEMENT

We thank Patrick Farrell and Esther Gray of the Office of Academic Affairs and Martha Bonney at the Center for Policy Research, at Syracuse University for helping to prepare this manuscript.

15. Developing new employment and compensation policies in higher education

Robert L. Clark and
Madeleine B. d'Ambrosio

American colleges and universities face a series of important challenges as they strive to remain the best in the world. We are all familiar with reductions in state appropriations, financial market fluctuations and their impact on institutional endowments and pension funds, and the limited growth in federal research funds. Academic administrators must seek to maintain high quality faculties in the face of rising salaries in non-academic employment and the escalating costs of health benefits for active and retired faculty. Changing faculty demographics also present institutions with new issues in the cost of retaining older professors, the flexibility to respond to changes in student preferences, research and teaching productivity, and the ability to hire and promote a more diverse workforce. The impact of these trends varies by academic discipline, implying that there may be a shortage of faculty in some areas while other disciplines may have an excess of potential faculty.

The chapters in this volume provide an in-depth assessment of the current state of the academic labor market and how it is evolving in response to the changing economic, demographic, and social environment. The rapid aging of university faculties is described for the academy at large and for specific institutions. Faculty aging, changes in mandatory retirement policies, and new retirement policies have fundamentally altered the ability of institutions to recruit, retain, and retire quality faculty. The implications of an aging professorate for institutions of higher education are examined in detail throughout the volume.

Our analysis indicates that in response to these demographic changes, universities are altering their employment and compensation policies. It is essential that presidents and chancellors, provosts and deans understand the response of faculty to these changes, recognize the effects on academic productivity, and assess the cost of alternative HR policies. It is important to remember that changes in compensation policies directly affect the well-being of faculty, and that consideration must be given to both the interests of the institution in providing high quality education and to the welfare of faculty. Reducing the value of a career in higher education will ultimately make recruiting and retaining faculty more difficult.

This volume addresses many of the key issues associated with recruiting, retaining, and retiring faculty as they were explored at Recruitment, Retention, and Retirement: the Three R's of Higher Education in the 21st Century, a national conference sponsored by the TIAA-CREF Institute. The objective of any institution is to provide the best possible teaching and research programs, given its mission and available resources. The preceding chapters shed new light on the impact of employment and compensation policies in higher education. In this final chapter, we summarize the primary contributions of the research and analysis and speculate on the need for new and innovative compensation policies.

15.1   RECRUITMENT

A priority of any institution of higher education must be to recruit high quality faculty in order for the university to successfully fulfill its mission. While the emphasis institutions place on teaching and research varies, an appropriately qualified faculty is necessary for a university to remain competitive in the academic marketplace. Employment and compensation policies must be given higher priority as competitive compensation and working conditions are needed to attract a new generation of scholars. In the present economic environment, institutions must assess the various options of having sufficient instructors to staff needed classes for both undergraduates and graduates. In addition, universities must have the right mix of faculty to provide required service to the institution, and have faculty who are at the forefront of their disciplines who can demonstrate state of the art research to their students. The generation of new knowledge and the transfer of existing knowledge to students are at the heart of any college or university.

Two major changes are occurring in the employment decisions of institutions of higher education. The first is the increasing reliance on contract or fixed-term instructors and the second is the growing use of post-doctoral fellows in many areas of science and engineering. These trends are documented and statistical analysis is used to explain the causes of the decline in hiring of full-time, tenure-track faculty. Let us consider each of these changes.

The movement away from full-time, tenure-track faculty can be decomposed into two main components. First, there has been an increase in the proportion of full-time, non-tenure-track faculty to total full-time faculty. In private institutions, this ratio increased from 14.2 per cent in 1989 to 19.7 per cent in 1999. The shift to non-tenure-track faculty was somewhat smaller in public institutions where the increase during the same period was from 11.0 per cent to 13.7 per cent. Second, the ratio of part-time faculty to full-time faculty increased even more rapidly. Among private institutions, the proportion of faculty composed of part-time instructors increased from 49.9 per cent in 1989 to 68.6 per cent in 2001, while the ratio for public institutions rose from 26.9 per cent to 37.7 per cent.

What caused this sharp shift in the composition of faculties? Academic administrators have the option of filling vacant positions with part-time faculty, non-tenure-track faculty, or tenure-track faculty. The relative salary or cost of each of type of appointment can be determined and, hopefully, academic administrators can also measure any differences in the contributions to the teaching and research programs of the various types of new hires. Based on costs and productivity comparisons of different types of faculty, hiring decisions can be made.

Research indicates that a major reason for the increased use of non-tenure-track faculty is a decline in the relative salaries of non-tenure-track faculty compared to the compensation of tenure-track faculty. As non-tenure-track instructors have become relatively less expensive compared to standard tenure-track appointments, colleges and universities have decreased their reliance on tenure-track faculty. This shift may also be the result of budgetary pressures that emphasize teaching students today versus the longer-run contributions of research and service that tenure-track faculty can provide. While cost savings are apparent, the impact of this change in the mix of faculty on university productivity is less visible. New research is needed to determine whether students learn less, graduate more slowly, drop out more often, and become less interested in research as the proportion of tenure-track faculty erodes.

In summary, it is important to assess whether the greater use of part-time and contract instructors adversely affects the ability of the institution to fulfill its teaching and research missions. Some institutions are now beginning to adopt long-term employment policies that include the use of non-tenure-track faculty to provide a different mix of skills and experiences. These faculty, who are sometimes referred to as Professors of the Practice, often lack terminal degrees and are not interested in research; however, they are well versed in their discipline and have spent their careers addressing and solving more practical problems. They can provide a different type of enrichment for students. The use of fixed-term faculty also provides a greater degree of flexibility to institutions as they attempt to respond to changing student preferences and budgetary restrictions. Each institution must assess these benefits along with the cost advantages against the loss of research potential and dedication to the university that comes with the use of tenure-track faculty. The ability to attract well-qualified contract faculty is much easier for institutions in large urban areas, and the labor market for contract faculty also varies by academic discipline.

In science and engineering, more new PhDs are accepting post-doctoral positions instead of faculty positions. In addition, the length of post-doctoral appointments has been increasing. The average duration of a post-doctoral appointment increased from two years for PhDs awarded in 1965 to three years for PhDs awarded between 1982–92. The use of post-docs is concentrated in the disciplines of science and engineering. The concentration of post-doctoral appointments in these fields is closely tied to the need for large research teams and well-trained laboratory assistants to conduct leading edge research. These appointments are often financed by grants and contracts by the federal government and industry. Most of these grants are awarded to faculty at the nation's leading research institutions.

Most young scholars view post-doctoral positions as further investment in their human capital. These positions are accepted as a method of continuing the learning experience and enhancing the prospect of finding desirable employment in the future. Graduates from the very best universities spend several additional years learning their profession by working in the laboratories with nationally prominent scientists at other top research universities. In many cases, these transitional appointments have become part of the normal career paths.

Labor market conditions influence the supply of and demand for post-docs. When a greater number of individuals receive PhDs in a specific discipline, the supply of graduates seeking faculty positions rises. With the number of new faculty positions being relatively stable in many areas, more graduates means that many new PhDs will not immediately find faculty positions, and therefore will tend to accept post-doctoral positions that pay much lower salaries. Similarly, when research funds are cut, the demand for new faculty declines and more new PhDs accept post-doctoral appointments.

Labor market conditions and general economic conditions affect the employment policies of institutions and the employment prospects of new entrants into the academic labor market. In adverse economic times, colleges and universities must decide how to continue to provide teaching services with reduced budgets. Budgetary restrictions clearly influence employment choices. New graduates seeking employment ultimately must decide whether to remain in academe as contract employees, post-docs, or part-time instructors or choose some other career. Recent trends suggest that colleges and universities will have fewer full-time, tenure-track faculty in the future. The impact of a change in the composition of university faculties on educational quality remains to be seen. This volume indicates the need for new research on how these employment trends will affect the quality of higher education in the coming decade. Short-term budgetary problems must be addressed but we must understand the long-run implications of alternative employment policies.

15.2   RETENTION

Having recruited a high quality faculty, each college and university must attempt to retain these valuable employees. Competitive salaries and benefits are essential. Without competitive levels of compensation, some institutions will have their best faculty bid away by peer universities, while others will find their faculty leaving the academy entirely for more lucrative employment in other sectors of the economy. Molly Broad, President of the University of North Carolina, noted the difficulty of retaining high quality faculty at the University of North Carolina after three consecutive years without a salary increase. She also expressed the need to continue to offer competitive health benefits when these costs are rising more rapidly than inflation.

Understanding the preferences and attitudes of faculty is central to the adoption of appropriate employment and compensation policies to retain productive faculty. The TIAA-CREF Institute has funded several surveys in an effort to ascertain faculty preferences and attitudes toward compensation and employment policies of their universities. Faculty aged 50 and older at member institutions of the Associated New American Colleges, the University of North Carolina, and the University of Minnesota were asked about their work patterns, professional interests, institutional relationships, and compensation preferences. The faculty were interested in flexible workload policies and they were very concerned about health insurance while working. In addition, they worried about the ability to maintain university-provided health insurance if and when they leave the university. The surveys indicated that senior faculty in these institutions were 'hard-working, institutionally-motivated, and flexible'. Review of the responses illustrate that senior faculty provide universities with a resource 'that institutions could benefit from taking advantage of faculty interests in new roles and their seeming willingness to cooperate in retirement transitions beneficial both to institutions and to faculty members'.

Surveys combined with other areas of institutional research could provide the basis for developing future compensation and employment policies. It is important that organizations provide their employees with the most value for each dollar of compensation. With faculties continuing to age, understanding the preferences of senior faculty for flexible assignments, phased retirement, and their willingness to continue to contribute to their university is very important. Knowledge of faculty preferences is important to those institutions seeking to facilitate the orderly retirement of senior faculty, and also to those colleges and universities that are anticipating increases in enrollments, and who would like to entice senior faculty to delay retirement to meet the growing student demands.

Changes in the economic environment and faculty aging are requiring institutions to reassess rigid employment rules to be more consistent with faculty preferences and to reevaluate employee benefits. Institutions must reform employment and compensation policies to meet new budgetary realities, but they must also continue to pay competitive salaries and benefits if they are to maintain the quality of their faculty. Chapters in this volume illustrate the importance of faculty participation in reviewing existing policies, determining the need to amend them, and developing new benefit plans. Financial pressure of rapidly escalating health care costs is requiring many institutions to reduce the generosity of their health plans and to shift more of the cost to faculty participants. Acceptance of these policy changes requires faculty buy-in, and the inclusion of faculty in the developmental phase of policy changes enhances the chances that such modifications will be accepted. Equally important is the introduction of new employment policies such as phased retirement and family benefits. Institutions should develop a process for faculty participation and policies should be based on faculty preferences as well as institutional needs.

Many colleges and universities have prominent faculty members who are experts on compensation policies, employment practices, and health and retirement benefits. Using these faculty as a resource can facilitate the adoption of optimal compensation packages for a changing workforce. Amending compensation policies to provide less generous benefits should be done carefully with substantial faculty input. The process will be smoother if it is transparent and the decisions are based on surveys of faculty preferences.

15.3   RETIREMENT

The aging of faculties is requiring colleges and universities to consider the cost and benefits of older faculty, the need for planned retirements to allow hiring of new faculty, and the need to have flexibility to meet student preferences. Retirement decisions are influenced by a variety of family, health, and economic considerations. University compensation and benefit policies significantly affect the value of remaining on the job and the ability to have an adequate standard of living in retirement. The differences between health insurance coverage for active and retired professors are a major consideration for many older faculty considering retirement. The value of their retirement accounts or annual annuities also directly affect faculty work and retirement choices. Understanding the incentives that are imbedded in these policies is essential if colleges and universities are to develop cost-effective retirement policies that enable institutions to achieve their HR objectives while providing faculty with the resources to enjoy retirement.

A key factor in retirement policies in the coming years is the trend toward greater use of defined contribution pension plans and a decline in the reliance on defined benefit plans. This trend is not as yet as pronounced in public institutions of higher education as it is in the general economy; however, defined contribution plans have long been the standard among private colleges and universities. When faculty are given a choice between plan types, as they are in many public institutions, they overwhelming select the defined contribution plans. While defined benefit plans have a number of very significant age-specific retirement incentives, defined contribution plans are more age-neutral in their retirement effects, and age-specific retirement rates are lower for faculty covered by defined contribution plans. Thus, in the future, many universities could face even lower retirement rates for faculty in their 60s. These pension effects are another reason why institutions must reconsider their retirement policies.

Two of the most significant policies that universities are now considering are amending or ending retiree health plans and the adoption of alternative transitions from work to retirement. Health insurance premiums that are rising at a rate more than twice the increase in consumer prices are forcing institutions to reevaluate their health plans for active and retired faculty. Universities concerned with employment costs and the age structure of their faculties are establishing phased retirement plans while others have adopted early retirement plans to increase retirement rates. Changes in health and retirement plans require academic administrators to consider the direct cost effects of amending these plans, the response of senior faculty to changes in employee benefits, and the productivity and cost effects of changes in faculty behavior.

15.4   RETIREE HEALTH INSURANCE

Institutions of higher education do not operate apart from national events. The soaring cost of health insurance is a national problem and will require national solutions. However, the rising cost of medical care has led employers throughout the economy to adopt policies aimed at reducing costs. These policies include cost shifting to employees in the form of higher premiums, larger deductibles, and higher co-payments. In addition, employers have begun adopting health saving accounts, dropping health insurance in some cases, and terminating retiree health insurance programs.

University faculties tend to be older than the labor force in general and the pace of aging has been faster in the educational sector of the economy. As a result, the cost pressures of health insurance for active workers and retirees has been greater. A national survey of colleges and universities shows that some institutions are now freezing their retiree health plans while others are reducing benefits or terminating them.

Reducing or eliminating retiree health plans may reduce employer health care expenditures but it can also result in professors remaining on the job until older ages. Each faculty member considering retirement must assess the value of staying employed versus the welfare they will have in retirement. Economic models predict, and available evidence indicates, that reductions in the retiree health plans will delay retirement for many older professors. This response will tend to exacerbate the aging of the faculty. Faculty surveys clearly indicate that retiree health plans are important employment benefits that help universities recruit, retain, and retire faculty. Institutions must consider the implications of reductions in, or the elimination of, retiree health plans.

15.5 PHASED RETIREMENT PLANS

Institutions concerned about an aging of their faculty have adopted new and innovative retirement plans. Phased retirement plans offer senior faculty the opportunity to move from a full-time appointment to a reduced workload. These plans may be cost-neutral or provide specific incentives to older faculty to relinquish tenure and accept a fixed-term appointment. Phased retirement plans can also be thought of as a new employee benefit that allows faculty to gradually retire instead of moving directly from full-time work to full-time retirement.

Phased retirement plans have spread rapidly among institutions of higher education. Surveys indicate that phased retirement has been extremely popular among faculty, and that many senior faculty are choosing phased retirement as their preferred method of ending their career. Several case studies have found that institutions adopt phased retirement plans to facilitate orderly retirement, to assist in faculty planning, and to provide a new benefit to loyal employees. Some administrators are not convinced that phased retirement plans are effective policies. Department chairs are often concerned about the loss of resources and their ability to manage phased retirees.

15.6   EARLY RETIREMENT PLANS

Many colleges and universities have adopted early retirement plans in an effort to reduce faculty size by enticing older faculty to retire, with the hope that this will reduce employment costs. While early retirement plans have been widely used, relative few universities have examined the cost-effectiveness of adopting these plans. A series of early retirement plans at the University of California produced large take-up rates that substantially reduced the number of senior faculty. Evidence suggests that large reductions in tenured faculty employment can be achieved by offering individuals inducements to retire, and that less productive faculty were more likely to accept these offers. Despite these findings, it is important that the costs and benefits of early retirement plans be determined before such plans are introduced.

Individual faculty members decide on the age at which they want to retire. For the faculty as a whole, age-specific retirement rates depend on the retirement policies of the institution. Universities seeking to increase retirement rates can adopt policies that raise the incentive to retire. However, institutions attempting to reduce employment costs by reducing or eliminating retiree health plans should expect that age-specific retirement rates will decline. It is important that administrators consider the direct and indirect effect of altering retirement policies.

15.7   DEVELOPING NEW COMPENSATION POLICIES

The chapters in this volume describe the serious challenges confronting academic institutions as they attempt to recruit, retain, and retire highly skilled faculty. The analysis presented in the preceding chapters identifies the difficulties that lie ahead and the factors that will influence future decisions by academic leaders. The chapters also show how changes in compensation and employment policies affect the well-being of faculty and their decisions to remain with an institution, leave for non-academic jobs, or retire. The chapters illustrate the importance of research in evaluating the current state of the academic labor market. The analysis also notes the importance of employment and compensation policies in achieving the desired faculty of the future.

This volume is based on the premise that institutions of higher education need high quality faculty to achieve their missions. The ability of universities to recruit and retain a new generation of outstanding faculty is threatened by adverse economic conditions, an aging faculty, and rapidly rising health care costs. As institutions seek to respond to their new environment, academic decision makers need to understand both the short and long-run implications of modifying their employment and compensation policies. Institutional research units should review and evaluate proposed policy changes and changes in human resource policies should be based on this research among other factors.

At the conference on which this volume is based, a panel of academic leaders led by Deborah Freund, Provost of Syracuse University, provided a clear call for more research that would be directly helpful to provosts, presidents, and chancellors. Institutional research can and should be done. Each campus can conduct its own research on its needs and requirements but there is also a need for research using data from many institutions. A plan for sharing of university data, agreements to conduct evaluations of new policies, and a willingness to share evaluation reports is needed to guide universities in the twenty-first century.

Colleges and universities are facing a changing academic labor market. It is one in which the professoriate is aging, retirement rates are low, health care costs are skyrocketing, competition for talent is intense, and revenue sources are shrinking. In this new environment, significant choices must be made concerning what types of faculty to hire, what levels of benefits and salary are needed to retain the best faculty, and how the retirement of older faculty can be made more predictable and consistent with university objectives. The conference sponsored by the TIAA-CREF Institute, and this volume, represent a significant step toward providing new and important information that is necessary for academic administrators to make these key decisions.

Index

academic institutions, financial
    pressures 135–7
academic job contract, life-cycle model
    see ARM
Academic Retirement Model see
    ARM
accounting standards
    and higher education sector 120–21
    and retiree benefits 116–20
administration, by senior faculty 83–4
adult education 24–5
adverse selection problem 225, 230–31,
    263
aging cross 4
aging of faculty 1–6, 26–7
agriculture post-docs 65, 68
Allen, Steven G. 13, 198, 203, 204, 219,
    234, 237, 243
ANAC see Associated New American
    Colleges
Anderson, Eugene L. 10, 16, 19, 32
Arellano, Manuel 40
ARM (Academic Retirement Model)
    advantages 139–40
    definition and assumptions 140–45
    uses 138–9
ARM health insurance change
    simulation
    base case 147–52
    case-0 153–5
    case-1 155–60
    case-2 160–64
    case-3 164
    case comparisons 164–7
    case definitions 153
    caveats 167
    data creation 145–7
Ashenfelter, Orley 6, 7, 11, 210, 237
Associated New American Colleges
    (ANAC), senior faculty 82–93
astronomy, PhD production 26
astronomy post-docs 65, 68

Atkins, G. Lawrence 115
Austin, Anne E. 97

baby boomer retirement 25, 131
Bains, Mandeep 115
Baldwin, Roger G. 32
basic retirement plans 10–12
benefits see health benefits
Benjamin, Ernst 18
Bergquist, William H. 81
Bettinger, Eric 49
biological sciences, PhD production 26
biological sciences post-docs 55–6, 65,
    68–9
Bland, Carole J. 81
Blodget, Henry 30
Bolge, Robert D. 49
Bond, Stephen 40
Brown, Charles 212, 222
buyout programs
    appeal for university 224, 226
    case study 224–32
    concerns over 225
    retirement incentives of 221–4

California State University (CSU) 254
Canadian faculty 4–5
Card, David 6, 7, 11, 210, 237
chemistry, PhD production 26
chemistry post-docs 65, 68–9
China, investment in education 27
Chronister, Jay L. 32, 235
citizenship, and post-doc position
    takeup 62
citizenship of potential faculty pool
    26–7
Clark, Robert L. 4, 5, 6, 7, 11, 12, 17,
    20, 210
compensation package design see
    ARM
computer sciences, PhD production 26
computer sciences post-docs 65, 68

Conley, Valerie Martin 32, 250
consumer driven health care plans,
    rejected at SU 174
contract faculty *see* non-tenure-track
    faculty
contribution caps *see* employer
    contribution caps
Cool, Kenneth E. 81, 91
cost reduction 10
cost-sharing of retiree health benefits
    119, 124–5, 165–6
Costello, Declan 115
CSU *see* California State University

DB plans *see* defined benefit (DB)
    plans
DC plans *see* defined contribution
    (DC) plans
declining enrollments 10
Deficit Reduction Act (1984) 117–18
defined benefit (DB) plans
    compared to DC plans 213
    defined 212
    and early retirement plans 259–60
    and private/public institutions 213
    and retirement decisions 10–12, 198,
        213
    trend away from 282
defined contribution (DC) plans
    and buyout programs 224
    compared to DB plans 213
    defined 212–13
    and phased retirement policies 192,
        220–21
    and private/public institutions
        213–14
    and retirement decisions 10–12, 187,
        213
    trend toward 282
    see also early retirement plans, in
        DC environments; notional
        defined contribution plans
DEFRA *see* Deficit Reduction Act
departmental impact, of phased
    retirement 244–5
dependents, number of, and post-doc
    position takeup 62
Dertouzos, J.N. 234
disclosure requirements *see* accounting
    standards

doctoral institutions
    and buyout programs 224
    early retirement plans 14–15
    expected preference for phased
        retirement 189–90
    and phased retirement policies 221
    see also research and doctoral
        institutions
Dopkeen, Jonathan C. 119
d'Ambrosio, Madeleine 12

early and mid-career faculty
    defined 95
    issues influencing retention 97
    research project on 93–8
early retirement plans 14–16, 284
    see also pre-65 retirees; retiring at 70,
        probability of
early retirement plans, in DC
    environments
    bonus size 263
    design features 259–61
    potential benefits 262–3
    potential drawbacks 263–4
earned doctorates, taking post-doc
    positions on graduation 56–67
earned doctorates, trends in 26–7
earth science and oceanography post-
    docs 65, 68
economic conditions, and retirement
    rates 11, 265–6
Ehrenberg, Ronald G. 11, 12, 13, 14,
    15, 16, 19, 48, 49, 191, 208, 213,
    214, 215, 217, 218, 219, 220, 223,
    234, 236
employer contribution caps 119, 124–6
employer-sponsored health insurance
    see health benefits
engineering, PhD production 26
engineering post-docs 55, 65, 68–9
enrollments and retirements 10
ERISA (Employee Retirement Income
    Security Act, 1974) 120
explicit retirement incentives 216–18

faculty
    compensation preferences 280
    composition changes 33–7
    employment levels *vs.* for-profit
        sector 128–9

proportion over 50 *vs.* industry
129–30
retirement patterns 240–41
Faculty Early Retirement Program
(FERP) 254
Faculty Family Leave Benefits policy
177–9
faculty-planning model 8–9
Faculty Retirement Incentive Program
(FRIP) *see* Stanford University
early retirement plan
family-friendly policies 177–9
family leave policy *see* Faculty Family
Leave Benefits policy
Farber, Henry S. 230
FASB (Financial Accounting
Standards Board) 116–20
FERP *see* Faculty Early Retirement
Program
Financial Accounting Standards
Board (FASB) 116–20
financial advice for faculty 262
Finegan, T. Aldrich 49
Fischer, Stanley 112
flexible health benefit plans 106
forecasting, severance behavior 227–30,
232
Freudenheim, M. 17, 143
FRIP (Faculty Retirement Incentive
Program) *see* Stanford University
early retirement plan
Fronstin, Paul 107
full-time faculty, and health insurance
16
future retirement plans 12, 14

gaining acceptance for policies 182–3
Garrison, Howard H. 77
GASB *see* Governmental Accounting
Standards Board
gender differences 83
generational turnover 80
Gerbi, Susan A. 77
Ghent, Linda S. 4, 5, 7, 11, 13, 198,
203, 208
Giroux, Robert 4, 5
global change 23–5
Governmental Accounting
Standards Board (GASB)
standards 120–21, 131

graying of America 25
GSS (Graduate Student Survey) *see*
Survey of Graduate Students and
Postdoctorates in Science and
Engineering

Hamermesh, Daniel S. 235
Hammond, Brett 19
Hansen, Lee 19
Harrington, Charles 49
HCAC *see* Health Care Advisory
Committee, Syracuse University
health benefit costs, and worker
productivity 112–15
health benefits
as part of compensation package
110–12
and post-doc positions 72
and senior faculty 90, 91
see also retiree health insurance
health care
costs 107–10
HR practices at SU 170–76
spending 107–8, 114–15
Health Care Advisory Committee,
Syracuse University (HCAC)
173–6
health insurance
and academic institutions 16–18
cost control 106–7
coverage of population 107–8
history of employers' role 105–7,
115–16
importance as retirement incentive
217
see also Medicare
health sciences, PhD production 26
HMOs (health maintenance
organizations) 103, 106–7
Holden, Karen 19

implicit retirement incentives 216
income levels for retirement 87–8
India, investment in education 27
inflation, of health care costs 109
institutions of higher learning
and accounting standards 120–21
market pressures *vs.* corporates 121
survey of benefits provided 122–4
Ireland, investment in education 27

job prospects, and post-doc positions
66

Karoly, L.A. 234
Kepple, Thomas R., Jr. 235
Kim, Seongsu 230, 236
Klaff , Daniel B. 48
Kotlikoff, Laurence 20

laboratory space for retired faculty
217–18, 242, 256
see also office space for retired
faculty
late-career faculty (age 50+)
benefiting institutions 98, 242–3, 243
demographic profile 82–3
as highly productive 91–2
motivators 86–7
plans for retirement 87–93
professional profile 83–4
proportion of faculty 81
survey 81–2
work patterns 84–6
Lazear, Edward P. 235
Leslie, David W. 250
Levin, Sharon G. 235
limiting retiree health benefit liabilities
methods used by academic
employers 124–6
methods used by corporates 118–19
pressure on corporates to 121
see also retiree medical accounts
Long, Bridget Terry 49
Lumsdaine, Robin L. 234
Lyman, Peter 30
Lynch, Gerald J. 49

management style, and phased
retirement plans 192–3, 195
mandatory retirement, ending of 6–7,
136, 209–12
mass retirements/hirings 80
maternity leave, at SU 178
mathematics, PhD production 26
mathematics post-docs 65, 68
McDermed, Ann 11
McDevitt, Roland D. 118, 119, 120,
124, 126
McGill, Dan M. 129
McPherson, Michael S. 234

Medicaid 102–4
see also Medicare
medical fields post-docs 65, 68
Medicare
and ARM predictions 166–7
background 102–4
and employer obligations 132
faculty retiree costs 130
incomplete cover 16
and retirees 17
see also post-65 health care
Medicare wrap-around coverage
174–5
merit pay 86–7
mid-career faculty *see* early and mid-
career faculty
Mitchell, Olivia S. 234
Moe, Michael T. 30
Morgan, Harriet 19
motivators
for retirement 87–91
for senior faculty 86–7
Mueller, Marjorie Smith 107

National Survey of Postsecondary
Faculty (1998) 240
NIH (National Institutes of Health)
budget, and post-doc positions 66
non-profit institutions of higher
education, and accounting
standards 120
non-tenure-track faculty
concern over 47
demand for 37–43
see also faculty, employment levels
vs. for-profit sector
increase in 18–19
new hires 43–6
proportion of 33–5, 37, 51
notional defined contribution plans
118–19

OBRA *see* Omnibus Budget and
Reconciliation Acts
oceanography *see* earth science and
oceanography post-docs
office space for retired faculty 90, 92,
205, 217–18, 261
see also lab space for retired faculty
Oi, Walter Y. 237

Omnibus Budget and Reconciliation
  Acts (1989/90) 118
Oster, Sharon M. 235

parental leave, at SU 178–9
part-time faculty
  growth of 35–6, 277–9
  and health insurance 16
  sponsored health care plan at SU
    174
pay-as-you-go retiree benefits 121–2
Pencavel, John 15, 236
pension benefits, and post-doc
  positions 72, 74
pension plans, and retirement patterns
  212–15
permanent personnel policies 215–16
  see also phased retirement plans
phased retirement plans 283
  as humane 243
  incidence of 12–14, 189–95, 220–21
  and on-campus workloads 200–201
  outcomes for individuals 246–8
  problems addressed by 185–6
  questions institutions should ask 250
  and retirement decisions 91–2, 202–4
  at Syracuse University 179–81
  at University of California 252–7
  University of North Carolina case
    study 195–206
  value for faculty 186–7, 200–202,
    206
  value for universities 188–9, 202–7,
    241–6, 248–9
  see also Stanford University early
    retirement plan, half-time jobs
PhDs *see* earned doctorates, trends in
Phelan, C. 139
physical sciences, postdoctorate
  population 55
physics, PhD production 26
physics post-docs 65, 68–9
Pikrell, Jesse F. 105
planning, role of institutional research
  7–9
Plus 5 program 226–7
post-65 health care 174–5
postdoctoral position duration 67–76
postdoctoral position takeup 56–67
postdoctorate associations 53

postdoctorate population growth 53–6,
  279–80
pre-65 retirees 115
private institutions
  and buyout programs 224
  and DB/DC pension plans 213–14
  early retirement plans 14–15
  and phased retirement plans 13, 192
  and phased retirement policies 221
  proportion of non-tenure-track
    faculty 33–5, 37, 51
  proportion of part-time faculty 35–6
  proportion providing retiree health
    benefits 122–4
  retirement plan types 10–11
probit analysis 193
productivity of faculty, and phased
  retirement 188
Professors of the Practice *see* part-time
  faculty
promotional prospects 6
public institutions
  accounting standards 120–21
  and buyout programs 224
  and DB/DC pension plans 213–14
  and phased retirement policies 221
  proportion of non-tenure-track
    faculty 33–5, 37, 51
  proportion of part-time faculty 35–6
  proportion providing retiree health
    benefits 122–4
  retirement plan types 10–11
Purcell, Pat 11

Quinn, Joseph 20

recruitment, developing new policies
  277–80
Rees, Albert 19
research (into Three Rs), need for
  267–75, 285
  data user needs 271–2
  faculty demographics 268–9
  impact of funding variation 269–71
  model for collaborative research
    274–5
  standardizing measures 272–3
research and doctoral institutions 13
  see also doctoral institutions
restructuring faculty 10

retaining senior faculty 89
retention, developing new policies
    280–81
Retire Then Phase-In (Stanford
    University) 235
retiree dependency ratios 130
retiree health accounts *see* retiree
    medical accounts
retiree health benefits
    and accounting standards 116–20
    eligibility requirement at SU 173–4
    future of provision of 128–32, 282
    for higher education faculty 120–28
    history of employers role 115–16
    risks of reducing 137–8
retiree health insurance 17, 104, 282–3
retiree medical accounts 126–7
retirement, developing new policies
    281–2
retirement age, senior faculty plans for
    29, 87–8, 91
retirement incentives
    of buyout programs 221–4
    and employment after retirement
        212
    of pension plans 212–13
    personnel policies types 215–18
    of phased retirement programs
        218–21
    of retiree medical accounts 127
retirement patterns 240–41
retirement planning 12
retirement plans 9–16
    see also defined benefit (DB) plans;
        defined contribution (DC) plans;
        early retirement plans
retirement rates
    and phased retirement 188
    and the stock market 11, 265–6
    at UNC 197–9
retirement scheme design *see* ARM
retirement windows *see* buyout
    programs
retiring at 70, probability of 7
Rice, Dorothy P. 102, 115
Rice, R. Eugene 93, 94, 96, 97
Rust, J. 139, 141, 142

S&P500, and retirement rates 11,
    265–6

Sass, Steven A. 116, 131
SCFRP *see* Survey of Changes in
    Faculty Retirement Policies
Schapiro, Morton Owen 234
Schibik, Timothy 49
SDR *see* Survey of Doctorate
    Recipients
SED *see* Survey of Earned Doctorates
senior faculty *see* late-career faculty
severance behavior forecasting 227–30,
    232
Shapiro, Mark 18
Siegfried, John J. 49
Smallwood, Scott 49
Smith, Sharon 19
stable enrollments 10
Stanford University early retirement
    plan 264–6
    adverse selection problem 263
    bonus size 263
    call-back status 235, 261
    eligibility 260
    financial advice for faculty 262
    half-time jobs 264
state defined benefit plan 11–12
Stein, Herb 112
Stephan, Paula E. 235
stock market performance, and
    retirement rates 11, 265–6
Strong, Jay V. 105, 107
SU *see* Syracuse University
Supported Resignation Program 179
    see also Tenured Faculty Voluntary
        Phased Retirement Program
Survey of Changes in Faculty
    Retirement Policies (SCFRP)
    12–13, 189–95, 211
Survey of Doctorate Recipients (SDR)
    67
Survey of Earned Doctorates (SED)
    56
Survey of Graduate Students and
    Postdoctorates in Science and
    Engineering 54–5
surveys, of faculty attitudes 8–9
Switkes, Ellen 15, 236, 253
Syracuse University (SU)
    Family Leave Benefits policy 177–9
    gaining acceptance for policies
        182–3

health care HR practices 170–76
phased retirement 179–81

Take 5 program 226–7
technology changes, and health care
   costs 110
temporary personnel policies 215–16
tenure
   and phased retirement policies
     190–92, 193–5
   relinquishment of, *vs.* retirement 212
Tenured Faculty Voluntary Phased
   Retirement Program 179–81
Thompson, Lawrence H. 117
Three Rs 267
TIAA-CREF Institute 29, 81, 93, 189,
   274, 280
TIAA-CREF Institute Three Rs
   conference 267, 285
Trotman, Carroll-Ann 97
Trower, Cathy A. 97

UC *see* University of California
UCFW *see* University Committee on
   Faculty Welfare
UM *see* University Minnesota
UNC *see* University of North Carolina
universities *see* institutions of higher
   learning
University of California (UC)
   administration-faculty retirement
     program discussions 252–7

buyout program case study
   224–32
early retirement plans 15
University Committee on Faculty
   Welfare (UCFW) 254–7
University Minnesota (UM) 82–93,
   88
University of North Carolina (UNC)
   age structure of faculty 3–5, 28
   faculty growth needs 28–9
   faculty income levels 88
   phased retirement plans 14, 29–30,
     195–206, 219
   retiring at 70, probability of 7
   senior faculty 82–93
US health care financing 102–4

Varian, Hal 30
verips (Voluntary Early Retirement
   Incentive Programs) 225–32,
   253

Watts, Michael 49
Weiler, William C. 237
Wergin, Jon F. 87
window policies 216
   see also buyout programs
Wise, David 20
wrap-around coverage *see* Medicare
   wrap-around coverage

Zhang, Liang 49